SUBCONTINENT ADRIFT

SUBCONTINENT ADRIFT

Strategic Futures of South Asia

Feroz Hassan Khan

Rapid Communications in Conflict and Security Series
General Editor: Geoffrey R.H. Burn

CAMBRIA
PRESS

Amherst, New York

Requests for permission should be directed to:
permissions@cambriapress.com, or mailed to:
Cambria Press
University Corporate Centre, 100 Corporate Parkway, Suite 128
Amherst, New York 14226, U.S.A.

Library of Congress Cataloging-in-Publication Data

Names: Khan, Feroz Hassan, 1952- author.
Title: Subcontinent adrift : strategic futures of South Asia / Feroz Hassan Khan.
Other titles: Strategic futures of South Asia
Description: Amherst, New York : Cambria Press, [2022] |
Series: Rapid communications in conflict and security series |
Includes bibliographical references and index. |
Summary: "While several books have examined the security challenges faced by India and
Pakistan in isolation, as well as the strategies they have each adopted in response, this
book places the two sets of clashing outlooks, policies, and strategies together and analyzes
the causes and consequences of the drift in South Asia. This study maps out and explains
India and Pakistan's respective interests, motivations, and long-term objectives from a
contemporary perspective. Much has happened in the intervening period since the nuclear
tests in 1998 that has shaped the rivalry between these two countries, including advances
in their strategic capabilities, domestic political shifts, and changes in the global balance
of power. Hence the book considers to what extent the "drifting" Subcontinent is affecting
the political, military, and economic dynamics on the international stage and causing a
"global drift." This study identifies the latent and emergent drivers behind the mounting
acrimony in South Asia-notably, India's ambitions as a "rising power" coupled with the
resurgence of China and Pakistan's strategic anxiety as the United States unmoors itself
from Afghanistan and embraces India. India is similarly concerned as China advances its
Belt and Road Initiative (BRI) across the region, developing a network of economic and
strategic hubs and bringing India's neighbors into China's embrace through its strategy of
peripheral diplomacy. The aim of this book is to conduct a detailed analysis of the India-
Pakistan impasse without losing sight of the regional complexities and sensitivities that
are often ignored or subsumed in purely comparative works"-- Provided by publisher.

Identifiers: LCCN 2022021001 (print) | LCCN 2022021002 (ebook) |
ISBN 9781621966487 (library binding) | ISBN 9781638570639 (paperback)
ISBN 9781621966661 (pdf) | ISBN 9781621966678 (epub)

Subjects: LCSH: India--Relations--Pakistan. | Pakistan--
Relations--India. | National security--South Asia.

Classification: LCC DS450.P18 K46 2022 (print) | LCC DS450.P18 (ebook) |
DDC 327.5405491--dc23/eng/20211027

LC record available at https://lccn.loc.gov/2022021001

LC ebook record available at https://lccn.loc.gov/2022021002

TABLE OF CONTENTS

ACKNOWLEDGEMENTS

I wish to acknowledge the contributions and hard work of several colleagues, mentors, friends, and family involved in the genesis and production of this book.

Ryan French initially joined this project as co-author but was unable to continue due to other pursuits and commitments. His intellectual input and research contributions were invaluable. Suzelle Thomas completed her research thesis under my supervision, which allowed me to crystallize many of my thoughts. I am grateful for her hard work and for sharing her research.

Several sponsors facilitated many of the research projects over the years, including conference attendance and visits to the region. The participants in these projects comprised top scholars as well as former civil and military officials from the United States, India, and Pakistan. I owe sincere thanks to each of them for enriching my knowledge, shaping my thoughts, and helping me conceptualize the themes and develop the narrative of this book.

Above all, this work is the outcome of encouragement proffered by a great many colleagues and academics as well as those with a passionate interest in peace and security and the strategic future of South Asia. Here I would like to make special mention of my mentor and friend, the late Professor Stephen P. Cohen, who initially planted the idea for this book some two decades back and provided constant encouragement.

Catherine L. Grant helped with extensive editing of the first draft of the manuscript, while Rene Bailey coaxed and cajoled the text into its final shape. Without their input this manuscript would have been less polished, for which I am very grateful. Special thanks to Dr. Sharad Joshi for his inputs and myriad discussions on Indian politics. Many thanks also to Geoffrey Burn and his team at Cambria Press for their patience with the tedious process of reviews, editing, and keeping me on track to maintain the standards of scholarly conventions required for this publication.

Finally, I wish to thank all members of my family—Mahreen, Mahvish, Sarem, and Haider—who bore the brunt of my distractions in the difficult times of shelter-in-place during the COVID-19 pandemic and displayed a great deal of understanding, patience, and support, without which I would have been unable to complete this work.

INTRODUCTION

The idea for this book emanated in 2001–2002, when I was a visiting scholar at the Woodrow Wilson Center and the Brookings Institution in Washington, DC. At Brookings, Professor Stephen Cohen, the late American doyen of South Asia, was supervising my research. It was less than a year since the United States, the "world's paramount power," had suffered an asymmetric terror attack on its soil in September 2001, which had brought South Asia into the center of world politics.[1] The situation in the region at the time was very volatile: on the one hand, US forces had overthrown the Taliban regime in Afghanistan, enflaming the tribal borderlands between Pakistan and Afghanistan in the process, and on the other, India and Pakistan were in a military standoff following a terrorist attack on the Indian parliament in New Delhi in December 2001. The prospect of catastrophic nuclear war on the Subcontinent could no longer be regarded as purely hypothetical. For the second time in just two decades, Pakistan found itself in a two-front situation. Previously, in the winter of 1986–1987 while the war raged against Soviet occupation in Afghanistan, the armies of India and Pakistan had been similarly engaged in a military standoff (known as the Brass Tacks Crisis). This time, however, the character of the crisis was very different: India and Pakistan had demonstrated their nuclear capabilities; the Kashmir separatist insurgency was more than a decade old; the region was a hub for entrenched non-state actors and violent extremist groups; and the United States had replaced the Soviet Union in yet another asymmetric war in Afghanistan (this time against global terrorism). The world was worried.

In 2001–2002, Professor Cohen and I participated in a Stanford University conference titled "South Asia in 2020: Future Strategic Balances and Alliances," which examined the possible pathways the two new nuclear powers, India and Pakistan, might take in the first two decades of the new millennium. Three common positions emerged from that conference, and the findings were later published in an edited volume.[2] The first position was one of cautious optimism about the future, arguing that with the advent of nuclear capabilities, India and Pakistan would likely turn away from hostilities toward détente and seek cooperation to bring an end to the conflict. The second position was skeptical of the future, pointing to the political, economic, and social complexities in the region—given the uncertainty around future political alignments and what stance the various nuclear-armed powers would take—and leaning toward India and Pakistan continuing to muddle through in a series of intermittent crises. The third position, based on the importance of the region for the United States, argued that US involvement was inevitable for reasons which were both negative (terrorism, military crisis, and the nuclear arms race) and positive (the region being home to a quarter of the world's population, its economic potential, and geopolitical significance). I was in the first group of guarded optimism, Cohen in the second group, expressing skepticism, while most participants concurred with the third position that the United States was in a pivotal position to stabilize the nuclear balance and possibly change the course of future developments in South Asia.[3]

Cohen advised me to broaden my research on the strategic future of the region. In my numerous discussions with him and several other scholars at various think tanks in DC, we would debate the causes and consequences of the continuing conflict between India and Pakistan. Why has the Subcontinent, with its immense pool of talents and resources, its rich history and geostrategic significance, been unable to find peace and harmony? While many scholars have analyzed the India-Pakistan conundrum from varying perspectives, Cohen thought that the only way South Asia's puzzle could be resolved would be for Pakistan to accept the primacy and inevitable rise of India, and for India to accept the improbability of having a compliant Pakistan as its neighbor—a "West Bangladesh" of sorts.[4] The real question, then, is why what appears to be such a logical solution has not come to pass after nearly three quarters of a century since these countries gained independence from Britain.

India and Pakistan are both hostages to stubborn fixations—one of a rising power seeking its place in the sun, and the other of a nation seeking parity with its mightier neighbor; in the process, both have lost their bearings and caused the drift in their relationship. Even after two decades of demonstrating and developing their nuclear capabilities, both sides are unable to overcome these fixations that continue to aggravate their rivalry at a time when the rest of the world is looking for economic interdependency, connectivity, and regional integration.

My research on this subject has continued for two decades since that conference at Stanford, drawing on numerous seminars, workshops, bilateral Track II dialogues, and crisis simulation tabletop exercises that I participated in or organized as principal investigator. For a time, this study was put on the backburner while I prioritized research for my book on Pakistan's nuclear-bomb program,[5] but I came back to the manuscript in 2015, a year after a new government under Prime Minister Narendra Modi first took office in India. There were early signs that the Modi government was adopting a new proactive approach in the region that was both aggressive in its security policy and bold in its diplomacy. Given that there were two nuclear powers in a region with a deep history of animosities and broken relationships, any belligerent shifts in regard to security policy could set the Subcontinent on a path to a dreadful future. Conversely, assertive diplomacy marked by positive determination could help resolve the conflict and eliminate the roots of discord, which would dramatically pave the way toward a brighter future.

Whereas much academic literature has been published on India and Pakistan's rivalry, the last major surge of books came hot on the heels of the 1998 nuclear tests, the 1999 Kargil War, the September 11 attacks, and the 2001–2002 military standoff. These books, though masterful, are now somewhat dated.[6] As for more recent works on South Asia, they have tended to focus on Pakistan-centric explanations for the regional security conundrum. By focusing on one country over another, these books forego a holistic analysis of the factors driving security competition in South Asia.[7]

Before continuing, a word about terminology. The terms "Subcontinent" and "South Asia" are often used synonymously in this book. The former refers to a geographical space, whereas the latter is a regional construct based on the former British Raj. A third term, "Southern Asia," is also often used, that expands the geographical scope to include parts of China bordering India (i.e., Xinjiang and Tibet) and connotes the triangular rivalry in the region. I do not use that term here because it suggests that the rivalry between India and Pakistan is just one problem amongst several. As this book will show, my argument is that the rivalry between India and Pakistan represents the crux of the whole security dilemma in the region and is the cause of the Subcontinent's continued drift. Essentially, "Subcontinent," "South Asia," and "Southern Asia" are all loaded terms, denoting specific connotations, psychological fears, and hidden political imperatives.

Stephen Cohen—who had encouraged me earlier—sought the answer to the future of the region with his own book on the India-Pakistan conundrum.[8] Another exceptional work is that of Moeed Yusuf,[9] which is the first of its kind to examine the role of a third party (the United States) in Indian-Pakistani brinkmanship. Yusuf analyzes the crisis behavior of two nuclear-armed countries in the absence of any clear policy or strategy within the international community. While several books have examined the security challenges faced by India and Pakistan in isolation as well as the strategies they have each adopted in response, the current work places the two sets of clashing outlooks, policies, and strategies together and analyzes the causes and consequences of the drift in South Asia.

Subcontinent Adrift maps out and explains India and Pakistan's respective interests, motivations, and long-term objectives from a contemporary perspective. Much has happened in the intervening period since the nuclear tests in 1998 that has shaped the rivalry between these two countries, including advances in their strategic capabilities, domestic political shifts, and changes in the global balance of power. Hence, the book considers to what extent the "drifting" Subcontinent is affecting the political, military, and economic dynamics on the international stage and causing a "global drift," described by Chester Crocker as a "disorderly mixture of turbulence and drift in relationships among the leading powers and key regional states."[10]

This work identifies the latent and emergent drivers behind the mounting acrimony in South Asia—notably, India's ambitions as a "rising power" coupled with the resurgence of China and Pakistan's strategic anxiety as the United States unmoors itself from Afghanistan and embraces India. India is similarly concerned as China advances its Belt and Road Initiative (BRI) across the region, developing a network of economic and strategic hubs and bringing India's neighbors into China's embrace through its strategy of peripheral diplomacy. Countries in the region are attracted by the new opportunities offered through the BRI, which in turn undercuts India's national objectives and provides new incentives for Pakistan to balance against India.

China and the Subcontinent form a confluence of three nuclear-armed countries comprising two asymmetric dyads. The China-India dyad is typified as a rivalry between two rising Asian powers at the international level, whereas the India-Pakistan dyad represents a deep-seated conflict at the regional level. These two dyads meet at the conjuncture of three disputed and volatile sub-regions (Tibet, Xinjiang, and Kashmir), which has consequently become the locus for sporadic armed clashes over contested borders in a mountainous terrain. In the current context of great power competition, where power rebalancing and strategic realignments are shaping geopolitical outlooks, a number of scholars have suggested viewing the conflict in South Asia in terms of a strategic triangle between China, India, and Pakistan.[11] Whether or not such a triangular construct is possible, it is clear that the two sets of rivalries are characterized by deep ideological underpinnings, territorial claims, and asymmetries of power. This book primarily focuses on the India-Pakistan dyadic conflict, but it also charts the region's future from the perspective of a changing global power construct that necessarily includes China as well.

Chapter 1 traces the complex history of the India-Pakistan conundrum to explain how the partition of the Subcontinent into two nations in 1947—intended to *resolve* a communal problem—instead prepared the ground for enduring hostilities that would become deeply entrenched. A combination of cognitive biases and structural issues caused the region to drift further with the passage of each decade. The failure of India and Pakistan to resolve their differences early on meant that the bitter wounds suffered during the 1947 Partition became a festering sore, at the heart of which lies each of these countries' right to exist.

Chapter 2 provides an overarching appraisal of the situation on the Subcontinent by examining Indian-Pakistani security competition through three tiers of analysis: international system-level dynamics, bilateral relations, and domestic undercurrents. At each level of analysis, I identify and discuss the historical and emergent factors that imperil strategic stability in the region, offering an all-inclusive account that is missing from many recent publications on South Asia.

Chapters 3 and 4 seek to make sense of India and Pakistan's divergent grand strategies—defined as each state's "vision" in terms of its national objectives and the course of action needed to pursue its national security, along with specifying the requisite instruments to achieve them.[12] I examine India and Pakistan's strategic interests and map out how these interests translate into each country's current foreign and military policies, and the challenges they face in developing and executing coherent grand strategies. India and Pakistan's grand strategies are difficult to assess at the best of times, but today's geopolitical complexities and technological advances make this even harder. As we move into the third decade of this century, India's grand strategy remains caught between the push and pull of pragmatism and idealism. India continues to dogmatically embrace a policy of non-alignment—adopted by its founding fathers in the early years of independence—but now feels compelled to partner with the United States to contain a resurgent China. Meanwhile, India's archrival Pakistan is hedging its bets by cozying up to its trusted ally China. From Pakistan's standpoint China is a strategic partner that helps balance against India and is also a full-fledged global power that compensates for Pakistan's diminished alliance with the United States.

Chapter 5 examines the Subcontinent's tenuous deterrence stability by analyzing the dialectic of opposing military and nuclear doctrines. More than two decades since the 1998 nuclear tests, neither India nor Pakistan is able to fully appreciate the other's doctrines and standpoint or discern the true intentions and capabilities of the other. Both are likely to misread the other and underestimate the other's resolve to use violence, possibly leading to use of the nuclear option. The chapter examines the dynamics of conflict escalation that are inducing crisis instability and accentuating the regional drift.

Chapter 6 outlines in detail the trajectory of the ongoing military and nuclear competition on the Subcontinent, positing new challenges to the present arms race stability. Military and nuclear modernization and other technical advances have resulted in India and Pakistan reevaluating their strategies vis-à-vis the other. For example, India has adopted a new gray zone approach through which it aims to isolate Pakistan politically and diplomatically, raise the economic and military costs for Pakistan to compete with India, and counter Pakistan in the same asymmetric manner that it believes Pakistan is deploying to "defeat India with a thousand cuts." Simultaneously, India is daring Pakistan to engage in a debilitating arms race with the objective of exhausting its archrival.

The final chapter examines the failure of several peace initiatives in the past and their impact on overall crisis stability. It then explores three potential scenarios for the rivalry between India and Pakistan to play out in the years and decades ahead. The first—and most desirable—scenario is for South Asia to achieve a good future. This scenario assesses the prospects for a détente between India and Pakistan and the potential for achieving some kind of grand bargain, which might also involve China in building the architecture for peace and security on the Subcontinent. The second is the bad future, which projects a perpetuation of the existing regional cold war. The third is the ugly future, which foresees a deterioration of existing conditions and the rise of extremist forces, leading to state failure, enhanced military competition, and wars involving not just India and Pakistan, but China as well. The chapter concludes by proposing a regime of strategic restraint to cool the arms race between India and Pakistan.

In short, the aim of this book is to conduct a detailed analysis of the India-Pakistan impasse without losing sight of the regional complexities and sensitivities that are often ignored or subsumed in purely comparative works.

NOTES

1. Zbignew Brezezinski, *The Grand Chessboard: American Primacy and Its Geostrategic Imperatives* (New York: Basic Books, 1997), xiii.
2. Michael Chambers, ed., *South Asia in 2020: Future Strategic Balances and Alliances* (Carlisle, PA: Strategic Studies Institute, 2002).
3. Chambers, *South Asia in 2020*, 1–5.
4. I am indebted to Stephen P. Cohen for the term "West Bangladesh," implying a pliant state to India's west that is dependent on India.
5. Feroz Hassan Khan, *Eating Grass: The Making of the Pakistani Bomb* (Palo Alto, CA: Stanford University Press, 2012).
6. Sumit Ganguly, *Conflict Unending: India-Pakistan Tensions since 1947* (New York: Columbia University Press, 2002); Ashley Tellis, *Limited Conflict under the Nuclear Umbrella: Indian and Pakistani Lessons from the Kargil Crisis* (Santa Monica, CA: RAND Corporation, 2002); S. Paul Kapur, *Dangerous Deterrent: Nuclear Weapons, Proliferation, and Conflict in South Asia* (Palo Alto, CA: Stanford University Press, 2007).
7. T. V. Paul, *The Warrior State: Pakistan in the Contemporary World* (Oxford: Oxford University Press, 2014); C. Christine Fair, *Fighting to the End: The Pakistan Army's Way of War* (Oxford: Oxford University Press, 2014); Aqil Shah, *The Army and Democracy: Military Politics in Pakistan* (New Haven, CT: Harvard University Press, 2014).
8. Stephen P. Cohen, *Shooting for a Century: The India-Pakistan Conundrum* (Washington, DC: Brookings Institution Press, 2013).
9. Moeed Yusuf, *Brokering Peace in Nuclear Environments: US Crisis Management in South Asia* (Palo Alto, CA: Stanford University Press, 2018).
10. Chester A. Crocker, "The Strategic Dilemma of a World Adrift," *Survival* 57, no. 1 (February/March 2015): 7–30. That essay is from Chester A. Crocker, Fen Osler Hampson, and Pamela Aall, eds., *Managing Conflict in a World Adrift* (Washington, DC: US Institute of Peace, 2015).
11. Monish Tourangbam, "The China-India-Pakistan Triangle: Origins, Contemporary Perceptions, and Future," South Asian Voices Project, Henry L. Stimson Center, June 25, 2020, https://www.stimson.org/202 0/the-china-india-pakistan-triangle-origins-contemporary-perceptions-and-future/.
12. See Robert Art, *A Grand Strategy for America* (Ithaca, NY: Cornell University Press, 2004), 1-2; S. Paul Kapur, *Jihad as Grand Strategy: Islamic*

Militancy, National Security and the Pakistani State, (New York: Oxford University Press, 2017), 8.

SUBCONTINENT ADRIFT

CHAPTER 1

WOUNDS THAT FESTER

The chronic rivalry between two nuclear powers—India and Pakistan —exemplifies the kind of deep-seated religious enmity and unresolved political, strategic, and economic antagonisms which lie at the heart of the drift in South Asia. It was this unique type of conflict that led President Bill Clinton to describe this region as the "most dangerous" in the world.[1]

The troubled history of India and Pakistan's relations is fueled by a combination of two phenomena: cognitive bias and unresolved issues. It is vital to understand both the difference between these factors as well as their nexus in order to comprehend the conundrum that is South Asia from the perspective of its bitter post-Partition history (rather than focusing on its symptoms). The absence of any structural framework for peace and security contributes to the problem. In the decades since the 1947 Partition, new sources of distrust have eroded whatever confidence-building measures existed, so that they have either become defunct or no longer offer a sufficient convergence of interests. Although both sides recognize the need to overcome the prevailing cognitive biases and resolve the main issues between them, the strategies adopted by each have only compounded the conflict and driven them further from their common history and shared cultural heritage, and thus reduced any hopes for peace and security.

COGNITIVE BIAS

The roots of conflicts based on cognitive bias tend to be buried deep in a long history of animosity and past injustices between tribal societies or nations locked in perpetual conflict. Cognitive bias fuels mistrust and often gives justification to violence for no apparent reason other than mere spite or mutual hatred. While seldom supported by rational discourse, a cognitive bias confirms prejudices, allows for a selective interpretation of history, and imputes evil intent to the other in any disagreement.

Stephen Cohen described the India-Pakistan conflict as a "paired-minority conflict." In other words, it is a conflict based on intractable disputes and psychological fears "rooted in perceptions held by important groups in both states" that are not the minority but nonetheless feel "threatened from [the] weaker party."[2] He adds, "paired-minority conflicts are fomented by strong-weak identity," whereby a powerful state feels vulnerable and acts to subdue its weaker neighbor; this then reinforces the sense of victimhood of the weaker state and prompts it to seek additional security measures, leading to a classic security dilemma. This phenomenon is not specific to the rivalry between India and Pakistan; it also applies to the Israeli-Palestinian and Iranian-Arab rivalries.[3] Indian and Pakistani insecurities are rooted in the perceived treachery, deceit, and evil imagery of the other. These shared myths about "the other" have formed part of their respective national narratives for three generations, complicating attempts at communication and conflict resolution and becoming an engine of this enduring rivalry between the two nations.[4]

Hindus and Muslims have not just lived together for centuries; both cultures have intermingled and synthesized to create a common ethos on the Indian Subcontinent. Yet each culture maintains its respective values, with an emphasis on what separates them rather than what they have in common. Moderate Hindus and Muslims do not have a visceral consciousness of the differences between the two communities; it is only when viewed through a political lens or with religious fervor that the sense of separate identities becomes perceptible.

Until the last quarter of the twentieth century, religious forces in both India and Pakistan were on the fringes of politics. By the turn of the new century, however, far-right Hindu fundamentalists in India had entered the political mainstream, gradually achieving near-absolute power—which now threatens India's secular polity. Fundamentalist trends in Pakistan began even earlier, in the 1970s, under the regime of Muhammad Zia-ul-Haq that transformed Pakistan's hitherto moderate Muslim society into a more conservative one, so that over time the Pakistani state gradually provided more and more space in which radical forces could incubate. Although religious forces in Pakistan do not have the capacity to win mainstream elections—unlike in India—they wield enough street power to influence both the state and society, forcing successive civil and military governments to appease them.

Exacerbated by the rhetoric of nationalist governments and radical elements within society, from the 1990s onward, the attitudes of Hindus and Muslims vis-à-vis the other have become ever more discriminatory. This deep cognitive bias, which stems from the bitter experiences of Partition, colors the whole regional dynamics. Although not self-sustaining, this phenomenon is almost completely entrenched in the national psyche of each country.

The Vision of the Founding Fathers

As the steam clouds of the trains that traveled between Amritsar, Delhi, and Punjab in 1947 slowly cleared, what they revealed was the decimation of Hindu and Muslim communities and families, standing in stark relief against the vision of harmonious coexistence, or perhaps a peaceful parting of the ways, that had been conjured up pre-Partition. The tragic irony is that the idea of partitioning India was meant to offer a solution to the communal problem, but it has instead produced an intractable conflict between two nation-states.

The creation of a separate Muslim nation-state was intended to usher in a new age of Muslim-Hindu relations on the Subcontinent; it was to be an era characterized by coexistence and mutual harmony. Pakistan's founding fathers—the poet-philosopher Muhammad Iqbal and politician Muhammad Ali Jinnah—repeatedly presented their vision of a Muslim state as one that, rather than being inimical toward India, offered protection to its larger neighbor. In his epochal address at Allahabad in 1930, Iqbal announced that the idea of a new Muslim state should not worry the Hindus because "the North-West Indian Muslims will prove the best defenders of India against a foreign invasion, be that invasion one of the ideas or of the bayonets."[5] He never visualized a theocratic state. Rather, Iqbal asserted:

> Nor should the Hindus fear that the creation of autonomous Muslim states will mean the introduction of a kind of religious rule in such states ... I, therefore, demand the formation of a consolidated Muslim State in the best interests of India and Islam.[6]

Muhammad Ali Jinnah echoed Iqbal's sentiment. In the early 1940s, Jinnah argued that a separate Muslim state would ensure security in the northwestern zone, leaving India just the southern and western areas to protect. He declared, "We join together as good friends and neighbors and say to the world, 'Hands off India.'"[7] In October 1944 and again in November 1946, Jinnah said that India and Pakistan would "proclaim a 'Monroe Doctrine' of their own for the defense of the Subcontinent against all outsiders."[8] Shortly before he died in 1948, Jinnah reiterated his wish for a cooperative security framework for the region. When asked about cooperation with India in international affairs and defense, he replied:

> Personally, I have no doubt in my mind that our paramount
> interests demand that the dominion of Pakistan and India should
> coordinate for the purpose of playing their part in international
> affairs ... but this depends entirely on whether Pakistan and India
> can resolve their own differences and grave domestic issues in the
> first instance. In other words, if we can put our issues in order
> internally, then we may be able to play a very great part externally
> in all international affairs.[9]

The early loss of both Jinnah (who died on September 11, 1948) and his successor Liaqat Ali Khan (assassinated on October 16, 1951) did not simply leave a political vacuum in Pakistan; it signified a foreboding start for a nation-state riven by political instability from which Pakistan has never fully recovered. The Muslim League that created Pakistan remained fractured and repeatedly failed to form a stable government. Both the lack of national infrastructure and the all-encompassing strategic and political threats which threatened Pakistan's survival from the very beginning created an environment where national institutions were unable to reach maturity. Eventually, the system fell victim to the military-bureaucratic nexus, which overthrew the fledgling democracy that had barely manifested itself under the 1956 constitution. Jinnah's vision of a peacefully coexisting Subcontinent could no longer be realized. Alongside the military's ascendency in Pakistan and the effect this has had on national security thinking there, speculations about Pakistan's viability in India have continued to this day, dominating India's thinking and approach toward Pakistan.

Pakistan's Existential Question
There are several reasons for the idea that Pakistan's status is purely provisional, but all these essentially stem from three sources: the refusal of right-wing Hindu nationalists to accept the partition of India, the challenges associated with uniting a religiously homogenous but ethnically and linguistically diverse nation, and Pakistan's initial composition

in two geographically separate wings with their structurally imbalanced institutional development.

At the time of Partition, many Indians saw the creation of Pakistan as a temporary measure—a view which was shared by the British viceroy, who apparently perceived it as if it were "like pitching a tent or a Nissen hut."[10] It is also widely believed that the communalists in India, who opposed the creation of Pakistan in 1947, continue to be well-represented within India's ruling elite. For example, in 2012—more than six decades after Partition—a prestigious think tank in New Delhi expressed concerns about Pakistan's continued existence and analyzed India's options accordingly.[11] Even more recently, in 2019, public discourse within domestic politics in India manifested sentiments such as: "Pakistan is an accident of history, and must be 'forced to its knees,'" or India must "hold the [Pakistan's] feet to the fire."[12] Such blustering permeates strategic thinking in Pakistan and reinforces the insecurity and mistrust that has characterized Pakistan's relations with India to date.[13]

The second source for concern about Pakistan's long-term viability derives from the major faultlines running through its core which hamper its ability to coalesce as a nation-state: that Pakistan is an amalgam of ethnically diverse peoples; that despite being a Muslim country, it is subject to heterogeneous ideological interpretations of Islam; and that its institutions are structurally unbalanced and vulnerable to a hostile India ready to exploit these schisms within Pakistan.

Ethnically, the Pakistani polity consists of Punjabis, Pathans, Sindhis, Baluchis, Bengalis, and a vast number of Urdu-speaking immigrants from India. Unifying so many ethnically disparate groups—especially difficult in the case of the Bengalis before 1971, given the geographical separation of more than a thousand miles—became the foremost challenge for Pakistan's creation. Jinnah's answer to this challenge was to declare Islam as the national religion, Urdu as the national language, and the polity as democratic, plural, and tolerant of all faiths. Jinnah emphatically endorsed this vision in his famous speech to the Constituent Assembly in

1947, emphasizing freedom and equal rights for all faiths and minorities in Pakistan.[14]

Islam was already the most common religion in the territory that became Pakistan, and this was the essence of its creation. While Muslims generally do not dispute the fundamentals of Islam, interpretations are not doctrinally homogenous, and they split along sectarian lines (Sunnis and Shias) as well as in the way Islam is practiced (ranging from strictly orthodox legalist to syncretistic mystic to Sufi interpretations). For a newborn nation-state in the twentieth century, a critical question for Pakistan at the time was the political interpretation of "Islamic state." Added to this were questions concerning the compatibility of the fundamentals of Islamic faith with a modern nation-state and the place of a modern progressive Muslim state in the global context. Pakistan's founder, Jinnah, had categorically rejected any notion of theocracy in the new state's legal framework, partly in recognition of the country's minorities. However, the intrinsically pluralistic Muslim society has faced constant challenges from the religious right in Pakistan. For example, the leading Muslim critic of Pakistan, Maulana Abulala Maududi, opposed the campaign for Pakistan from its earliest inception, fearing that "it would not become an Islamic state and maintain[ing] that 99.9% of the Indian Muslims were thoroughly unregenerate."[15] This type of philosophical opposition within the Muslim community, compounded by ethnic and linguistic diversity, posed a formidable challenge to national solidarity and integration for the new nation-state.

Lastly, not only were East and West Pakistan geographically distant, but ethnic Bengalis in East Pakistan also had a litany of grievances against West Pakistan over their language and perceived inequality and discrimination. The territorially contiguous state of West Pakistan (modern-day Pakistan) was based on the province of Punjab, and it dominated the smaller, ethnic-minority-populated provinces within its territory. This inevitably created problems in terms of interprovincial harmony and national unity, which was compounded by structural imbalances in the development of Pakistan's national institutions. Pakistan's political leaders blame the frequent military takeovers and the army's domineering role in governance for the country's lack of mature civil institutions and the resulting political instability. The military instead points to the multiple challenges posed by India, which, combined with the chronic internal disorder in Pakistan, border insecurities, and Cold War imperatives, created a highly securitized environment. Regardless, the growth of Pakistan's military institutions outpaced that of other national institutions in the country.

Given these significant challenges inherent since Pakistan's birth, the main question was what would act as the glue to hold the many parts of the nation together. The immediate answer lay with the military, which was the only institution strong enough to prevent the nascent nation from becoming a failed state. Stephen Cohen described Pakistan thus:

> It is a state that has an army that cannot govern but that will not allow civilians to rule ... Pakistan's army is strong enough to prevent state failure, but it is not imaginative enough to impose the changes that might transform the state.[16]

The stage for the two-nation debate was set in the second half of the nineteenth century when the British Raj began contemplating the inclusion of "natives" in the political process after having persistently fanned ethnic and religious rivalries under its policy of divide and rule. As a result, both Hindus and Muslims began to see how their two cultures differed, rather than considering what they had in common as Indians. Chaudhry Muhammad Ali sums up the duality of Hindu-Muslim relations in India: how two peoples are able to share the same cultural roots yet remain so distinct. He explicates:

> They [Hindus and Muslims] have met at a thousand points, on battlefields and at festivals, around market places and in homes, on spiritual heights and in the lowlands of mundane affairs ... their tongues have mixed to produce new and rich languages; and in ways of living they have left their mark on each other. And yet they

have remained distinct with an emphasis on their separateness. They have mixed but never fused; they have coexisted but have never become one.[17]

With this, Chaudhry Muhammad Ali captures the tension that has always existed between Pakistan and India and that underlies the two-nation debate. Before 1947, the debate centered around two very different visions of reality. On the one hand, Indian Muslims, led by Jinnah, believed that as a minority populace, Muslims would be without any security or rights amongst the majority Hindus. The leaders of the Indian National Congress (INC)—Mohandas Karamchand (Mahatma) Gandhi and Jawaharlal Nehru—on the other hand contended that as a pluralistic and secular democracy, India would be able to incorporate all Indians, regardless of race or religion.

However, it was the rhetoric of some Hindu leaders such as the INC's hawkish leader Sardar Vallabhbhai Patel that intensified the Hindus' fears of the Muslims. Patel expressed sentiments that aligned with those of the general population—different from the English-speaking intellectual urbanites—who regarded India as an exclusively Hindu state. Amid the bitter violence that pitted neighbor against neighbor, Patel "suggested that there was little point in the army trying to protect Muslim citizens."[18] Such anti-Muslim attitudes exacerbated insecurities amongst Muslims and strengthened the demand for a separate Muslim state. In 2018, the Indian government built a "Statue of Unity"—a colossal statue of Sardar Patel in the Indian state of Gujarat— believed to be the world's tallest statue.[19] For Muslims of the Subcontinent, however, such symbolism harks back to the two-nation debate and adds fuel to the question about the future state of India as either a pluralist and secular state, or a Hindu-dominated conservative one. Noting the political rise of Hindu nationalists, widely respected scholar Sunil Khilnani has dubbed such developments as the "saffronization of India."[20]

Ostensibly, the Indian National Congress was secular, but Muslims believed its nationalism to be, at heart, Hindu chauvinism, the first indications of which had appeared long before the Muslims demanded separate statehood in the 1940s. As far back as 1867, in fact, when the Indians moved to replace Urdu with Hindi Muslim leader Sir Syed Ahmed Khan predicted there would be a need for separation; even though, historically, Urdu was a manifestation of the process of cultural synthesis in Indian history and is still widely spoken across northern India today. More than a century later, right-wing Hindu nationalist discrimination has become an integral part of twenty-first-century Indian politics.[21] Nor does the vision of the forefathers of the two-nation idea stand in doubt any longer—Pakistan is a sovereign Muslim nation-state with their blessing.

The wounds of Partition reopened in December 1992 when thousands of Hindu nationalists stormed and destroyed a 500-year-old mosque known as Babri Masjid at Ayodhya in Uttar Pradesh because it was believed to have been at one time a temple and birthplace of the revered Hindu god, Ram. In 2019, after nearly three decades of controversy and debate, the Indian Supreme Court accepted the case made by the Hindus and handed over the disputed land for them to build the temple Ram Mandir. The Supreme Court's verdict essentially vilifies Muslims in India and sanctions their plight.[22] In March 2002, extremist violence in the Indian state of Gujarat resulted in the massacre of hundreds of Muslims. In the same vein, Hindus point to the Muslim ambush of Hindu pilgrims on the Sabarmarti Express in Godhra (Gujarat, India) in February 2002 as an example of minorities seeking to destabilize the nation of India. Today, open vigilantism against Muslims in India rekindles the same fears amongst Muslims that existed when the two-nation solution was first proposed.

By this time, in Islamic Pakistan, extremist forces were not only operating within the country but across the whole region as well—in part due to the clandestine use by different intelligence agencies of militant religious groups (jihadis) for asymmetric wars in Afghanistan and Kashmir. Under the influence of such a jihadi culture, various segments within Pakistan's society gradually became more and more intolerant toward minorities.[23] For example, in January 2011, Salman Taseer, a sitting governor of Pakistan's largest province Punjab, was killed by his own bodyguard in broad daylight in Islamabad. Taseer was an outspoken, secular-minded politician, who opposed Pakistan's blasphemy law and stood up for the fundamental rights of a minority Christian woman accused of blasphemy in her village. Taseer's assassin was tried in the court and executed after being handed a death sentence, but he is feted as a hero and martyr. The judge who convicted him fled the country after receiving death threats, and the assassin's burial site on the outskirts of Islamabad has become a shrine to his sympathizers.[24] Another example of intolerance toward minorities took place in Karachi on May 13, 2015, when more than forty people were killed and many wounded in a gun attack on a bus carrying members of the minority Ismaili Shi'i sect.[25] Between 2008 and 2014, more than 200 people were killed as noted by Farahnaz Ispahani during her Woodrow Wilson Center discussion.[26] In sum, both sides present diametrically opposed explanations for the drift between Hindus and Muslims, based on inimical and mutually exclusive perceptions.[27]

Unresolved Issues

The preceding section has sketched out the many strands woven into the persistent cognitive bias that impedes the development of an equal and harmonious relationship between India and Pakistan. This next section focuses on the many unresolved issues that also impact the troubled history of India-Pakistan relations. A legacy of unresolved issues is an invariable feature in most postcolonial regions of the world. Nonetheless, with the passage of time, the prevailing intractability of the conflict between India and Pakistan has grown more complex and much more difficult to resolve.

Most of these issues (which virtually all stem from the messy implementation of Partition) are relatively minor in scope. They encompass such matters as boundary adjustments, water distribution, and rights of navigation. The issue of Kashmir, however, is a major exception that stretches into the domains of both unresolved issues and cognitive bias. It is an issue that seems to resist settlement at every juncture. Of the three major wars which have been waged on the Subcontinent since 1948, two have been over the disputed region of Kashmir, and almost all the military crises have their origins in the ongoing Kashmiri separatist campaign.

After India gained independence from Britain, Jawaharlal Nehru led the country for the next 17 years. His chance to cement Mahatma Gandhi's vision of India was at hand, especially given the leadership vacuum in Pakistan. All India needed was to resolve the various disputes and security issues with its smaller neighbors. In fact, India remained under the rule of a single party (the INC) and single-family rule for most of the first four decades of its existence. The vision Nehru held for India and South Asia was characterized by stability and goodwill; however, he had to face tough choices, and his vision did not translate into reality. Nehru adopted unpopular policies of conciliation and reconciliation and was swayed by the influence of hawkish elements within the Indian parliament and mainstream Indian polity.[28]

India's size, resources, and strength advantage obligated it to take the initiative in settling border disputes. The Nehruvian vision of a "Great India" could have gained credence had India pursued a policy of reassurance and magnanimity toward its smaller sibling nations, and having thrown off the yoke of colonialism, the stage was set for just such an initiative. Unfortunately, the embers of animosity and division permeated Indian parliamentary debate. The conservative elements saw to it that the years of opportunity were squandered without settling the border disputes, which would come back to haunt India. With the passage of time, the conflict inherited at independence became ever more complex and difficult to resolve.

Borders and Boundaries, Demarcation and Division

The borders of Pakistan and India were not drawn in a way that was conducive to security for the two countries. The boundaries between Afghanistan and Pakistan, India and Pakistan, and China and India are all plagued with ambiguity over their demarcation, religious cleavage, irredentist claims, or, in many cases, all three. A review of how these borders came into being reveals the nature of the inherited problems that created the security issues between India and Pakistan, already bedeviled by ideological differences.

The Radcliffe Boundary Award

In the dying days of the Raj, the departing British established the Radcliffe Boundary Commission to partition India and Pakistan, and it was this body that created the border between West Pakistan (modern-day Pakistan) and India. From its inception, the question of where to align the border was already compounded by the unresolved fate of Kashmir, and the division of Pakistan into two territories also had serious implications. The border alignment in the Punjab resulted in chaos and mass migration, which further divided the Hindu, Sikh, and Muslim communities. It cut across the Punjab watershed and created land corridors between the major rivers flowing into Pakistan from India and Kashmir. These divisions enabled mechanized military operations to cross the border with ease. The border between West Pakistan and India runs roughly parallel to the existing rail and road communication lines on the Indian side. Across the border in Punjab and Sindh, the terrain presents miles of open and flat land that could be easily severed at several points by a simple mechanized operation. Any offensive from India along the elongated border in the Punjab-Sindh region would slice Pakistan in two.

Because of Pakistan's inception as a Muslim nation settled in two geographically separate territories, it has given its defense planners a perpetual strategic nightmare since its birth. In its western half, the country's major communication centers—such as Lahore, which is also Pakistan's major political-cultural hub—lie perilously close to and dangerously exposed to India. East Pakistan (modern-day Bangladesh), in contrast, would eventually protest its subordination and fight to break free of West Pakistan entirely. The lack of strategic depth in Pakistan's security policy, aggravated by the perception of a two-front threat from Afghanistan and India, poses a constant security challenge for Pakistan's military. This has necessitated keeping a standing army with a forward defense posture, strong fortifications, and carefully layered lines of defense using rivers and canals as obstacles against potential Indian invasion.

The Durand Line

Agreed upon after negotiation in 1893, the Durand Line was the porous and unsettled western border of over 1,400 miles between British India and Afghanistan, which made the latter a buffer state between the erstwhile Russian and British empires. The border cut across the territory of the ethnic group of the Pashtuns. The Durand Line border was challenged by "successive Afghans as imposed upon the Pashtuns as if it were a 'line drawn on water.'"[29] Afghan kings and tribal Pashtuns had persistently clashed with British rulers throughout the time of the British Raj, and this was the legacy inherited by Pakistan. Post-Partition, the ethnic tensions generated by the Durand Line in the nineteenth century engendered harsh relations between Pakistan and Afghanistan from the outset and gave India occasion to foment sub-nationalist discord in Pakistan. Afghanistan cast the sole vote against the admittance of Pakistan into the United Nations (UN) in 1947, and India's Congress Party supported separatist movements among the Pashtuns in what was then Pakistan's North-West Frontier Province (now Khyber Pakhtunkhwa) and Baluchistan, which immediately challenged the legitimacy of Pakistan's borders with Afghanistan.

The sub-nationalist movements were made up of Pashtun nationalists known as Khudai Khidmatgar ("Servants of God," also known as the Red Shirts) demanding a free Pashtunistan and independent Baluchistan. Pakistan firmly believed these movements had the backing of several intelligence agencies—Soviet, Indian, Afghan—that were aiding and abetting dissenting tribes in the volatile western provinces to destabilize the country. Following a series of coups in Afghanistan in the late 1970s, Soviet occupation in the 1980s, and Taliban rule in the 1990s, the Pashtunistan and Baluchi separatist movements and the Afghanistan-Pakistan border problem seemed to have disappeared, but the issue resurfaced again in 2003 once the Taliban regime was ousted from power. This history of Afghanistan's territorial claims, its perpetual meddling with centrifugal elements, and its active collaboration with hostile intelligence agencies against Pakistan eventually gave birth to the concept of "strategic depth" in response, which will be analyzed later in chapter 4. In addition, each time there was trouble with Afghanistan, Pakistan chose to retaliate by strangling its landlocked economy, which continues to bedevil relations between these two countries.[30]

The Johnson and McMahon Lines

In the middle of the Himalayas, in the north of the Subcontinent, the British drew the Johnson Line (1865) and the McMahon Line (1914) that left in dispute the border areas between China and India/Pakistan. Beyond these boundaries lay the Tibetan plateau and Xinjiang—China's troubled western provinces. Because of the volatile regional politics in this area, the border became highly contested for two reasons. One was the fact that in the past this region had served as a second buffer zone for the British Raj in India, coming under its sole control. The other was the political dynamics created by the Chinese military occupation on Xinjiang's indigenous Muslim population, with its inherent potential for spillover into the disputed territory of Kashmir.

While Pakistan inherited the rough borderlands with Afghanistan in the northwest, India was now responsible for dealing with the complex northeastern tribal region. The difficult tropical geography complicated the security problems for India with neighboring Burma (now Myanmar) and East Pakistan (now Bangladesh), while China claimed parts of the territory known as the North-East Frontier Agency (NEFA, now the Indian state of Arunachal Pradesh). India's northeastern region—connected to India via the Siliguri Corridor—comprises seven sister states (Arunachal Pradesh, Assam, Manipur, Meghalaya, Mizoram, Nagaland, and Tripura), many of which wanted to secede and demanded the right to self-determination. In sum, while India's heartland was geographically protected (or constrained), Pakistan represented a gateway into the Subcontinent in a new world order balanced between the Soviet Union and the United States, dancing to the tune of the superpowers' geopolitical competition. From the very start, then, an extremely complex set of security issues lay on the doorsteps of newly independent India and Pakistan, all of which have become more complicated over time, aggravating the internal security situation as well as relations with neighboring states.

Throughout the Cold War, the bipolar international system had an enormous impact on South Asia. India and Pakistan were unable to resolve any of their conflicts, and—rather than healing—the wounds of Partition festered and settled deeper with the passing of each decade.

New Conflicts, Old Enmities

For the first two decades after independence, India remained preoccupied by its need to use force internally for domestic consolidation, and it also pushed its borders outward to assert its claims. On its northern disputed borders with China, India's aggressive forward policy resulted in a short war in October 1962, ending with the humiliating defeat of the Indian forces in the Himalayas. The 1962 war has left a huge scar on India's psyche, damaging its national pride, and laying the foundations for bitter rivalry between China and India; this has had profound implications for the regional balance of power and alliances within South Asia.

The outcome of the border war between China and India alarmed the smaller nations in South Asia that were looking to India for leadership. India's dismal handling of the crisis with its stronger neighbor and its failure to resolve conflicts with its weaker ones, especially Pakistan, set the pattern for India's neighborhood security policy into the future.

As the next 70 years would show, India's regional policies drove South Asian states toward external major powers as they searched for a power balance against dominating India, rather than embracing India as their South Asian brother with a shared historical and cultural heritage.

Distilled to its most salient essence, behind the backdrop of conflict between India and Pakistan lies a history of mutual exploitation and opportunism, which has been both the cause and the result of an environment of animosity and suspicion.

Kashmir, Junagadh, and Hyderabad

Under the broad principles of Partition were two conflicting concepts: (1) the geographical contiguity of Muslim areas with Pakistan; and (2) the choice given to the princely states of Jammu and Kashmir to join with either India or Pakistan. Both Jammu and Kashmir (treated as a single region) were majority Muslim states and their territory was contiguous with that of Pakistan. For Pakistan it therefore seemed natural that Kashmir, with its majority Muslim population, should choose to merge with its neighbor. Nonetheless, the last Hindu maharaja of Kashmir, Hari Singh, procrastinated on joining either side.[31] India claims that the maharaja eventually chose to join India under the "instrument of accession," a decision which Pakistan rejects, accusing India of coercing him to sign the agreement. As a result, war erupted in 1948, leading to the division of Kashmir. Nearly two-thirds of the region (in the east and south) became the Indian-administered state of Jammu and Kashmir, while the remaining third (in the west and north) became Pakistan-administered Azad Kashmir. The northeastern portion of Indian Kashmir (Ladakh) and the northern portion of Pakistani Kashmir (Gilgit-Baltistan) border China, where territorial disputes continue. China is thus a nominal third party in the Kashmir dispute, but only regarding limited territories along the line of the border and not as a claimant on Kashmir. Ever since, the struggle over Kashmir and various intrigues have continued to fuel tensions between India and Pakistan.

Just as Kashmir was a majority Muslim state with a Hindu ruler, the states of Junagadh and Hyderabad were the opposite—states with a majority Hindu population and a Muslim ruler. When the Muslim princes of Hyderabad Deccan (in southern India) and Junagadh and Manavadar (in western India) opted to join Pakistan, the Indian army swiftly moved in and forced them into a union with India. Consequently, Pakistan has lived with the rancor of this perceived injustice and double standard ever since.

The First Kashmir War 1948
Whereas the issues of Junagadh and Hyderabad were ephemeral, Kashmir was to become the enduring bone of contention between India and Pakistan. Kashmir was strategically important for Pakistan. At the time of Partition, Kashmir was 77% Muslim, and all the major rivers flowing into Pakistan emanated from Kashmir, linking them geographically. Further, India's occupation of Kashmir would make Pakistan's North-West Frontier Province (NWFP), which had already been claimed by Afghanistan, vulnerable to incursions by the Indian military. Hearing stories of violent oppression by Indian soldiers directed against the Muslims of Kashmir from people fleeing the territory into Pakistan, tribesmen from the border regions of Afghanistan and Pakistan entered the Kashmir Valley in 1947 to wrest back control.[32] At the same time, the Indian army also entered the Kashmir Valley. In the ensuing battle, the Indian forces managed to evict the invading tribesmen from the Kashmir Valley. As the Indian forces moved westward and the tribesmen retreated, they encountered the newly created Pakistani army defending the area, and this resulted in the first Kashmir War. That war eventually ended in a ceasefire in 1948, and the ceasefire line (CFL) was established in 1949 under the aegis of the UN, with Indian and Pakistani forces deployed along both sides. The CFL—or Line of Control (LoC) from 1971—marks the division of the erstwhile princely states of Jammu and Kashmir.

By forcing the accession of Kashmir, India put a population with a Muslim majority under Indian rule. From the Pakistani perspective, such coercion negated the principle of Partition and usurped the right to self-determination for the people of Kashmir. This act sowed the seeds of animosity with Pakistan that led to war in 1948 and again in 1965 as well as a series of military crises that persist to this day. Whereas Pakistan believes it has a moral justification and right to Kashmir, India considers Kashmir to be an integral part of the nation of India and testimony to India's secular credentials.[33]

After the 1962 war between India and China, President John F. Kennedy sent Ambassador Averell Harriman to visit the region to commence a process of resolving the Kashmir dispute, but this went nowhere. Between December 1962 and May 1963, the Indian and Pakistani foreign ministers held six rounds of bilateral talks to reach a settlement on Kashmir. Simultaneously, Pakistan and China quietly engaged in settling their own border dispute. While India and Pakistan failed to reach a settlement, in a dramatic move in March 1963, Pakistan announced that it had reached a border agreement with China, under which Pakistan agreed to cede some 2,050 square miles of Gilgit-Baltistan (also known as the Shaksgam Valley or the Trans-Karakorum Tract) to China. Pakistan's bold diplomatic move upset the United States, which had earlier made it clear to Pakistan that the "US cannot stand by idly while China tries to expand its power in Asia."[34] The US warned Pakistan that it was risking its alliance with the West and that "the sympathy that Pakistan enjoyed from other governments on Kashmir in the United Nations and elsewhere would be dissipated."[35]

The territorial transfer agreed to by Pakistan enabled China to build road links across its western province of Xinjiang and (eventually) road access into Pakistan. Even more importantly, it established an all-weather friendship between Pakistan and China, much to the dismay of India.[36] Meanwhile, across the eastern end of the Himalayas, India remained doggedly defiant of China's desire to unify its western provinces with the NEFA/Arunachal Pradesh. Hence, a negative precedent toward conflict resolution was set in the 1960s, and relations between India and Pakistan have been characterized by coercion and mistrust ever since, complicated by China's significant, albeit indirect, involvement in the South Asian imbroglio.

The Second Kashmir War 1965

On March 30, 1965, India changed Kashmir's status by replacing its local head of state (*sadr-i-riyasat*) with a governor, which implied direct rule from New Delhi and a major step toward Kashmir's absorption into the Indian polity.[37] This removal of Kashmir's legislative authority signaled to Pakistan that India was attempting to accelerate the process of unification. Emboldened by its new alliance with China, Pakistan laid plans to foment an uprising in Kashmir (Operation Gibraltar), to be followed with a military operation (Operation Grand Slam). These operations failed and instead triggered a second war over Kashmir in September 1965. The border drawn by the Radcliffe Commission gave West Pakistan an elongated geography arching northwest of India, leaving it exposed and susceptible to attacks by India. Unlike the 1948 war that was confined to the disputed territory of Kashmir, this time India crossed the international border and attacked Lahore in Pakistan's heartland. The 17-day war ended with a ceasefire, but it greatly heightened the animosity between the two countries.

India's suppression of Kashmiri Muslims and Pakistan's ability to stir up nationalist sentiment and support the periodic Kashmiri uprisings set the pattern for subsequent military crises between the two countries. Pakistan's vulnerability was not only due to the exposure of its western wing to incursion by India but also because India surrounded its eastern wing on the Bay of Bengal from three directions. While Pakistan obsessively focused on uniting Kashmir with itself, the 1965 war proved that its combined geographical weaknesses were greater than the power of its military to defend it. As the crisis over Kashmir waged in the west, East Pakistan was left abandoned, disenchanted, and exposed to the Indian threat.

The Bangladesh War 1971

The 1971 war over East Pakistan (Bangladesh) stands out to Pakistan as proof of India's refusal to accept the terms of Partition and India's determination to further truncate its "ill-created and temporary" neighbor whenever possible. The division of Pakistan into two ethnically divergent wings (East Pakistan and West Pakistan) provided India with the perfect opportunity to exploit the geographical and demographic gaps in the precarious situation. In 1970, Pakistan's military regime held general elections across both parts of the country that resulted in an absolute majority win for the Awami League, led by Sheikh Mujib-ur Rehman, in East Pakistan. In West Pakistan, the Pakistan People's Party, led by Zulfiqar Ali Bhutto, won the majority. The military regime under President Yahya Khan, a general, was unable to bring the two leaders to agreement, and the regime's refusal to hand over power resulted in a rebellion in East Pakistan. The Pakistan army's subsequent crackdown led to a civil war that lasted throughout 1971, causing thousands of refugees to flee to India and giving India cause to support the rebels against the military regime.

At the peak of the crisis in August 1971, India signed a "treaty of friendship" with the Soviet Union, enabling India to intervene in East Pakistan with impunity. The situation in East Pakistan was one of social turmoil, during which the army's refusal to hand power to the elected representatives of East Pakistan's ethnic majority combined with years of anger and unhappiness over the unequal distribution of resources between Pakistan's two halves. This was what India had seemingly been waiting for, as renowned strategist K. Subrahmanyam described it, "an opportunity the like of which would never come again."[38]

In November 1971, tens of thousands of Mukti Bahini (Freedom Force) fighters alongside the Indian military invaded East Pakistan. Pakistan's beleaguered military garrison defended East Pakistan for nearly three weeks, but in the end it was overwhelmed. On December 3, 1971, Pakistan then opened fire on its western front in West Pakistan and the CFL in

Kashmir, hoping to reverse Indian advances into East Pakistan. For two weeks India and Pakistan were engaged in total war, which ended with a humiliating surrender by Pakistani troops in East Pakistan and an exchange of territories across the CFL. East Pakistan ceased to be part of Pakistan, and the new country of Bangladesh was born. India achieved a resounding success in its desire to dismember and humiliate Pakistan.[39]

Whether the 1971 war resulted from the flood of Bengali refugees streaming into India from Bangladesh (as India claims), or India's ambition to (literally) cut its rival down to size, does not actually matter. As a result of the debacle, Pakistan lost a sizeable amount of territory, Bangladesh became an independent country, and one more indelible mark was added to Pakistani threat perceptions, with significant consequences for the subsequent history of the Subcontinent.

NUCLEAR SHADOWS, TERRORIST THREATS

India and Pakistan signed a peace accord in July 1972 at Simla, which heralded an era of relative peace and improved relations between India and Pakistan (for a brief period). Under the accord, the 1949 Ceasefire Line (CFL) was renamed the Line of Control (LoC). Unlike the end of the 1965 war, when both forces returned to their previous position on the CFL, this time India refused to return to the same position and instead forced Pakistan to agree to the new positions held at the end of the 1971 war. The LoC represented the new defense positions of the Indian and Pakistani militaries in Kashmir. Both the CFL and the LoC demarcated an arc stretching from near Chamb (Jammu) in the south for about 500 miles north and northeastwards to a point on map coordinate NJ 9842. At its southern end, there is a stretch of about 124 miles that in pre-independence days formed the boundary between the princely state of Kashmir on its eastern side and the state of Punjab (now Pakistan) to the west. In Pakistan, this stretch of land is referred to as the "working boundary," whereas India regards it as an international border.

The CFL/ LoC was not extended beyond NJ 9842 and stopped well short of the border with China that lies some 40 miles to the north. Beyond this point are glaciers and high mountainous terrain that was assumed to be inaccessible; for this reason, a vague terminology "thence northwards" was inserted into the new LoC boundary under the 1972 Simla Agreement. Overall, there are three distinct boundary issues in the division of Kashmir that continue to vex India and Pakistan: 40 miles without demarcation north of the border with China; 500 miles of the CFL/LoC; and 124 miles of "working boundary."[40]

Under the terms of the 1949 Karachi Agreement and the 1972 Simla Agreement, certain "ground rules" were established to regulate activities along the LoC. Accordingly, in high-altitude locations along the LoC and in non-demarcated areas both sides are to temporarily withdraw from their untenable posts during the winter months, which they then reoccupy in the summer. Nevertheless, ambiguities around the non-demarcation of the LoC sowed the seeds for future conflicts in these areas.

The Siachen Glacier and Kargil Conflicts

In 1984, Indian forces occupied the Siachen Glacier, a frozen area beyond NJ 9842, located in the non-demarcated area. India justified the action as a preemptive operation before Pakistan did the same. Pakistani forces rushed to occupy the remaining part of the glacier, and since then both sides have been locked in a face-off on the frozen heights of the Saltaro range in the Karakorum Mountains. India's operation was the first of its kind that ended the unspoken agreement by which both sides had upheld the inviolability of the LoC in Kashmir and respected the spirit of the 1972 Simla peace accord. As a sequel to the occupation of the Siachen Glacier, Indian and Pakistani forces continue to jockey for improving their defensive positions, always keeping a vigilant eye on the posts vacated during the winter retreat or poorly held locations anywhere along the LoC.

The (mutual) nibbling at remote posts set a new precedent of tactical opportunism and a new norm of hostility: creeping forward and over-powering weakly guarded areas (irrespective of treaties and agreements), which would previously have been completely out of character for the two otherwise disciplined armies. As far as India was concerned, it was retaking areas that belonged to "Indian Kashmir." To the Pakistanis, this was yet another manifestation of Indian aggression against Pakistan, and it reaffirmed the notion that India would exploit any gap or weakness if the opportunity arose. The occupation of Siachen added another layer to the bedrock of future crises.

A few years later, India would be confronted with the same type of opportunism it had itself patented in the Siachen Glacier.[41] In 1999, groups fighting for Kashmir's independence from India (Mujahidin), backed by the Pakistan Northern Light Infantry, exploited the gaps and vacant positions left by India in the Kargil sector of Kashmir, resulting in a limited war. The Kargil conflict resulted in many casualties on both sides and was eventually halted through US intervention. More significantly, however, it brought a new dimension to the nature of military crisis and war in the region, in that it was the first high-intensity conflict to occur since India and Pakistan had carried out their nuclear tests.

Cross-border Terrorism: Military Standoffs and Doctrinal Shifts

In the debates on nuclear proliferation, optimists hypothesized that nuclear weapons would decrease the incidence of conflict between the two states, pointing to the fact that the last major war between India and Pakistan occurred in 1971, long before either country wielded an operational nuclear deterrent. However, the nuclearization of the Subcontinent has instead been correlated with an increased incidence of militarized crises, starting with the 1999 Kargil conflict and continuing with the 2001–2002 "Twin Peaks" standoff. The latter was ignited when terrorists attacked the Indian parliament building in New Delhi in an operation that was traced to the Pakistan-based terrorist organization

Jaish-e-Muhammad (JeM). The crisis extended over ten months with two "peak" periods: the first from December 2001 to January 2002, and the second from May to June 2002.

A second militarized crisis manifested after the 2008 Mumbai terrorist attacks on India's financial capital, which was traced to another Pakistan-based group, Lashkar-e-Tayyaba (LeT), and which New Delhi blamed on Pakistani malfeasance. Unlike the "Twin Peaks" crisis, the Mumbai terror attack did not result in mass military mobilizations or cross-border retaliation. Nonetheless, it derailed the backdoor channels for negotiating peace and security deals. Since then, frequent ceasefire violations (e.g., small arms fire and artillery shelling) along the LoC have continued. After the Modi government came to power in 2014, a series of crises across Kashmir—in Pathankot, Uri, and Pulwama-Balakot—which were greater in intensity and frequency, brought the two nuclear-armed countries close to the brink.

Terrorist attacks did not only occur in India but caused mayhem all over Pakistan as well. Hundreds of grisly suicide attacks on the security forces, military bases, hotels, and bazaars (including, for example, the Islamabad Marriot Hotel in 2008, Karachi Airport in 2014, and the Peshawar Army Public School in 2014) were carried out with impunity across the country and were traced to homegrown extremists and cross-border attacks from Afghanistan with links to the Indian intelligence services operating from Iran and Afghanistan.

HEADS I WIN / TAILS YOU LOSE

Perceptions, formed through often painful experiences, can persist and become even more intense when the experiences are accompanied by a sense of injustice, especially if the weaker victim is given to believe that the stronger perpetrator has "gotten away with it." Over time, such perceptions turn into cognitive constructs which breed intolerance, hatred, and a refusal to compromise.

Since the end of the British Raj, security perceptions on the Subcontinent have been shaped by the staunch belief of victimhood and injustice. In the Indian narrative, Great Britain looted it of its wealth and unfairly partitioned the country, leaving it weaker post-independence. Within this same narrative, the Western powers emboldened India's archrival Pakistan by bolstering its military power—threatening India in the process and undercutting democracy and civilian rule.

From Pakistan's perspective, the unjust Partition is equally to blame for creating, as famously expressed in Jinnah's words, a "truncated or mutilated moth-eaten Pakistan," that Britain and India set up to fail.[42] The fate of Muslim-majority Kashmir was decided on the whim of a Hindu maharaja, and the decisions concerning the fates of Hyderabad and Junagadh were also not in Pakistan's favor. India's role in the breakaway of East Pakistan in 1971 heightened Pakistan's mistrust of India and its perceived sense of injustice. In the Pakistani narrative, it has consistently seen India getting away with aggression, exploitation, and destabilization. It is a case of India winning and Pakistan losing.

As each decade passed, Pakistan saw its major Western allies move closer to India. Pakistan's collective memory is steeped in the subjectivity and consistency with which Pakistan is penalized, but never India. The regularity with which the international community has dismissed Pakistan's concerns on a wide spectrum of political and security questions has left Pakistan bitter, exacerbating its sense of injustice and pushing Islamabad toward hyperrealist policies. Disappointed by the capriciousness of the West's international system, which seemed to favor the strong (India) while caring little for the weak (Pakistan) amongst its allies, Pakistan abandoned relying on Western allies for its national security and set out to acquire its own nuclear capability to guarantee its national survival.

Despite its inherent structural weaknesses, geophysical vulnerabilities, and smaller size and power, Pakistan is the only country in South Asia that challenges India's hegemony. Meanwhile, smaller South Asian powers are looking beyond the region to other major powers to safeguard their security, as they attempt to steer clear of getting entangled in the India-Pakistan competition or getting pressured by their "big brother," India.[43]

Each of the crises outlined in this chapter has influenced the military strategies and technical military advances of both Pakistan and India, with profound implications for the strategic stability of South Asia. Subsequent chapters will further analyze the grand strategies and evolution of these military doctrines as the two countries adapt to the changing characteristics of war in the twenty-first century. What seems clear in 2022, however, is that nuclear weapons have failed to prevent coercion or armed conflict between India and Pakistan; both countries continue to invest heavily in their conventional and nuclear arsenals, while the triggers that could set off a major military crisis under the nuclear shadow continue to multiply.

NOTES

1. Peter Popham, "The World's Most Dangerous Place Is Already at War," *The Independent*, March 18, 2000, https://www.independent.co.uk/news/world/asia/the-worlds-most-dangerous-place-is-already-at-war-282458.html.

2. Cohen later introduced the "paired minorities" concept in two of his books: Stephen P. Cohen, *Shooting for a Century: The India-Pakistan Conundrum* (Washington, DC: Brookings Institution Press, 2013), and Stephen P. Cohen, *India: Emerging Power* (Washington, DC: Brookings Institution Press, 2001), 198.

3. Cohen, *Shooting for a Century*, 130–131.

4. For an examination of the enduring rivalry, see T. V. Paul, "Causes of the India-Pakistan Enduring Rivalry," in *The India-Pakistan Conflict: An Enduring Rivalry* (New York: Cambridge University Press, 2005), 3–24.

5. Cited in Waheed uz-Zaman, *Towards Pakistan* (Lahore: Publishers United, 1969), 132.

6. It was in this speech to the All-India Muslim League at Allahabad on December 29, 1930, that Iqbal first propounded the idea of Pakistan. Muhammad Iqbal, "Sir Muhammad Iqbal's 1930 Presidential Address," in *Speeches, Writings, and Statements of Iqbal*, 2nd edition (revised), ed. Latif Ahmed Sherwani (Lahore: Iqbal Academy, 1977 [1944]), 3–26, http://www.columbia.edu/itc/mealac/pritchett/00islamlinks/txt_iqbal_1930.html.

7. Samuel M. Burke and Lawrence Ziring, *Pakistan Foreign Policy: An Historical Analysis* (Karachi: Oxford University Press, 1973), 55.

8. Burke and Ziring, *Pakistan Foreign Policy*, 56.

9. Personal interview with Muhammad Ali Jinnah by Eric Strieff, special correspondent of the *Neue Zürcher Zeitung*, March 11, 1948, cited in Sharif Al Mujahid and Liaquat Merchant, eds., *Quotes from the Quaid* (Karachi: Oxford University Press, 2007), 133.

10. Waheed uz-Zaman, *Towards Pakistan*, 132.

11. Ashok K. Behuria and Sushant Sareen, "Pakistan: Chronic Instability and India's Options," in *India's Neighbourhood: Challenges in the Next Two Decades*, ed. Rumel Dahiya and Ashok K. Behuria (New Delhi: Institute for Defence Studies and Analyses, 2012), xxvii–xxviii, 163–164, https://idsa.in/system/files/book/book_IndiaNeighbourhood.pdf.

12. "Simla Agreement Resulted in 'Revanchist' Pak, J&K Problems," NDTV, November 15, 2019, https://www.ndtv.com/india-news/external-affairs-minister-s-jaishankar-says-simla-agreement-resulted-in-revanchist-pakistan-problems-2132747.

13. Shirin Tahir-Kheli, *India, Pakistan, and the United States: Breaking with the Past* (Washington, DC: Council on Foreign Relations, 1997), 30.

14. Muhammad Ali Jinnah, *Jinnah Speeches and Statements 1947–1948* (New York: Oxford University Press, 2000), 25–29.

15. Anwar Hussain Syed, *Pakistan: Islam, Politics, and National Solidarity* (New York: Praeger, 1982), 34.

16. Stephen P. Cohen, *The South Asia Papers: A Critical Anthology of Writings* (Washington, DC: Brookings Institution Press, 2016), 186.

17. Chaudhry Muhammad Ali, *The Emergence of Pakistan* (Lahore: Research Society of Pakistan, 2009), 4.

18. Sunil Khilnani, *The Idea of India* (New York: Farrar, Strauss & Giroux, 1999), 31.

19. Sardar Patel, however, had no respect for the Rashtriya Swayamsevak Sangh (RSS) organization, which was behind the assassination for Mahatama Gandhi. The current Bharatiya Janata Party (BJP) regime, however, attempts to use Patel as their icon to counter Nehru and Gandhi as the leaders of the freedom struggle. I am indebted to Dr Sharad Joshi, professor at Middlebury Institue for International Studies, Monterey, California, for this insight.

20. The term "saffronization" is borrowed from Khilnani, *The Idea of India*, 9. See also Snigdha Jain, "BJP and Its Hindutva Politics: The Slow Saffronisation of India," *Week*, April 25, 2018, https://www.theweek.in/news/india/2018/04/25/bjp-and-its-hindutva-politics-the-slow-saffronisation-of-india.html.

21. Bilal Kuchay, "Hate Campaign in India against Urdu for being a Muslim language," Aljazeera, October 27, 2021, https://www.aljazeera.com/news/2021/10/27/india-urdu-hindu-groups-hate-campaign-muslim-language-fabindia ; Mina Anand, "Urdu is not the enemy, bigotry is", *The Indian Express,* Octocber 24, 2021, https://indianexpress.com/article/opinion/columns/urdu-is-not-the-enemy-bigotry-is-7585665/

22. See "Ayodhya Verdict: Indian Top Court Gives Holy Site to Hindus," BBC News, November 9, 2019, https://www.bbc.com/news/world-asia-india-50355775.

23. Khaled Ahmed, *Sectarian War: Pakistan's Shia-Sunni War and its Links to the Middle East*, 2011; Alizeh Kohari, "Acts of faith: Why people get

killed over blasphemy in Pakistan," *Herald*, September 11, 2016; C. Christine Fair, "Explaining Support for Sectarian Terrorism in Pakistan: Piety, Maslak, and Sharia," *Religions* 6 (2015): 1137–1167.

24. Salman Masood and Carlotta Gall, " Killing of Governor Deepens Crisis in Pakistan," *New York Times*, January 4, 2011, https://www.nytimes.com/2011/01/05/world/asia/05pakistan.html; "Pakistan Courts hangs Mumtaz Qadri for Murder of Salman Taseer," Al Jazeera, February 29, 2016, https://www.aljazeera.com/news/2016/2/29/pakistan-hangs-mumtaz-qadri-for-murder-of-salman-taseer. See also Madeeha Anwar "Convicted Murderer's Grave in Pakistan Becomes Shrine for Some," VOA Extremist Watch, March 25, 2017, https://www.voanews.com/a/convisted-murders-grave-becomes-pakistan-shrine/3781717.html.

25. Niloufer Siddiqui, "Sectarian Violence and Intolerance in Pakistan," Middle East Institute, Policy Analysis, May 26, 2015, https://www.mei.edu/publications/sectarian-violence-and-intolerance-pakistan.

26. Farahnaz Ispahani, "Religious Intolerance in Pakistan and the Plight of Religious Minorities," Woodrow Wilson Center, discussion, June 4, 2014, https://www.wilsoncenter.org/event/religious-intolerance-pakistan-and-the-plight-religious-minorities.

27. Stephen P. Cohen, *India: Emerging Power* (Washington, DC: Brookings Institution Press, 2001), 198–199.

28. Sunil Khilnani, personal communication, December 4, 2001. Khilnani was writing a biography of Jawaharlal Nehru at the time.

29. For a commentary, see Vartan Gregorian, "The Yearnings of the Pashtuns," *New York Times*, November 15, 2001, A31. See also Vartan Gregorian, *The Emergence of Modern Afghanistan: Politics of Reform and Modernization, 1880–1946* (Palo Alto, CA: Stanford University Press, 1969).

30. Feroz Hassan Khan, "The Durand Line: Tribal Politics and Pakistan-Afghanistan Relations," in Thomas H. Johnson and Barry Scott Zellen, eds., *Culture, Conflict, and Counterinsurgency* (Palo Alto, CA: Stanford University Press, 2014), 148–175.

31. Stanley Wolpert, *Jinnah of Pakistan* (New York: Oxford University Press, 1984), 135.

32. From the mid-nineteenth century, Kashmir was ruled by a despotic regime which enforced Hindu religious laws among the predominantly Muslim population. Oppression of Muslims continued throughout the British Raj, during Partition, and then into the Indian occupation.

33. Both India and Pakistan consider the portion of Kashmir under the other's control as "occupied territory." Thus, in Indian literature it is

referred to as "Pakistan-occupied Kashmir," and in Pakistani literature it is "Indian-held Kashmir."

34. Dennis Kux, *The United States and Pakistan 1947–2000: Disenchanted Allies* (Washington, DC: Woodrow Wilson Center Press, 2001), 133.

35. Kux, *Disenchanted Allies*, 139.

36. The Pakistani leadership believed it had China on its side in the event of conflict with India. As Foreign Minister Zulfiqar Ali Bhutto stated in parliament, "An attack from India on Pakistan involves the territorial integrity and security of the largest state in Asia." Cited in John W. Garver, *Protracted Contest: Sino-Indian Rivalry in the Twentieth Century* (Seattle: University of Washington Press, 2001), 192–193.

37. Sumit Ganguly, *Conflict Unending: India-Pakistan Tensions since 1947* (New York: Columbia University Press, 2002), 35.

38. K. Subrahmanyam in *National Herald*, New Delhi, April 5, 1971, cited in Kux, *Disenchanted Allies*.

39. For a detailed account, see Richard Sisson and Leo E. Rose, *War and Secession: India, Pakistan, and Bangladesh* (Berkeley: University of California Press, 1990).

40. Robert G. Wirsing, *India, Pakistan, and the Kashmir Dispute* (New York: St. Martin's Press, 1994) 75–76.

41. Zafar Cheema, "The Strategic Context of the Kargil Conflict: A Pakistani Perspective," in *Asymmetric Wars in South Asia: The Causes and Consequences of the Kargil Conflict*, ed. Peter Lavoy (New York: Cambridge University Press, 2009), 41–63.

42. "Jinnah on Partition," Text of Mr. Jinnah's Statement on Move to Partition Punjab and Bengal, I and B Department, New Delhi, May 4, 1947, *The National Archives*, https://www.nationalarchives.gov.uk/education/resources/the-road-to-partition/jinnah-partition/.

43. Remarks of a senior Sri Lankan participant in a Track II dialogue on the Indian Ocean in Hua Hin, Thailand, in November 2019. The term "big brother" colloquially refers to India's interference and intervention in Sri Lankan domestic affairs and its encroachment in Sri Lankan territorial waters. Indian participants rejected the allegations.

CHAPTER 2

THE DRIFT

AN APPRAISAL OF INDIA AND PAKISTAN'S SECURITY COMPETITION

By May 1998, when India and Pakistan shocked the international community by conducting back-to-back nuclear tests, both countries had enjoyed only five decades of independence. Nonetheless, despite their tumultuous history of three major wars and several military crises, the 1998 nuclear tests spawned a forlorn hope that the sheer destructive power of nuclear weapons might foreclose the possibility of a future armed conflict between these enduring rivals and force them to reach some form of *modus vivendi*. At a minimum, some believed that the promise of mutually assured destruction would have a sobering effect on their respective foreign and domestic security policymaking and prompt New Delhi and Islamabad to adopt a more circumspect approach toward their bilateral affairs.

Unfortunately, these hopes were dashed just a year later with the eruption of the Kargil conflict in the disputed heights of Kashmir. Although casualties were high on both sides, the hostilities remained geographically limited. The lessons that India and Pakistan took away from Kargil were distressing, in that India reassured itself that it could fight and win a limited conventional war against its nuclear-armed opponent, whereas Pakistan reinforced its belief that possession of nuclear weapons successfully deterred India from escalating the conflict.[1]

In the two decades since the Kargil conflict, there has been a series of further military crises, the most recent of which occurred in February 2019, leading to an aerial dogfight and the shooting down of two Indian aircraft, coupled with veiled Indian threats of escalation and deployment of India's sea-based nuclear deterrent (there was the widespread belief that both India and Pakistan put their nuclear forces on standby). Such volatility in a nuclear-armed region beset with a complex history of conflict poses a significantly different set of challenges for the concept of strategic stability, as compared to the Cold War era. Consequently, the concept has been somewhat redefined in the India-Pakistan context, epitomizing what is often called the "second nuclear age."[2]

STRATEGIC STABILITY IN THE SECOND NUCLEAR AGE

Strategic stability does not have a universal definition. During the Cold War, the term had many contending interpretations.[3] Among others, Thomas Schelling and Morton Halperin defined strategic stability as a dyadic contest where the risk of war is low and "neither side has an incentive to strike first," and where both are "reasonably secure against shocks, alarms and perturbations."[4] More recently, Lawrence Rubin and Adam Stulberg described strategic stability as a common frame of reference that recognizes the destructiveness of nuclear weapons among rivals possessing them. Rather than seeking surprise and victory, the "crux of strategic stability rests with reducing the need and incentives for *arms racing* or delivering a devastating first blow in a *crisis*" (emphasis added).[5]

Some Indian strategic thinkers have proposed three conditions for stability between nations: (1) the absence of conditions to be the first to use nuclear weapons (crisis stability); (2) the absence of incentives to build a nuclear force (arms race stability); and (3) the absence of armed conflict between nuclear-armed states where the states enjoy peaceful and harmonious relations.[6] The situation in South Asia defies all three conditions for stability. Given the entrenched ideological differences between India and Pakistan, the intensity of the conflict over Kashmir, and the frequency of militarized crises, relations are perpetually tempestuous and both countries on the brink of war. India and Pakistan could easily stumble into a nuclear war through the escalation of a conventional one.

While both countries continue to expand and modernize their nuclear arsenals, the India-Pakistan conflict is compounded by several variables that do not exist in other parts of the world: wild cards in the form of non-state actors (mostly religious extremists); the use of proxies to fight sub-conventional wars; a conventional military imbalance in a geographically asymmetric environment; and variance in their respective nuclear doctrines. The intersection with a third nuclear power—China —further complicates these conditions by creating a strategic triangular context in South Asia which is even more complex and difficult to define, especially when twenty-first-century technological innovations are also added into the mix. As South Asia drifts further from the ideal type in international relations, the security competition between the two nuclear-armed rivals continues to intensify. Fissile material production is expanding rapidly in both countries, and a suite of new delivery systems with nuclear capability—including sea-based deterrence and tactical nuclear weapons—is in the pipeline.

Even as nuclear weapons capabilities are increasing and both sides are doubling their investment in nuclear deterrence, neither side seems willing to dissuade the other from conflict or to reach détente. The truth is that operational nuclear deterrents have signally failed to resolve the fundamental irritants in the bilateral relationship. At the same time, global strategic shifts do not bode well for stability in the region. India and Pakistan's security competition can only be expected to intensify as Pakistan watches Washington's strategic overtures to India and, fearing abandonment, strengthens its strategic relationship with China. To make matters worse, the Subcontinent's proximity to the Middle East and Asia Pacific means that every tension, crisis, and conflict between India and Pakistan will invariably influence the strategic dynamics and balance-of-power calculations in these wider regions. Amongst others, South Asia's precarious drift away from the international mainstream could potentially affect—and even disrupt—US intentions to rebalance toward the Asia Pacific.

Turning now to an examination of the roots of India and Pakistan's strategic (in)stability, I adopt a "levels of analysis" approach to identify the systemic, bilateral, and domestic-level irritants in this relationship. At the system level, the evolving international balance of power indicates that two adversarial coalitions are in the offing—the United States and India on the one hand, and China and Pakistan on the other. Such a pairing, if it emerges, would severely impact the entrenched India-Pakistan rivalry that has become increasingly caustic over the past few years, which neither the United States nor China would want to be drawn into. Discussion of bilateral factors is kept deliberately brief here, as the rest of the book delves more deeply into the causes and consequences of the Subcontinent's nuclear contest. The analysis of factors at the domestic level reveals how cognitive biases, organizational pathologies, and domestic politics all work to stimulate security competition in South Asia. Of particular significance is the role of strategic enclaves in both countries that contrive to control the narrative, enhance nationalist sentiment, and stymie all prospects for alternative futures.

System Level

The outlook for stability between India and Pakistan is dampened by the evolving balance of power in Asia. China's meteoric economic growth has catapulted it to great power status. Beijing is investing heavily in its military—particularly its navy—to project power, exert influence, and protect its seaborne energy and commercial shipping lanes, many of which traverse the Indian Ocean. Developing alongside Beijing's expanding power is its growing confidence to uncompromisingly assert its claims to disputed territories on China's periphery—prominent among these are territories in Aksai Chin and the entire Indian province of Arunachal Pradesh. Recalling India's defeat in its 1962 border war with China, Indian security managers observe these developments with alarm.

Meanwhile, China-Pakistan relations are closer than ever. The two countries are cooperating on a host of development projects, collectively known as the China-Pakistan Economic Corridor (CPEC), which is touted as the flagship of China's Belt and Road Initiative (BRI) linking landlocked Central Asia with outlets through the Arabian Sea into the Indian Ocean. China's major investments include infrastructural expansion in Pakistan's northern hinterlands and southern provinces, defense research and development, and support for Pakistan's civil nuclear energy program. Whereas Pakistan hails its relationship with China as "deeper than the oceans" and "higher than the Himalayas," New Delhi interprets the partnership as collusion—a deliberate effort to encircle and contain India. In this analysis, Beijing is essentially a wedge driving India and Pakistan further apart. As China continues to rise and deepen its cooperation with Pakistan, India-Pakistan and China-India relations will likely deteriorate further.[7]

Another ongoing development which has a significant bearing on India and Pakistan's stability is the broadening of US-India relations. Islamabad is alarmed at Washington's determination to deepen its strategic relationship with India. One sign of this occurred a decade or so ago, when the United States spearheaded the mainstreaming of India's nuclear ambitions by creating a new "exceptional status" for a non-Nuclear Proliferation Treaty member under the Hyde Act of 2008. US-India relations were further cemented during President Barack Obama's visit to New Delhi in early 2015, and topics for discussion included a 10-year defense framework agreement (signed in June 2015) and the operationalization of the US-India Civil Nuclear Agreement. The Trump administration (2017–2020) took the US-India strategic partnership to a new level with the signing of several strategic agreements. These included the US-India Logistics Exchange Memorandum of Agreement (LEMOA) in 2016 and the Communications Compatibility and Security Agreement (COMCASA) in 2018 that "will facilitate access to advanced defense systems and enable India to optimally utilize its existing US-origin platforms."[8] In October 2020, India and the United States signed the Basic Exchange and Cooperation Agreement (BECA) for geospatial cooperation. These developments significantly shift the offense-defense balance further in favor of India, that in turn will push Islamabad even deeper into the Chinese camp to offset this imbalance.

For many years, the United States has been a key provider of aid—both economic and military—to Pakistan. However, Islamabad now fears its strategic relevance to the United States is waning, as Washington turns its attention toward the Asia Pacific amid mounting geopolitical tensions with an assertive China and revanchist Russia. Signs of Pakistan's declining importance for Washington began with President Donald Trump's policy speech on Afghanistan on August 21, 2017, publication of the US national security strategy in December 2017, and a public reprimand of Pakistan in a presidential tweet on January 1, 2018, which coincided with an intense military operational surge to defeat the Taliban in Afghanistan.[9] The surge eventually failed and forced the United States to commence talks for a negotiated settlement and eventual withdrawal from Afghanistan.[10]

The Trump administration also asked India to step up its support for the United States to help it achieve its goals, signaling to the world that India is the linchpin for the United States' balancing strategy in the Asia Pacific theatre.[11] The growing coziness between Washington and New Delhi has prompted Pakistan to hedge its bets and double down on enlisting China as an alternative benefactor, much to India's annoyance. The Biden administration that took office in early 2021 will likely review all the pieces on the global chessboard, and this could include revisiting US priorities in the wider Asian context.

Bilateral Level

At the bilateral level, two key factors undermine the outlook for long-term stability between India and Pakistan. The first is the two nations' enduring rivalry, spawned during the ugly experience of Partition in 1947, maintained by competing ideologies, reinforced through unresolved territorial disputes and sporadic militarized crises, and continued through the covert deployment of violent and increasingly autonomous militant groups as proxy tools behind state lines—allegedly a tactic used by the intelligence agencies of both countries.

The second significant factor is the poor economic connectivity between India and Pakistan. There is a rich body of academic literature that empirically establishes that economically interdependent countries are less likely to go to war with one another than those with fewer economic ties. Unfortunately for South Asia, trade between India and Pakistan is woefully curtailed and undercapitalized. The international border and the Line of Control between India and Pakistan are heavily militarized and mostly closed off to civilian traffic. Despite its rapidly growing economy and need for access to external markets and natural resources, India abstains from anything that would link it culturally to Pakistan—including trade routes—as a punitive policy to isolate Islamabad. Seeking access to the resource-rich Central Asian republics, Indian commerce does not take the obvious way through Pakistan. Instead, it routes through alternate pathways, particularly through the Iranian port of Chabahar, which provides India with an overland link to Afghanistan, Kazakhstan, Tajikistan, and the broader region. India is also looking to expand its trade relationships with Southeast Asia in a renewed push to develop its decades-old "Look East" policy and turn it into the "Act East" initiative that reflects current priorities in New Delhi.

It seems, then, that India is looking to expand economic cooperation with everyone but its western neighbor. India and Pakistan are not completely devoid of bilateral trade, but the tonnage is anemic, and what little trade does flow between them is frequently throttled or cut off during periods of crisis and tension. In fact, India exports more merchandise to the city-state of Singapore (population 5.4 million) than to the *entire country* of Pakistan (population 220 million).[12] Similarly, Pakistan has a more prosperous commercial relationship with war-torn Afghanistan (population 30.6 million) than with India (population 1.25 billion).[13] These factors not only limit prosperity and economic interdependence in South Asia, but they also hinder the formation of interpersonal ties between Indians and Pakistanis. The Byzantine India-Pakistan visa regime serves a similar stonewalling function. So long as India and Pakistan remain commercially disjointed and socially estranged, future confrontation and conflict between the two is unlikely to be tempered by economic calculations.

It is common for rising powers to be concerned with their level of prestige in the international community. As their economies and militaries grow, so does their sense of political entitlement, and they often seek deference from their smaller neighbors. Some rising powers are inclined to cast a wide net of diplomatic and military muscle in their neighborhood (and beyond) to proactively safeguard their perceived national interests. Viewing itself as a rising power, India believes that its rightful sphere of influence spans the whole of the Indian Ocean, from the Gulf of Aden to the Strait of Malacca. It seeks primacy over this maritime domain and a leadership role in South Asia. In this worldview, India regards China as its peer in the great power competition and Pakistan as a lesser power —the proverbial thorn in the tiger's paw.

India pays close attention to Beijing's actions and directs the bulk of its resources and strategic faculties toward countering China. For example, India's modernization of its nuclear forces is aimed primarily at deterring aggression from the increasingly capable army, navy, and air force of the People's Republic of China. Even as India increases its nuclear stockpile, it shows little concern for how Pakistan might react. New Delhi's dismissive hubris vis-à-vis Pakistan is rooted in India's rising power status, its military dominance over Pakistan, and its historical record of prevailing over its rival in every armed conflict since 1971.

Pakistani strategic thinking tends to view everything through an India-centric lens. Pakistan sees itself as an underdog, awkwardly juxtaposed against a hostile and dominant military power on its doorstep. This guarded worldview paints India as a regional hegemon itching for an opportunity to inflict a major military defeat on Pakistan. Pakistanis view their armed forces as the heroic vanguard against Indian and foreign encroachment, and they are generally skeptical of their elected civilian government, which is seen as corrupt and disconnected from the struggles of everyday people. Four times in its history, Pakistan's populace welcomed the military seizure of power from the elected civilian government during a crisis. In line with this disposition, Pakistanis perceive their nuclear arsenal as a monumental feat of national resolve and technical mastery that has guaranteed the survival of the Pakistani state against a determined enemy bent upon its subjugation.

In the final analysis, these cognitive biases strongly suggest that India will continue to develop its nuclear and conventional arsenals to hedge against China's growing military might, with little regard for Pakistan's strategic anxieties. Meanwhile, fearing the worst of Indian intentions, Islamabad will augment its own nuclear arsenal to keep pace with New Delhi in the hope of deterring hostilities. In short, the mutually perceived prejudice is steering both India and Pakistan toward security-centric policies that serve only to exacerbate their rivalry and mutual mistrust.

Domestic Level
At the domestic level of analysis, the examination reveals a plethora of additional irritants in the India-Pakistan relationship. As already noted, and as the next chapters will illustrate, both New Delhi and Islamabad tend to perceive their surroundings and each other through unique cognitive filters. India views itself as a rising power seeking its rightful place in the world, and India's intelligentsia, think tanks,

Bollywood movies, and domestic political campaigns constantly drive home this point to garner public support, especially during election campaigns. India's narrative describes Pakistan as being singularly intent on thwarting India's rise through the strategy of a thousand cuts. Pakistan, in contrast, views itself as a unique sovereign Muslim nation that separated from India after an ideological struggle for independence. Successive generations of Pakistani leaders have viewed India as a Hindu-dominated country. Within two decades of achieving independence, Pakistan had demonstrated its immense potential to become a progressive, moderate Muslim nation and a prospering state in Asia, but it lost its way due to internal dissent and perpetual conflict with India. These compulsions are deeply rooted and their effect is to actively steer the Subcontinent toward insecurity and detrimental economic outcomes.

Aside from these pervasive biases and anxieties over external threats, a plethora of India-specific and Pakistan-specific domestic factors are also contributing to South Asia's drift. In the case of India, these factors include (1) the preeminence of India's strategic enclave; (2) the undercapacity and rigidity of the Indian government's bureaucracy; (3) regional party pressures; and (4) competing foreign policy worldviews of idealism versus pragmatism. Taken together, these factors push and pull India in opposing directions and cause it to suffer from an incoherent grand strategy. In Pakistan's case, alongside some of the same pathologies as faced by India, specific domestic factors include: (1) the rise of violent religious extremism, which is partly compounded by the state's peculiar love-hate relationship with certain militant organizations; (2) the country's reliance on economic and military patronage from external powers; and (3) the Pakistan army's outsized influence over national security and nuclear policy. The next two sections outline in more detail how these internal dynamics impact India and Pakistan, respectively.

INDIA'S STRATEGIC ENCLAVE: COMPETING POLICY CHALLENGES

Originally identified by South Asia specialist Itty Abraham, the strategic enclave is the "subset of the Indian military-security complex" that is responsible for developing the country's missile and nuclear arsenal.[14] According to Gaurav Kampani, another analyst, the enclave "enjoys a considerable degree of organizational autonomy and its activities are kept secret from the scrutiny of the parliament, media, and rival bureaucratic agencies."[15] The relative autonomy and preeminence of the strategic enclave ensures that nuclear and missile capabilities feature prominently in India's national security strategy—a dynamic that has intensified the security dilemma on the Subcontinent. At every step, India's strategic modernization has elicited countervailing responses from neighboring China and Pakistan (and has even incentivized a degree of collusion among them).

Meanwhile, India's democratically elected political leaders frequently make pronouncements in favor of nuclear disarmament, reminiscent of the Gandhian tradition of non-violence, only to have their calls muted by hawks and elites within the strategic enclave and ultranationalists within domestic politics. Indeed, although India's civilian government professes the virtues of peaceful coexistence and nuclear disarmament (for example, in a 2014 speech in New Delhi by then prime minister Manmohan Singh endorsing a nuclear weapons–free world),[16] the security enclave continues to push for military and nuclear expansion. And whereas India's elected civilian governments come and go, the strategic enclave enjoys continuity and a critical role in shaping India's doctrinal thinking and armed forces posture.

India's second cause for concern is the chronic undercapacity within its national security institutions, particularly the National Security Council, the Foreign Service, and the Ministry of Defense. Although these institutions are known for their daily operational professionalism, they have shown an ineptitude for long-term strategic thinking, which hampers the formulation of a coherent and consistent Indian grand strategy. For example, the National Security Council is charged with developing an integrated national security strategy, but it lacks the authority to enforce any measures and is undercapitalized in terms of resources and manpower.[17] Undercapitalization is also an endemic problem within India's Foreign Service, which employs a corps of only 900 foreign service officers to manage the diplomatic affairs of a would-be great power with a billion-plus population and diverse global interests.[18] As for the Ministry of Defense, its principal problem (according to many Indian military officers) is its relative unfamiliarity with military matters, which is largely a consequence of staffing policy. Coming and going on a rotational basis, many of the Ministry of Defense's civilian staffers are temporary appointments, which hampers the development of institutional memory and expertise.[19] This disconnect within the Ministry of Defense has made it difficult for India to link its military doctrine and procurement strategy to long-term national goals, and the Indian bureaucracy's lack of strategic vision is also apparent in New Delhi's failure to promulgate an official national security doctrine. The lack of coherent, national-level strategic guidance severely reduces the ability of India's national security apparatus to make joint progress in identifying and acting on long-term diplomatic, economic, and military objectives.

The third factor behind India's strategic disjointedness is the propensity of regional officials and political parties to thwart national foreign policy efforts. For example, in 2011, Mamata Banerjee, Chief Minister of the Indian state of West Bengal, derailed an India-Bangladesh water-sharing agreement for the Teesta River, citing concerns that the terms of the deal favored Bangladesh. The Teesta River, which originates in Sikkim and cuts southeast through West Bengal before entering Bangladesh, is running dangerously low and endangering the livelihood of thousands of Bangladeshi villages downstream.[20] Since then, no further progress has been made on the water agreement.

Another instance of regional prerogatives dominating Indian foreign policy occurred in 2013, when the Indian province of Tamil Nadu successfully pressured New Delhi to censure Sri Lanka for human rights violations at a 2013 vote of the United Nations Human Rights Council.[21] This damaged India-Sri Lanka relations at a time when the Indian strategic community—alarmed at Beijing's economic overtures to the Rajapaksa regime in Colombo—was fearful that Sri Lanka was being slowly transformed into a forward operating base for the People's Liberation Army (PLA) amd People Liberation Army Navy (PLAN). Although Sri Lanka's next president Maithripala Sirisena, who assumed office in January 2015, sought to mend ties with India and balance Sri Lanka's relationship with both China and India, the point remains that regional parties in India occasionally steer foreign policy in ways that may conflict with India's broader security interests.

The fourth driver behind New Delhi's strategic myopia is the competition between idealism and pragmatism in its foreign policy. For one, India dogmatically embraces non-alignment as its foreign policy driver, yet simultaneously dabbles in *realpolitik*, as it attempts to build strategic "partnerships" with the great powers on its own terms. Similarly, India espouses the virtues of global nuclear disarmament while actively expanding its own nuclear arsenal; and it seeks permanent membership of the United Nations Security Council (UNSC) yet abhors the prospect of any external intervention in regional affairs.

Not only have these four factors had the first-order effect of complicating India's ability to formulate and prosecute a consistent grand strategy, but they have also undermined New Delhi's ability to achieve a leadership role in the region. Effective leadership is predicated on trust, but India's smaller neighbors interpret these mixed foreign policy messages as duplicity. The problem is compounded by the fact that India has been traditionally loath to give concessions to resolve issues and conflicts with neighboring states—whether weak or strong—and this perceived failure to meet surrounding states halfway on many issues has served to aggravate latent tensions.[22] This intransigence has hardened the already solid barrier to diplomatic engagement and détente with Pakistan.

The rise of Hindu extremists in India under the Modi regime has further aggravated this stance and given a new ideological twist to India's approach to its minorities, especially Muslims. India's changed character has not only permeated the domestic landscape, impacting bureaucratic structures and the strategic enclave; it has also given a new lease of life to the violent extremist forces operating in Pakistan, which the latter has been struggling to control and suppress for several decades.

PAKISTAN'S STRATEGIC ENCLAVE: THE CHALLENGE FROM RELIGIOUS EXTREMISTS

The history of religious extremism and insurgency in Pakistan dates to the late 1970s, when right-wing religious forces found support in a sympathetic military leader. In 1977 General Zia-ul-Haq overthrew the left-leaning civil government of Zulfiqar Ali Bhutto, later hanged him, and ruled for 11 years before dying in a plane crash. During the military rule of Zia in the 1980s Pakistan became a hub for jihadi forces that launched guerrilla attacks (with the assistance of the United States) on Afghanistan to defeat the occupying Soviet forces.

Pakistan has never recovered from the fallout of this eruption of religious bigotry that was unleashed on its soil to defeat the "godless" communists in Afghanistan, and this has had a lasting impact on its state and society ever since. Since 1989, Pakistan has attempted to replicate the success of the Afghan campaign by co-opting jihadist "freedom fighters" to wage an insurgency in Indian-administered Kashmir. For a while in the 1990s, the Kashmir insurgency proved strategically beneficial for Pakistan because it forced India to deploy significant military resources in an expensive counterinsurgency operation and gave Pakistan strategic depth in Afghanistan during the period of Taliban rule (1996–2001), which prevented India from opening a second front against Pakistan.

However, the strategy subsequently backfired. The jihadi outfits once trained for sub-conventional wars turned their guns on their erstwhile benefactors. As a result, the Pakistan army has spent the last decade and more battling an insurrection of its own making in the borderlands with Afghanistan as well as in Pakistan itself. Moreover, after September 11, 2001, Pakistan's security policy came under intense international scrutiny and the country experienced a dramatic shift in the international environment, whereby all insurgencies were now conflated with terrorism. On the first anniversary of the September 11 terror attacks, the United States' former national security advisor Zbigniew Brzezinski wrote the following in the *New York Times*:

> The rather narrow, almost one-dimensional definition of the terrorist threat favored by the Bush administration poses the special risk that foreign powers will also seize upon the word 'terrorism' to promote their own agendas, as President Vladimir Putin of Russia, Prime Minister Ariel Sharon of Israel, Prime Minister Atal Bihari Vajpayee of India, and President Jiang Zemin of China are doing. For each of them the disembodied American definition of the terrorist challenge has been both expedient and convenient.[23]

The proverbial chickens were coming home to roost in Pakistan, and it was India's opportunity to turn the tables. Since 2004, the Pakistan army has been mired in counterinsurgency operations in its mountainous northwestern borderlands with Afghanistan, the Federally Administered Tribal Areas (FATA), and the province of Khyber Pakhtunkhwa.[24] The insurgency formed as a backlash against the Pakistan army's efforts to root out al-Qaeda militants that had taken refuge in FATA following the US invasion of Afghanistan in October 2001. As the years went by, a profusion of new jihadist groups sprang up in FATA to oppose the Pakistan army, which eventually coalesced in December 2007 under an umbrella group known as Tehrik-i-Taliban Pakistan (TTP). Following this consolidation, the violence and combat losses for the army in the counterinsurgency campaign escalated considerably, and terrorist attacks such as suicide bombings proliferated throughout the country.[25]

After four decades of fighting and becoming battle-hardened, these militant outfits have grown increasingly autonomous and have demonstrated their capacity to precipitate a major bilateral crisis by unilaterally conducting terrorist attacks anywhere on the Subcontinent. Pakistan's ambiguous relationship with Islamist militancy writ large has led Western countries to accuse Pakistan of differentiating between "good" and "bad" militants within the tribal region, noting that it persecutes and combats militant groups opposing the state but tolerates and occasionally supports those groups that serve Pakistan's strategic interests. Elements of the Afghan Taliban sheltering in Pakistan's borderlands have allegedly been spared in the Pakistan army's counterinsurgency operations. The TTP has borne the brunt of the army's vengeance and its fighters have sought refuge across the border in Afghanistan, where the Afghan and Indian intelligence services have allegedly provided them with shelter and support.

Islamabad finally reached the limits of its patience with the militants on its northwestern flank and initiated Operation Zarb-e-Azb ("Sharp and Cutting Strike") in June 2014 after the terrorist attack at Karachi Airport and the horrific Peshawar school massacre perpetrated by the TTP in December that same year. Following the massacre, Pakistani Prime Minister Nawaz Sharif declared: "There will be no distinction between good and bad Taliban. The nation will continue this war with full resolve till elimination of the last terrorist."[26] Sharif's uncompromising declaration was a welcome change. Since then, the Pakistan military has waged a campaign to destroy its Frankenstein's monster—continually eliminating safe havens in FATA and other areas under the revised Operation Radd-ul-Fasaad ("Elimination of Discord") initiated by the incumbent Chief of the Army Staff, General Qamar Javed Bajwa, in 2017. As renowned journalist Declan Walsh acknowledges in *The Nine Lives of Pakistan*, "in 2013, Pakistan had forty-six suicide attacks and 2,400 deaths from militant attacks; in 2019 there were four suicide attacks and 350 deaths."[27]

The second factor compounding Pakistan's national security is the country's reliance on great power benefactors for strategic and economic support. With the withdrawal of the United States from Afghanistan and Washington's high hopes for an alliance with India, Pakistan is hedging its bets and looking to strengthen its friendship with China, which has pledged investment worth over US$ 72 billion under the CPEC projects. However, it is unclear whether China is willing to fully offset the economic and military aid vacuum that Pakistan will likely experience following the United States' withdrawal. With foreign aid wells running dry and under the impact of the coronavirus pandemic in 2020, Pakistan's economy has taken a major hit, which is exacerbating the security situation in the country and further inflating the allure of religious extremism.

The final domestic problem confronting Pakistan is the army's outsized influence over the country's national strategy and nuclear policy. Public perception, both domestically and abroad, is that Pakistan's democratically elected civilian government has only nominal control over its national strategy and the military. The Pakistan army remains the real power-broker in the country and can be regarded as a strategic enclave in its own right. It holds tremendous sway over the tools of national power— political, economic, military, and technological. Moreover, as the premier security institution, military exigencies directly influence Pakistan's security policy and grand strategy. With its fixation on the existential threat posed by India, Pakistan's security policy is based on the worst-case threat perceptions of New Delhi's intentions, resulting (unsurprisingly) in higher military budgets and more nuclear weapons to meet the Indian military threat. Meanwhile, the civilian government in Islamabad talks of confidence-building measures and economic connectivity with India but lacks a sufficient understanding of strategic affairs. The civil leadership gives its military-scientific apparatus a free hand to develop and deploy a surfeit of nuclear delivery systems while simultaneously failing to develop a cohesive grand strategy. As the old saying goes, when you have only a hammer, every problem starts to look like a nail.

Even within the military, there are autonomous enclaves that also have a decisive say in national policy. For instance, the Strategic Plans Division (SPD) now controls the nuclear-scientific bureaucracy, following the embarrassing revelation that A. Q. Khan, the infamous Pakistani scientist, had been running a nuclear black market. The SPD has become all-powerful within the Joint Services Headquarters (JSHQ), planning Pakistan's nuclear policy, posture, doctrine, and goals for the military forces. It functions as a secretariat to the civilian-led National Command Authority (NCA), but given the strict secrecy of nuclear matters, the SPD is relatively free from external oversight and criticism. Since its creation, the SPD has forged a military-scientific nexus which has legal and official authority.[28]

The other organization that enjoys significant autonomy within Pakistan is the directorate of Inter-Services Intelligence (ISI), whose powerful role in internal and external security policies overshadows the civilian and even military institutions. Like all intelligence agencies, ISI's functioning budget is shrouded in secrecy; however, it is widely believed that it has a hand in almost all policy matters in Pakistan. Both the SPD and ISI function under rules of strict secrecy and compartmentalization. Typically, military organizations are sensitive to critique and jealously guard their turf and control of the national narrative. Pakistan's military-dominated constituency—comprising former civil and military officials, academics, and think tanks—is euphemistically referred as the "establishment" and is somewhat analogous to India's strategic enclave.

As a result of this combination of factors, Pakistan is a state where religious extremism continues apace, the economy remains dependent on external fillips, security policy is immune to external influence, and the centrality of nuclear weapons and narratives of strategic deterrence permeate the organizational domain. Combined with the primacy of

Pakistan's military domestically and the country's pervasive mistrust of its elected politicians, it is not surprising that democracy in Pakistan remains on shaky ground. Taken together, these factors produce a toxic mix that constrains Islamabad's ability to develop a cohesive national security policy.

IMPLICATIONS FOR THE FUTURE

This snapshot of the various irritants in the India-Pakistan relationship at the systemic, bilateral, and domestic levels shows where the contemporary challenges to South Asian strategic stability lie. At the system level, the gap between India and Pakistan is growing as the United States and China each court them to be their offshore balancers. At the bilateral level, the lethal mix of acute mistrust, unresolved territorial disputes, and cross-border terrorism continues to poison the well for rapprochement and periodically ignites militarized crises. An array of domestic variables in both countries has also militated against serviceable bilateral ties. New Delhi's dismissive contempt of Pakistan combined with the ambitious influence of its strategic enclave has engendered a security posture that rapidly develops and fields new conventional and nuclear-capable weaponry, prodding Pakistan into a debilitating arms race. As for Pakistan, besides grappling with numerous challenges in forging domestic cohesion and a national identity, the central role of the military and nuclear-related bureaucracy has given rise to an India-centric foreign and national security policy. The fixations and stubbornness prevalent in both countries prevent any breakthrough in conflict resolution. As a result, India-Pakistan diplomacy tends to occur in short, perfunctory bursts and is always derailed by disagreement or crisis, rather than proceeding in a sustained and deliberate fashion.

The more shifts there are at the three levels, and the more military, technological, and social changes that occur, the farther the Subcontinent drifts from being able to forge détente and a sense of regionalism. It is my aim to explore the sources, causes, and outcomes of this drift by analyzing the grand strategies of India and Pakistan. Grand strategy is the expression of how a state advances its political, military, and economic agendas against the backdrop of its strategic environment. A great deal of literature has already been published in recent years on India's grand strategy, but the grand strategy of smaller states such as Pakistan is an emerging field.

Notes

1. Peter R. Lavoy, ed., *Asymmetric Warfare in South Asia: The Causes and Consequences of the Kargil Conflict* (New York: Cambridge University Press, 2009). For a recent Pakistani account, see Nasim Zahra, *From Kargil to the Coup: Events that Shook Pakistan* (Lahore: Sang-e-Meel Publications, 2018).
2. Paul Bracken, *The Second Nuclear Age: Strategy, Danger, and the New Power Politics* (New York: Times Books, 2012); Gregory D. Koblentz, ed., *Strategic Stability in the Second Nuclear Age,* Special Report No. 71 (New York: Council on Foreign Relations, 2014), 19.
3. Elbridge A. Colby and Michael S. Gerson, eds., *Strategic Stability: Contending Interpretations* (Carlisle Barracks, PA: Strategic Studies Institute, 2013).
4. Thomas C. Schelling and Morton H. Halperin, *Strategy and Arms Control* (New York: Twentieth Century Fund, 1961), 50.
5. Lawrence Rubin and Adam N. Stulberg, eds., *The End of Strategic Stability: Nuclear Weapons and the Challenges of Regional Rivalries* (Washington, DC: Georgetown University Press, 2018), 2.
6. Balraj Nagal, "Strategic Stability: Conundrum, Challenge and Dilemma: The Case of India, China and Pakistan," *Journal of the Center for Land Warfare Studies* (Summer 2015): 1–22.
7. Two recent publications highlight the emerging triangular strategic balancing and power rivalry in South Asia. See Jeff M. Smith, *Cold Peace: Sino-Indian Rivalry in the 21st Century* (Lanham, MD: Lexington Books, 2014); and Andrew Small, *The China-Pakistan Axis: Asia's New Geopolitics* (New York: Oxford University Press, 2015).
8. Ankat Panda, "What the Recently Concluded US-India COMCASA Means," *Diplomat*, September 18, 2018, https://thediplomat.com/2018/09/what-the-recently-concluded-us-india-comcasa-means/.
9. *IISS Armed Conflict Survey 2018* (London: Routledge-Taylor & Francis Group for the International Institute for Strategic Studies, 2018), 229–238.
10. *IISS Armed Conflict Survey 2018*, 230.
11. Salman Masood, "Trump Request for India's Help in Afghanistan Rattles Pakistan," *New York Times*, August 22, 2017, https://www.nytimes.com/2017/08/22/world/asia/pakistan-trump-afghanistan-india.html.

12. "India and Pakistan," WTO Statistics Database, http://stat.wto.org/ CountryProfile/WSDBCountryPFView.aspx?Language=E&Country=IN %2cPK.

13. "India and Pakistan," WTO Statistics Database.

14. Itty Abraham, "India's 'Strategic Enclave': Civilian Scientists and Military Technologies," *Armed Forces & Society* 18, no. 2 (Winter 1992): 233, https://doi.org/10.1177/0095327X9201800205.

15. Gaurav Kampani, "Stakeholders in the Indian Strategic Missile Program," *Nonproliferation Review* (Fall/Winter 2003): 51, https://doi.org/10.1080 /10736700308436943.

16. "Inaugural Address by Dr Manmohan Singh, Prime Minister of India, on a Nuclear Weapon-Free World: From Conception to Reality," Institute for Defence Studies and Analyses, 2014, https://idsa.in/keyspeeches/ InauguralAddressShriManmohanSingh.

17. Arvind Gupta, *A National Security Strategy Document for India* (New Delhi: Institute for Defence Studies and Analyses, 2011), http://www. idsa.in/idsacomments/ANationalSecurityStrategyDocumentforIndia_ arvindgupta_201011.

18. Happymon Jacob, "Brick and Mortar of Foreign Policy," *The Hindu*, June 12, 2015, http://www.thehindu.com/opinion/lead/brick-and-mortar-of-foreign-policy/article7306310.ece.

19. "Know Your Own Strength," *The Economist*, March 30, 2013, http://www. economist.com/news/briefing/21574458-india-poised-become-one-four-largest-military-powers-world-end.

20. Pinaki Roy, "Teesta River Runs Dry as India and Bangladesh Fail to Resolve Disputes," *The Third Pole*, https://earthjournalism.net/stories/ teesta-river-runs-dry-as-india-and-bangladesh-fail-to-resolve-disputes.

21. In a subsequent United Nations Human Rights Council vote in 2014, India reversed course and abstained from censuring Sri Lanka. See Indrani Bagchi, "India Abstains on Human Rights Vote on Sri Lanka, Rescues Foreign Policy," *Times of India*, March 27, 2014, http://timesofindia. indiatimes.com/world/south-asia/India-abstains-on-human-rights-vote-on-Sri-Lanka-rescues-foreign-policy/articleshow/32793377.cms.

22. See, for example, Vaishali Basu Sharma, "India's Lack of Respect for its South Asian Neighbours is Now Mutual," TheWire.com, August 20, 2020. https://thewire.in/diplomacy/india-south-asia-neighbours-foreign-policy-respect.

23. Zbigniew Brzezinski, "Confronting Anti-American Grievances," *New York Times,* September 11, 2002, https://www.nytimes.com/2002/09/01/opinion/confronting-anti-american-grievances.html.
24. In May 2018, FATA was merged with Khyber Pakhtunkhwa in an attempt to increase security in the region.
25. See "Fatalities in Terrorist Violence in Pakistan 2003–2015," South Asia Terrorism Portal, http://www.satp.org/satporgtp/countries/pakistan/database/casualties.htm.
26. Zulfiqar Ali, "Distinction between Good, Bad Taliban No More," *Dawn,* December 18, 2014, http://www.dawn.com/news/1151550.
27. Declan Walsh, *The Nine Lives of Pakistan: Dispatches From a Precarious State* (New York: W. W. Norton & Co., 2020).
28. Feroz Hassan Khan, "Nuclear Command, Control and Communication (NC3): The Case of Pakistan," Tech4Gs Special Reports. September 26, 2019, https://www.tech4gs.org/nc3-systems-and-strategic-stability-a-global-overview.html.

CHAPTER 3

INDIA'S SEARCH FOR A GRAND STRATEGY

Long years ago, we made a tryst with destiny, and now the time comes when we shall redeem our pledge, not wholly or in full measure, but very substantially ... there is no resting for any one of us till we redeem our pledge in full, till we make all the people of India what destiny intended them to be.[1]

—Jawaharlal Nehru,
speech on the eve of India's Independence,
August 14, 1947

Before the end of the Cold War or more specifically, before the September 2001 terror attacks in the United States, India's security strategic thinking did not feature particularly highly on the world's radar. Today in contrast, scholars and policymakers alike are questioning whether India has a grand strategy at all, and if so, whether it possesses the wherewithal to counter the new challenges presented by contemporary great power competition, particularly China's rising dominance.[2]

There are two schools of thought within India's strategic community. One camp believes that India lacks a coherent strategic direction and functions on an ad hoc basis, whereas the other camp believes that India has always had a grand strategy, even though it has not been articulated in a single document. This is how Shivshankar Menon, former Indian national security advisor, sums up the uniqueness of the Indian way of executing policymaking, for example:

> If there is an Indian way in foreign policy, it is marked by a combination of boldness in conception and caution in implementation, by the dominant and determining role of the prime minister, by a didactic negotiating style, by a fundamentally realistic approach masked by normative rhetoric, by comfort in a plural and diverse world or multiverse, and, most consistently, by a consciousness of India's destiny as a great power.[3]

India's premonition of its great power destiny was first conjectured at the beginning of the twentieth century. Lord George Curzon, Viceroy of British India, recognized the distinctiveness of India when he observed:

> The master of India must, under modern conditions, be the greater power in the Asiatic Continent, and therefore, it must be added, in the world. The central position of India, its magnificent resources, its teeming multitude of men, its great trading harbours, its reserve of military strength ... are assets of precious value.[4]

In the five decades between Lord Curzon and India's last viceroy, Lord Mountbatten, the strategic geography of British India was hugely transformed from what Lord Curzon had visualized when the British Raj was at its height. With the two wings of Pakistan on its eastern and western flanks, and communist China beyond the Himalayas to the north, India's geographical advantage at independence had contracted significantly, and it faced tough strategic choices in balancing these two potential rivals. In its quest for great power status, India has found itself competing with China, engaging in regional wars and crises, and wrestling with multiple internal security issues and secessionist movements. In the final analysis, despite its primacy and domination of the Subcontinent, India has failed to emerge as a regional leader and continues to face multiple threats from within and outside.

If we want to arrive at a deeper understanding of India's rise as an Asian power and the implications of this, we need to examine India's objectives and policy choices as it works to fulfil its tryst with destiny, as envisioned by its founders. Equally important is the question of how India approaches the strategic future of the Subcontinent as a whole.

A Guide to Indian Strategic Thinking

The ongoing rivalry in South Asia has prompted scholars to interpret the nature of the conflict and the resulting policy approaches in liberal or neoliberal terms in line with realist or neorealist theories of international relations. South Asian academics generally favor neorealist explanations that interpret states' behavior in terms of power and the national interest. Rajesh Rajagopalan, for example, explains that neorealists interpret conflict in structural terms (using Kenneth Waltz's structural theory), whereas hawks invariably trace the source of conflict to the aggressive behavior of adversaries.[5] The structural imbalance of power between India and Pakistan is obvious, but the narrative is usually easier to sell if it places the blame on one's opponent.

In South Asia, the realist prism alone is insufficient to fully explain the conflict, which needs to be viewed through the intervening lens of strategic culture. This perspective weaves historical experiences, cognitive bias, and unresolved issues into a fabric of "strategic beliefs," where the myths and genuine threats become intertwined and difficult (if not impossible) to separate.[6] Several theoretical explanations have been proffered for interpreting India's grand strategy, which I shall discuss in turn. This is followed by an analysis of the two major doctrines which emerged to direct India's grand strategy—the Indira Doctrine and the Gujral Doctrine, respectively. The chapter concludes with an assessment of India's strategic policy under Atal Bihari Vajpayee and Manmohan Singh prior to the election of Narendra Modi in 2014.

A Modern Arthashastra

In 1992, at the end of the Cold War, George K. Tanham, an American
scholar at the RAND Corporation, wrote a comprehensive essay interpreting India's strategic thinking. In the essay, he identified the progression of India's grand strategy up until the end of the Cold War, and
through an examination of varying perspectives he also provided a
prognosis of future Indian strategic policy.[7] Tanham noted that India's
strategic influences continue to follow an ancient "mandala system,"
whereby Indian rulers treat the Subcontinent as a single strategic whole
with a shared geography, history, and culture, and view the world
through the lens of concerted strategic circles.[8] The first circle relates to
India's primary security concerns at the core (domestic level). The second
circle (regional concerns at the periphery) comprises India's smaller
neighbors (Sri Lanka, Nepal, Bangladesh, and Maldives), but not its larger
adversarial neighbors. The third circle encompasses global concerns
in the extended neighborhood, and this is where India places Pakistan
and China.[9] Stephen Cohen agrees with Tanham that Indian strategic
thinking has continued to follow a modern-day form of *Arthashastra*,
from which the mandala framework is derived. In Cohen's assessment,
India's leaders consider the country's geographical location, size, and
population to be the basis of Indian dominance of the Subcontinent—
which Indian leaders believe they should rightfully control—and this lies
at the heart of Indian strategy.[10]

Despite this belief, past insecurities continue to influence contemporary Indian strategic thinking. The northwest passages (now part of
the Afghanistan-Pakistan border) historically allowed invaders to reach
India, and these long-held fears continue to permeate and affect India's
current strategic thinking.[11] Historical anxieties relate not only to physical invasions per se but also, perhaps even more, to the ideological
influences of such historical invasions—primarily by Muslims—on India.[12]
Indian strategic thinking therefore remains framed by a combination of
nostalgia for India's great past and an obsession with protecting India
against outside invaders and influences. Tanham and Cohen each observe

that India's foremost strategic goal of unifying the Subcontinent and protecting it against outside powers dates back 2,000 years.[13] Scholars also note India's strong belief that it is ordained to spread the idea of "Indianness"—of India as a progressive modern state—across Asia, and eventually around the globe.[14]

From a military strategic standpoint, the hangover of the British Raj has had a negative influence on Indian thinking as well; its legacy has been an army-centric military strategy and a shaky civil-military relationship. Although indigenous Indians joined the British military as soldiers, there was never a focus on naval forces.[15] Even today, India retains a large army but lacks commensurate naval power, and the Indian navy calls itself the "Cinderella service."[16] John Gill argues that officials have brought few reforms to India's army-centric strategy, and that, like the British Raj before it, modern-day India continues to be governed through a bureaucratic-military establishment—which is efficient in maintaining a strict order but oppressive against Indian civilians.[17] Such negative influences persist in India today, as evidenced by the inability of the current civilian and military leaders to work together effectively in the Indian policymaking process.

India's historical and cultural stimuli allow its leaders to galvanize the public around the idea of expanding Indian values and global influence.[18] Indeed, as Sunil Dasgupta and Stephen Cohen observe, Indian leaders and strategic thinkers tend to base their lofty aims on "ideological perception and not as much on their true capacity."[19] Viewed from the perspective of its historical aspirations, then, contemporary India continues to search for a clear grand strategy.

Principal Theories

In 2014, a study on Indian grand strategy examined the main principles behind India's strategic thinking and outlined three major and three minor schools of thought to explain India's somewhat anarchic approach to international relations.[20] The major schools are described as Nehruvianism, neoliberalism, and hyperrealism, and the three minor schools are Marxism, Gandhism, and Hindutva. The Nehruvian approach focuses on conflict avoidance, continued communication, and negotiated settlements with adversaries. For the neoliberals, economic power is the key to becoming an effective military power, whereas confrontation and wars are detrimental to the national interest. The worldview of the hyperrealists is diametrically opposed to these two approaches. From a hyperrealist perspective, threats are an unremitting reality that can only be met with strategic assertion and investment in military power, and the use of force is a natural instrument of statecraft in a world that finds itself in a constant state of war.

Amongst the three minor schools, Marxism and anti-imperialism have been present in Indian politics since the early twentieth century, providing the basis for India's non-alignment and autarkic economic and socialist policies—in accordance with the Nehruvian approach—for the greater part of India's post-independence history. Gandhism refers to the acceptance of pluralism, non-violence, and a social order based on welfare and strategic restraint; it was an effective tool peculiar to the Indian resistance against imperial rule and became the hallmark of the Indian independence movement. This approach offered little guidance on statecraft once India achieved independence, however. Hindutva is defined as "the Hindu way of life" and implies the supremacy of the Hindu religion over religious minorities in India; this challenges the secularism and pluralism espoused by Gandhism.[21] Hyperrealist thinking, however, does not always imply adherence to a Hindutva mindset alone.[22]

The gradual rise of Hindutva and the resultant change in India's character is intrinsically linked with the rise of Narendra Modi, who came to power in 2014. Specifically, the absorption of Hindutva—as distinct from the religious faith of Hinduism—within the hyperrealist school of thought has redefined India's grand strategy in a significantly aggressive manner.[23] While successive Indian leaders in the post–Cold War period embraced the non-violence espoused by Gandhi and gave primacy to the economy, trade, and connectivity over hard security, neither neoliberalism nor Gandhism succeeded in integrating the region, nor in resolving the enduring rivalries with India's principal adversaries.[24]

Several Indian scholars, such as Kanti Bajpai, assert that although India's neoliberal approach may not have resolved these conflicts, it had "softened the rough edges" and paved the way for their eventual resolution. Since the ascendency of the Modi regime, however, conflicts have hardened and the edges have become rougher than ever, both domestically and in India's neighborhood (including border clashes with China and Pakistan); the only visible "softening" has been in relation to the United States, with Modi's signature strategic embrace.[25]

Nehruvian Pillars: Non-Alignment, Socialism, and Secularism

Jawaharlal Nehru, the charismatic Indian leader, remained uncontested until 1964 to lead India's "tryst with destiny." He was the figurehead on whose leadership the course of the Subcontinent's post-independence history rested. Nehru decided on three fundamental policies that formed the pillars of Indian strategic thinking throughout the twentieth century.

The first was a policy of non-alignment and retention of India's strategic autonomy. India steadfastly refused to join any military alliances but selectively chose strategic partnerships with major powers when it was deemed to be in India's national interest; throughout the Cold War, India developed close strategic congruity with the Soviet Union. The second element had its roots in Nehru's fascination with socialism and self-reliance, leading to enforcement of an autarkic economic policy and a state-controlled economy as prerequisites for the alleviation of poverty. Consequently, for the first four decades after independence, India's economic growth was stunted and its structural modernization stalled, exhibiting what Prime Minister Manmohan Singh famously dubbed in the 1990s the "Hindu rate of growth." (The term was originally coined in 1978 by Indian economist Raj Krishna in reference to India's socialist approach and central planning that resulted in growth of no more than 3.5%.)[26] The third important pillar was to declare India a constitutionally secular state based on the principles of pluralistic federal democracy and constitutionalism. Nehru kept the military at arm's length from policy matters, strictly confined to its professional role of defense.

The Nehruvian policy of democratic self-rule, secularism, and non-alignment gave India a fundamental strength that helped it to consolidate, despite its poor economic growth and significant ethno-religious diversity. India survived through what Selig Harrison once described as its "most dangerous decades."[27] Harrison observed that Nehru was impressed with the Soviet Union's experience of consolidating a large population speaking multiple languages across a vast territory, but he predicted that in India's case: "The centrifugal forces will ultimately prevail and ... the nation may be compelled to go through a period of political anarchy and face the risk of fascism, which is Nature's way out of disorder."[28] However, India defied such prognoses and crushed any attempt at secessionism on the part of its territories (discussed elsewhere in this chapter). The excessive use of force against people with genuine grievances who were suffering from economic deprivation in a caste-based society turned the secessionist movements into sub-nationalist ones—a challenge that India is still dealing with today.[29]

There is an argument that by adopting the Nehruvian approach, India has exercised "strategic restraint" in dealing with domestic and regional crises to avoid all-out war. Proponents of this argument contend that the Nehruvian policy combines diplomacy with the selective use of force in order to achieve settlement while preserving India's core strategic interests.[30] India's weaker neighbors, however, have experienced India's penchant to strategically coerce them over disputes or policy differences, which is a fundamental reason why India's neighbors choose to balance with other major powers.[31] The failure to reach a lasting solution after each crisis or war continually comes back to haunt both India and Pakistan, with each new military encounter aggravating the wounds of the past—gradually turning simple rivalry into an enduring enmity, and transforming the region into an intermittently active war zone in a state of permanent instability.

The Swing State

Not all Indian analysts thought the Nehruvian approach made India's focus too inward-looking or stagnant, much less that India lacked a grand stratagem. K. Subrahmanyam, India's highly respected strategic thinker, certainly attributes India's success to the three Nehruvian pillars of non-alignment, secular democracy, and autarkic economic policy. He observed that India had recovered remarkably from a

> war-ravaged economy and downtrodden former colony after inheriting 80 percent poverty, life expectancy of 31, and food shortages and low literacy at independence to become the world's third largest economy, with 62 percent of the population above the poverty line, despite its having grown fourfold.[32]

Commenting on India's rise in the emerging world order of the twenty-first century, Subrahmanyam predicted: "If the US remains the world predominant power, and China is second, India will be the swing power."[33] Supporters of the Nehruvian approach believe that India's policy of non-alignment and strategic autonomy has enabled India to exploit both superpowers while avoiding entanglements with either.[34]

Debate on the foundations and future of India's grand strategy continues as India's star rises in an era of great power competition. Western experts on South Asia expect that India will live up to the "swing state" promise that Subrahmanyam predicted; however, India's lack of a coherent grand strategy remains an impediment for the role India has given itself in today's international system.[35] India's former foreign secretary and national security advisor, Shivshankar Menon, considers weak institutions and poor civil-military relations to be the main obstacles holding India back from developing a far-reaching grand strategy.[36] In a speech in November 2019, Subrahmanyam Jaishankar

(Modi's foreign minister and son of the late K. Subrahmanyam), who has had a long and distinguished diplomatic career, disagreed with his father's view. Instead, he censured the Nehruvian approach for the lack of a coherent external strategy and blamed the fixation with the three pillars —or "Delhi's dogma," as he called it—for constraining India's foreign policy.[37] For three decades since the end of the Cold War, New Delhi's strategic community has been trying to set India on a new pathway toward the destiny envisioned by its first prime minister at midnight on August 15, 1947.

Post–Cold War Strategic Adjustments

One of India's leading academics, C. Raja Mohan, identified three key strategic dilemmas facing India at the end of the Cold War: a closed economy, the consequences of the demise of the Soviet Union, and the legacy of Partition.[38] By the end of the twentieth century, India had freed itself from two of these—dependency on the Soviet Union and its autarkic economy. However, the persistent conflict with Pakistan and India's inability to resolve other conflicts in its neighborhood continued to negatively impact India's potential to become a great power. The post–Cold War shifts in the international system, including the hard reality of a unipolar world, meant India's leaders had no alternative but to reassess India's national objectives and strategic concerns, as it searched for an alternate strategy.[39]

For five decades, India had maintained the political consensus on non-alignment and cleaved to its left-leaning policies, which included Soviet influence over its economic system. Many Indian leaders believed that if India jettisoned socialism, it would be forced to rely on the imperialist West, thereby losing the strategic autonomy it was so accustomed to in its partnership with the Soviet Union.[40] Forward-looking Indian leaders were keen to develop a partnership with the United States, whereas traditionalists were worried the Western powers would be less compromising, and many considered Indian and Western interests too divergent to find common ground.[41] India decided to gradually adjust its policy of non-alignment by developing selective bilateral strategic partnerships with Western countries, especially the United States.

Under the direction of finance minister (and later prime minister) Manmohan Singh, India reversed decades of socialist economics and opened for business. This economic liberalization saw India's economy undergo a dramatic shift toward a liberal capitalist system. By 2010–2011, India's annual growth rate was 7.1%, up from 4.4% in the 1970s.[42] The next step was to transform India's economic prosperity into military power and expand its influence in the world.[43] According to some scholars, India had long been following its own version of the Monroe Doctrine, regarding itself as the sole guardian of security on the Subcontinent[44] and intervening in regional conflicts—such as supporting the secession of East Pakistan (Bangladesh) in 1971 and sending a peacekeeping force to intervene in Sri Lanka's civil war in 1987.[45] Now, however, India's ambition was to be recognized as a "major Asian power," not just a South Asian power.[46] Seasoned Bharatiya Janata Party (BJP) politician Jaswant Singh noted in 1999 that India had engaged in 32 military operations over a period of 50 years. He defended these actions as examples of India's "resolve" and resilience but also lamented that India did not take advantage of its true potential.[47]

India identified China as an emerging rival in Asia, posing a collective threat alongside Pakistan, yet India still did not commit to a formal military alliance with Western powers. This new position was dubbed "non-alignment 2.0."[48] India's key security concern today is centered on maintaining its preeminence on the Subcontinent by countering China's rising influence and finding a strategy to resolve the Pakistan problem.[49] For many observers, the best strategy for India to alleviate these security concerns is to encourage its neighbors to have a stake in India's interests and capabilities.[50]

Currency of Power

The final layer of India's grand strategy was a demonstration of its nuclear capability. In 1998, India conducted nuclear tests—for the second time since 1974—but this time it made no excuses; instead, it defiantly announced its arrival as a new nuclear power capable of acting independently. Pakistan's immediate response in the form of its own nuclear tests challenged India's claim to sole supremacy, with significant implications for the future stability of the Subcontinent.[51]

Under the astute leadership of Prime Minister Atal Bihari Vajpayee, Indian diplomats and strategic planners set out to convince the world —especially Washington—to treat India as an emerging power.[52] In particular, although regional tensions now had a nuclear dimension, India felt much more confident and assertive in its dealings with the major powers because it had demonstrated that it possessed the currency of power in the form of nuclear weapons. For C. Raja Mohan, this altered the "internal political balance in favor of realists and marked the end of the Nehruvians, who still held onto the legacy of non-alignment."[53] The late Indian Vice Admiral Varghese Koithara captured the impact of India's nuclear tests, commenting: "India found that going overtly nuclear in 1998 did not lead to any penalty but actually sizeable gains. The tests boosted both self-image and security assurances within the country."[54]

Before 1998, the United States viewed the Subcontinent through a nuclear non-proliferation lens, concerned that the advent of nuclear capabilities in a volatile and actively hostile region would pose unacceptable dangers to world peace. India's leaders, however, anticipated (correctly) that the world would eventually accept a nuclear-armed India as a *fait accompli*. US Deputy Secretary of State Strobe Talbott records how US-India relations began to develop when he led a diplomatic initiative to normalize relations with both India and Pakistan following the imposition of sanctions and international condemnation because of the nuclear tests. From this point onwards, each dramatic shift in the international environment brought new opportunities for the United States to deepen relations with its new strategic partner in Asia.[55]

Between 2000 and 2005, India signed three agreements with the United States that included logistics coordination and communications between the two militaries, though without a formal alliance.[56] In 2008, the United States and India concluded the Indo-US Civil Nuclear Agreement, which "normalized India's status as a de facto nuclear power" and ushered in a new era of strategic partnership which brought India to the center stage of great power competition.[57] One outcome was the Nonalignment 2.0 Policy published in 2012, that promised India's active engagement with the major powers without compromising India's strategic autonomy.[58] Although India has shown more willingness to compromise in dealing with the West since the nuclear tests, it remains resistant to the concept of alliances, with their connotations of entanglement and deeper commitment, and prefers instead to hold onto its independence and strategic self-sufficiency.

Successive Indian leaders have juggled to find a compromise between the idealist (Nehruvian, Gandhian, and/or neoliberal) approaches and the pragmatist worldview of the neorealists and hyperrealists—wrestling between a display of hard power and diplomatic concessions. The struggle to balance these competing dichotomies has created two major doctrinal streams within India's strategic thinking, known as the Indira Doctrine and the Gujral Doctrine,[59] which I analyze in the following sections. The term "doctrine" is defined in terms of the specific policy approaches adopted by different leaders in pursuit of national objectives and the way instruments of national power were applied at the domestic, regional, and global level.

The Indira Doctrine

As the new millennium dawned, India's grand objective was evident—to become a global power. To achieve this end, India had to choose between two competing pathways. One option was to overpower or ignore internal dissent and regional security in order to focus on competing at the global level; this was the Indira Doctrine. The other option, in the form of the Gujral Doctrine, was to adopt a policy of embracing one's neighbor and establishing regional leadership before seeking a seat at the global table. This latter doctrine will be discussed in detail in the next section.

The Indira Doctrine is based on the hard-core realist approach that began under the regime of Indira Gandhi and continued briefly under that of her son, Rajiv. Subsequent Indian leaders advanced this doctrine —some more pragmatically, others more aggressively—and eventually steered it toward hyperrealism. The thrust of this policy is that India should establish itself as an indispensable power on the Subcontinent and then project this power to subdue Pakistan and achieve parity with China. According to this perspective, India should maintain an aggressive posture in its neighborhood and on the periphery, forcing weaker states to succumb to Indian dominance.

Indira's Assertive Nationalism

Indira Gandhi, Jawaharlal Nehru's daughter, remained at the apex of Indian politics for twenty years after the death of her father in 1964. She served as prime minister twice. Her first period in office from 1966 until 1977 included the controversial state of emergency period from 1975 to 1977, after which she was ousted from power. Gandhi returned to power in 1980 but was assassinated in October 1984 by two of her Sikh bodyguards. Indira Gandhi was a strong woman—the only female Indian prime minister to date—who set a course of high-handed domestic policy (core) and an aggressive policy vis-à-vis India's neighbors (periphery), with the objective of enforcing India's regional dominance and setting India up to project its power into its extended neighborhood and beyond (the outer circle of the mandala model).

When Indira Gandhi assumed office in 1966, she understood that increasing India's national power would determine its status in international relations and that she needed to have a bold and aggressive policy in India's neighborhood.[60] Unlike her idealist father, Indira Gandhi would not shy from confrontation as she pursued the goal of confirming India as a preeminent regional power. She was willing to fight with Pakistan in 1971 over the secession of East Pakistan, and her victory in helping create an independent Bangladesh was the first major example of India using war as a policy instrument to achieve its strategic goals. Richard Sisson and Leo F. Rose note that Prime Minister Indira Gandhi desired India to become a "major Asian power—not just a South Asian power— and a victory over Pakistan was seen as a contribution to this objective."[61] This assertive stance continued under the premiership of Rajiv Gandhi (prime minister from 1984 to 1989 and Indira's son) and subsequent Indian governments, but many have severely criticized Indira Gandhi's high-handed domestic policies and their cross-border spillover, resulting in negative relations with India's immediate neighbors.[62]

Indira Gandhi recognized that she needed to be tough in dealing with domestic challenges—including charges of corruption and electoral fraud —as well as external ones. Therefore, in 1975 she declared a state of emergency to tighten her grip on power by suspending civil liberties and jailing her political opponents.[63] The state of emergency—the first of its kind in post-independence India—was not only extremely unpopular but also a huge setback for India's democratic credentials and internal stability. It heightened the alienation and disgruntlement felt by many religious and ethnic groups, sparking outbreaks of violence that spilled over into neighboring countries and affected regional security in the process. This tense situation was compounded by drought, famine, high levels of national debt, and decreased industrial output.[64]

Consolidating Internal Power

Indira Gandhi was certainly not the first of India's political leaders to adopt heavy-handed policies and utilize the military to consolidate power internally.[65] The precedent was set immediately after Partition, when Nehru and his deputy Vallabhbhai Jhaverbhai Patel (more commonly known as Sardar the "Strongman") did not hesitate to send the Indian army into three princely states—Hyderabad, Junagadh, and Kashmir—

as a means to consolidate India's territory.[66] And while the separatist movement in Kashmir remained relatively subdued during Indira Gandhi's time in office, the aggressive policies of her regime for crushing ethno-religious grievances managed to create new separatist movements, which did not remain confined to India but fanned out across the whole region.

The Naxalite Movement

In the late 1960s, a local communist party in West Bengal began protesting against a policy which benefited the wealthy buyers of land while forcing the lower castes to give up their land; the protestors (known as Naxalites) demanded a redistribution of land to the peasants.[67] The administration seriously mishandled the grievances, which quickly turned violent against the landowners and resulted in the spread of the Naxalite (Maoist) insurgency in eastern India.[68] The Gandhi regime's strategy for dealing with this domestic issue proved so counterproductive that decades later, in 2010, Prime Minister Manmohan Singh described Naxalism as the "greatest threat" to India.[69] However, even as the Naxalite movement metastasized through India's eastern states, a more dangerous crisis—the Sikh Uprising—was erupting in the western states bordering Pakistan.

The Khalistan Movement (Sikh Uprising)

Shiromani Akali Dal (SAD), a political party in the state of Punjab supported by Sikhs, won sufficient votes to form a regional government in the 1970s. When Indira Gandhi dismissed the Akali Dal government's demands for Sikh rights, they moved to demanding autonomy and a separate state—Khalistan—instead.[70] Not long after regaining power in 1980, Gandhi dismissed the Akali Dal-led government, resulting in the creation of a violent separatist movement that plunged Punjab into a decade of crisis.[71]

In 1984 a Sikh separatist group took over the holy Golden Temple in Amritsar, and the crisis came to a head. Gandhi authorized the Indian army to force the Sikh "terrorists" out of the holy site, and the ensuing military response—involving tanks, guns, and a final assault by the Indian army named Operation Blue Star—caused the deaths of hundreds of Sikhs.[72] The Sikhs' revenge came on the morning of October 31, 1984, when two Sikh bodyguards fatally shot Indira Gandhi as she walked across the compound from her residence to her office.[73] Gandhi's brutal assassination evoked mayhem in India, as Hindus retaliated against Sikhs in a frenzy reminiscent of the chaos at Partition, while the police stood by and watched.

The Tamil Crisis

As if these were not problems enough, far to the south of the Indian peninsula lay India's Dravidian civilizations with Tamil and Telegu populations and a litany of grievances of their own. For decades since India's independence, the states in India's south have had sub-nationalist tendencies stemming from the social consciousness of their unique cultures— the major call of the movement was to resist the imposition of Hindi over all India and the marginalization of the Tamil language. Eventually, what began as the scholarly pursuit of reestablishing Tamil influences turned into a united political struggle of non-Brahmins (including Telugu and Malayali ethnic communities) against the Hindu Brahmin elite. Thus, resistance to Hindi became central to the movement, which soon turned into a demand for political autonomy.[74] One major difference between this movement and India's other separatist movements, however, is that while Indira Gandhi dismissed the government in the Indian state of Tamil Nadu during the state of emergency in February 1976,[75] India nonetheless provided the Tamils of Sri Lanka facing repression from the majority Sinhalese with safe sanctuaries, arms, and political support in the late 1970s and at the start of the Sri Lankan civil war.[76]

Managing Regional Domination

Alongside the many centrifugal challenges to internal security, Indira Gandhi worried about the "growing strategic ties between China and Pakistan."[77] According to Indian strategic planners, Pakistan was the main obstacle that stood in the way of India achieving regional dominance and

having a greater strategic role in world politics.[78] Hence, undermining
Pakistan's power and influence became an important strategic goal under
Indira Gandhi's leadership, who believed the Indian military should be
prepared to fight a joint China-Pakistan offensive while simultaneously
subduing India's internal security threats.[79]

Gandhi's perfect storm arrived when Pakistan's military crackdown
in East Pakistan in March 1971 resulted in the flow of nearly 10 million
refugees into India. Gandhi provided sanctuaries and training camps for
the Bengali secessionists—the Mukti Bahini (Freedom Force)—and India
supported the insurgency and attacks on the Pakistani military and West
Pakistanis residing in East Pakistan. Civil war raged in East Pakistan
throughout the summer, and in late November 1971 Gandhi dispatched
Indian troops to East Pakistan, resulting in India's third all-out war with
Pakistan. Aided by the Mukti Bahini, the Indian army marched into the
capital Dhaka and forced the Pakistani troops to surrender; and so an
independent Bangladesh came into being on December 16, 1971.[80]

The dismemberment of Pakistan allowed Gandhi, who was now a
national hero, to proclaim the end of the two-nation theory and India's
regional primacy. India signed a peace accord with Pakistan at Simla in
1972 which paved the way for the return of territory as well as the 90,000
prisoners of war held by India.[81] Subsequently, in 1975, Gandhi signed
an agreement with the popular Kashmiri leader, Sheikh Mohammed
Abdullah, who allegedly agreed to accept the new reality of Indian
predominance after 1971. In return for Sheikh Abdullah's agreement
to forgo Kashmir's demand for independence, Gandhi agreed to make
the special status and autonomy of the states of Jammu and Kashmir
(Articles 35A and 370 of the Indian constitution) permanent.[82]

With the signing of the Simla Agreement in 1972 and the Kashmir
Accord in 1975, it appeared that Indira Gandhi had solved India's Pakistan
problem as well as the problem of Kashmir. India could bask in the glory
of its victory over Pakistan and its acceptance as a regional power. It
was at this point, in 1974, that India conducted what it called a peaceful

nuclear explosion—the first defiant signal that India's ambition was not restricted to regional power alone and that it sought to challenge China's position as a major power and the developing US-China détente. Three years later, despite her successes, Gandhi was ousted from power in the elections of 1977 and a new government was formed under the Janata Party and its leader Morarji Desai that lasted till 1980.

A Transformed Regional Landscape

Upon her return to power in 1980, Indira Gandhi found a changed regional security landscape on India's periphery. There were renewed tensions between Afghanistan and Pakistan following the 1973 coup in Afghanistan that overthrew King Mohammed Zahir Shah and brought President Sardar Dawood to power. For a decade or more under King Shah, political and border disputes between Pakistan and Afghanistan had been in abeyance, but a series of coups in Afghanistan in the 1970s drastically altered the dynamics in the borderlands as Afghan refugees started pouring into Pakistan—often with the Afghan military in pursuit.

The Soviet invasion of Afghanistan in 1979 transformed Pakistan into a frontline state. Zulfiqar Bhutto, who had signed the Simla Agreement with Indira Gandhi, was overthrown in a coup in 1977 and later hanged. For India, martial law in Pakistan was nothing new, except that this regime was of a different kind. Devoutly religious, Pakistan's new president, General Muhammad Zia-ul-Haq, was determined to transform Pakistan into a Sunni theocracy. That same year, in neighboring Iran, the Islamic revolution deposed and exiled the Shah. Hence, both Iran and Pakistan simultaneously transmuted from secular leadership and moderate societies into authoritarian Islamist states based on two different (and opposing) sectarian schools of thought. These transformations were happening concurrent to America's asymmetric war against the Soviet occupation in Afghanistan.

Enforcing India's Monroe Doctrine

Just a few months before her assassination, as Indian forces were storming the Sikhs' Golden Temple in Amritsar, Indira Gandhi approved another military operation code-named Operation Meghdoot, which was launched in April 1984 to capture the Siachen Glacier in the un-demarcated area above the Line of Control (LoC) in Kashmir. This triggered an India-Pakistan military standoff which has continued in that inhospitable terrain for nearly four decades. Another military crisis between India and Pakistan known as the Brass Tacks Crisis occurred two years later, which will be analyzed in chapter 5.

While tensions in the Siachen Glacier and along the LoC continued, in 1987 India held state elections in the Indian-administered state of Jammu and Kashmir; the elections were heavily rigged to install a political leadership favorable to India.[83] India met the resulting Kashmiri protests with strong-armed suppressive measures that failed to resolve the problem, and by 1989 Kashmir was experiencing a major uprising that continues to date. The Kashmiri uprising provided Pakistan with an excuse to launch a "full-scale proxy war in Kashmir," into which it diverted trained guerrilla fighters from the Afghan war.[84]

Meanwhile, in the south, the Tamil crisis in Sri Lanka spiraled into a civil war that lasted for nearly 30 years.[85] In mid-1987, Prime Minister Rajiv Gandhi strong-armed Sri Lanka into allowing an Indian Peacekeeping Force (IPKF) into Sri Lanka to quash the very Tamil rebellion that began under his mother's watch.[86] Rajiv Gandhi had two major concerns for sending the IPKF mission to Sri Lanka. First, India was concerned that the Tamil revolt in Sri Lanka would have a catalytic impact on India's Tamil population, which still nursed various grievances. Second, India was concerned that the Sri Lankan crisis could induce interference from external powers in what India always considered its own backyard.[87] In particular, India feared the United States might intervene in the conflict and gain a "geostrategic foothold" in the region.[88] Eventually, India's IPKF enterprise backfired as Indian forces became deeply mired in the Tamil insurgency, and in 1990 India withdrew completely from Sri Lanka after less than three years. Thus, India's first outside intervention since the 1971 Bangladesh war ended in failure and laid the foundations for mistrust with Sri Lanka.[89] And just as the mishandling of the Sikh Uprising cost Indira Gandhi her life, so too did the Tamil crisis cost that of her son's; Rajiv Gandhi was assassinated in a Tamil suicide attack in 1991.[90]

To India's north, the tiny landlocked Himalayan kingdom of Nepal is sandwiched between India and China. In 1989 Nepal sought to improve its economic and military ties with China and purchased Chinese air-defense weapons. India reacted swiftly by enforcing an economic blockade and increasing tariffs on some Indian goods, which succeeded in forcing the Nepalese government to backtrack.[91] Since then, Nepal has undergone several internal crises, including the overthrow of its monarchy. Hence, given its extreme vulnerability as a landlocked country, it remains a pliant neighbor of its southern "big brother."

In the Indian Ocean region, an attempted coup in November 1988 against Maldives president Maumoon Abdul Gayoom also prompted India to intervene. Approximately 200 mercenaries took control of key points in the Maldives capital, and the distressed Gayoom regime sought military assistance from world powers.[92] Rajiv Gandhi seized the opportunity and responded by sending naval warships to the Maldives, successfully overpowering the rebels and restoring government control.[93] The major powers lauded India's maritime intervention, which reinforced India's objective of gaining acceptance for New Delhi's "zone of influence," as well as the notion that an assertive policy pays dividends.[94]

These examples portray a realist strategy that guided India's interventions in other states to increase its power and achieve hegemonic status. As the Cold War waned, however, India's heavy-handed polices were themselves becoming a threat to Indian democracy and security.[95] India therefore began to nuance its policy approach from hard-core realism toward a more neoliberal approach of reaching out to its neighborhood, restoring communications, and developing confidence-building measures with both China and Pakistan, which will be analyzed in later chapters.

End of the Line for the Indira Doctrine

New Delhi is often criticized for lacking a grand strategy; however, the Indira Doctrine represents the first indication of a well-thought-out, coherent concept of national security. Indira Gandhi's strategy extended her father Nehru's "broad doctrine," and her son furthered the projection of India's power beyond the Indian Subcontinent into the Indian Ocean region.[96]

By 1989, however, it was clear to Prime Minister Rajiv Gandhi that the thrust to consolidate power through harsh internal measures and aggressive external policies was weakening India's position, even as it sought to take up its place in the international hierarchy.[97] Rajiv Gandhi and his successors therefore began seeking dialogue and inclusiveness in a process of healing the multi-directional crises on the Subcontinent— an indication that the Nehruvian and Gandhian approaches still had a role to play (if only partially) in settling disputes. Hence, the policies of Indira and Rajiv Gandhi laid the foundations that have shaped India's grand strategy for subsequent generations.[98]

At the same time, India also needed a major remodeling of its closed economy (which had been a contributing factor for several of its domestic crises) and to give up its fascination with socialist and Marxist economic models. The Cold War was ending, and new opportunities were knocking on India's door—just as India was becoming mired in the insurgency in Kashmir.

The Gujral Doctrine

Inder Kumar Gujral was India's prime minister for only a short period, from April 1997 until March 1998, but he was the first to present an alternative strategy to the Indira Doctrine. The Gujral Doctrine attempted to reverse Indira Gandhi's hardline approach and move toward the

Nehruvian approach of accommodation, compromise, and negotiated settlement, both domestically and in the region. Before becoming prime minister, Gujral had served as minister of information and broadcasting under Indira Gandhi, and he was minister of external affairs under two administrations in the 1990s.[99] Gujral was convinced that for India to sustain its power at the global level, it must stabilize itself internally and have good relations with its immediate neighbors to give them confidence and a stake in India's rise.[100] Under this precept, Gujral insisted India must follow the enduring principles of respecting sovereign equality and adhering to universal non-interference in the South Asian region.[101] The Gujral Doctrine is therefore a blend of Nehruvian and neoliberal approaches to India's grand strategy that transforms India's image from one of seeking hegemony to that of assuming a leadership role in the region.

Chatham House Speech

In a famous speech at Chatham House in London in 1996, while still minister of external affairs, Gujral formally articulated the basic principles of his foreign policy. The premise of his vision stems "from the belief that India's stature and strength cannot be divorced from the quality of its relations with its neighbors."[102] Hoping to mitigate the fears of India's smaller neighbors, Gujral was creating a new climate of "close and mutually benign cooperation in the region."[103] Gujral set out his five key principles:

> First, with the neighbours like Nepal, Bangladesh, Bhutan, Maldives and Sri Lanka, India does not ask for reciprocity but gives all that it can in good faith and trust. Secondly, no South Asian country will allow its territory to be used against the interest of another country of the region. Thirdly, none will interfere in the internal affairs of another. Fourthly, all South Asian countries must respect each other's territorial integrity and sovereignty. And finally, they will settle all their disputes through peaceful bilateral negotiations. These five principles, scrupulously observed, will, I am sure, recast South Asia's regional relationship, including the

tormented relationship between India and Pakistan, in a friendly, cooperative mould.[104]

Gujral used the speech not only to outline India's actions but also to clearly state India's expectations of its neighbors in return. The first principle, based on reciprocity, presents an opportunity for smaller countries in the region to expect concessions from India without worrying about respective sizes and power differences—Gujral sought to eliminate the historical fear of India, with its vast geography, casting a huge shadow of intimidation over weaker states to extract concessions. The second principle clearly states that no country in the region would permit its territory to be used against the interest of another country and that all states must respect the sovereignty of the others. The third principle emphasizes explicit agreement on non-interference in the internal affairs of India's neighbors. This was a significant promise for India's smaller neighbors, given India's previous track record of aggressive interventions.[105] The fourth principle endorses mutual respect for territorial integrity and sovereignty as the foundation of intrastate relations in South Asia.[106] The final principle is a reiteration of India's grand strategic thinking concerning the bilateral settlement of disputes, past and present. The emphasis on "bilateral" in the doctrine indicated India's disapproval of outside intervention in regional affairs.

The Gujral Doctrine employed a soft-power approach with an emphasis on cultural commonalities as the basis for understanding and cooperation. Under this view, South Asian fraternal development would follow a principle of states offering cross-border concessions to each other, which would help develop a sense of regionalism. The Gujral Doctrine would usher in a new era of cooperative security arrangements and enhanced confidence-building measures, replacing policies of coercion and the threat of force. Despite the differences in approach, the end goal was the same as the Indira Doctrine—raising India's status to that of a global power.[107]

Through this policy, Gujral sought to implement peaceful initiatives and make concessions with India's immediate neighbors, but not Pakistan and China. His intention was to maximize New Delhi's overall position in the region, which would in turn enable India to engage with Pakistan and China from a position of relative strength. By keeping Pakistan out of the policy of non-reciprocal concessions to neighbors, Gujral attempted to isolate Pakistan and dissuade South Asian countries from allying with it. Pakistan would then be left to choose between continued regional competition or submission to India. India would then be free to focus on projecting its influence outward and brace for competition with China.

Although he was only prime minister for a short time, Gujral's revolutionary policies laid the foundations for the liberal policies of his successors Atal Bihari Vajpayee and Manmohan Singh at the start of the twenty-first century, which transited India away from previous decades of autarkic economy. Liberalizing the economy gave India the diplomatic space to forge stronger bonds with its smaller neighbors and to bring South Asian states closer together economically, despite the absence of a regional framework like the European Union (EU) or the Association of Southeast Asian Nations (ASEAN).[108] (It should be noted in this context that although the South Asian Association for Regional Cooperation [SAARC] had emerged in 1985, this framework remained mired in tensions and crises, primarily between India and Pakistan, being the two largest states involved.)[109]

Renowned South Asian scholar Sandy Gordon echoes the centrality of the Gujral Doctrine for India's rise:

> If India can stabilize and consolidate its domestic and neighborhood environments, it will be more capable of meeting its own goal of strategic autonomy. If, on the other hand, it continues to remain mired in the problems of South Asia, its growth and stability will be impaired and its strategic reliance on the United States, especially vis-à-vis China, will be greater. Its potential role in any Asian Order will likely be restrained.[110]

India's Changing Power Dynamics
One of the founding principles of the Gujral Doctrine was to counter the impression of India as an expansionist power, although, given India's historical record, this was no easy task.

In January 1996, India and Bangladesh signed the Treaty on Sharing of the Ganges Waters at Farakka—the first treaty between the two countries in eight years. Bangladesh's economy relies heavily on the River Ganges, which flows from India into Bangladesh, and the absence of a treaty had hurt Bangladeshi rice farmers. The treaty was significant, in that Gujral sought no reciprocal concession from Bangladesh.[111] In the same year, India renewed the India-Nepal Treaty for five years, which allowed Nepalese manufacturing firms to trade freely on the Indian market.[112] Hence Gujral was able to implement his doctrine successfully, and in the process, he managed to change perceptions of India as a bully to that of a neighbor from whom the whole region could derive benefits.

India explicitly excluded Pakistan from its neighbors-first policy. One probable reason may be Pakistan's continued support for the Kashmir separatist movement that was in full swing in the 1990s. Nevertheless, Gujral decided on diplomatic engagement with Pakistan, increasing people-to-people contact to forge greater cultural ties and investment in confidence-building measures—including talks between the respective foreign ministers, which began in June 1997.[113] Pakistan's prime minister Nawaz Sharif also embraced the peace overtures from his Indian counterpart, and in May 1997 India and Pakistan initiated bilateral peace talks known as the Composite Dialogue Process (CDP).[114] In the spirit of Gujral's vision of settling disputes peacefully through dialogue and bilateral negotiations, the CDP identified eight areas for negotiation between the two countries, including discussion of Jammu and Kashmir.[115] Some experts cite these peace talks as a sign that both leaders sought increased harmony in their relations at this time.[116] Unfortunately, the CDP eventually dissipated because subsequent Indian and Pakistani governments—besides having different agendas and policies—vacillated between military crisis management and continuing diplomatic engagement with each other.

India's other nemesis was China, which was both a competitor on the periphery and a direct challenger in India's extended neighborhood. Gujral employed his strategic doctrine to improve relations with China by reaching out to President Jiang Zemin. In 1996, India and China also engaged in confidence-building measures to improve bilateral relations, and they agreed to freeze their long-contested border dispute;[117] as negotiations progressed, the China-India border was "significantly demilitarized and its tranquility reconfirmed."[118] Since then, India's policy toward China has been a mix of security competition alongside economic engagement.

India failed to convince its neighbors that its rise was purely benign —especially given the history of military intervention that Gujral's predecessors had preferred. Nor could it prevent South Asian states on its periphery from developing their own relations with external powers (most notably China and the United States), particularly in a period of increasing globalization and improved communications in the information age. Despite this, shifts in the international system, the major powers' interests in regional economic liberalization, and India's revised approach to non-alignment enabled India to position itself as an Asian bridgehead for Western powers to contain China's rise.

There are three reasons why the Gujral Doctrine did not become the mainstay of India's grand strategy. First, Gujral was unable to develop a consensus within the strategic enclaves, where entrenched bureaucratic elements resisted a grand strategy based on liberal foundations. Second, the strategy relied upon bilateral relations and shied away from creating a regional institutional framework.[119] Finally, the isolation of Pakistan increased tensions between India and Pakistan and was the main reason for regionalism's failure.[120] Nonetheless, even though the Gujral Doctrine did not take root in the way its originator had hoped, its key principles have continued to influence the grand strategy of subsequent Indian administrations—notwithstanding the jettisoning of its more liberal features, particularly after the 1998 nuclear tests.

The Vajpayee-Singh Era: Merging Realpolitik with Idealism

When the Bharatiya Janata Party (BJP) formed a new government in March 1998, Prime Minister Atal Bihari Vajpayee followed in the footsteps of the Indira Doctrine and its architect by conducting nuclear tests in May 1998. In doing so, he removed any doubts that India would continue to accept being left out as a major power. For New Delhi, the tests were a "symbol of India's multifaceted strength demanding international recognition for India's enhanced scientific and technological capability."[121]

Vajpayee was a true statesman. Rather than following the hawkish policy that the BJP manifesto promised, Vajpayee remodeled the Gujral Doctrine with a more aggressive form of diplomacy and a peace initiative toward India's neighbors, including Pakistan. Vajpayee displayed pragmatism throughout his five years in office.

From Bus Diplomacy to an Era of Crisis

Vajpayee's crowning achievement was his dramatic bus ride across the border to Lahore in Pakistan in February 1999 and the signing of the Lahore Declaration, setting a new precedent for bilateral engagement with Pakistan. The Lahore Declaration included provisions for deliberations to take place to achieve a peaceful resolution of the dispute over Kashmir, in addition to policies to manage nuclear relations and assure stability, including discussions on a framework to avoid the accidental or unauthorized use of nuclear weapons.[122] Vajpayee's bus expedition showed the world that India could advance the Gujral Doctrine aggressively and decisively with Pakistan.[123]

Nonetheless, the 1999 diplomatic offensive failed when it was discovered that Pakistani soldiers had infiltrated areas on the Indian-administered side of the LoC in the high mountainous region. The infiltrators were intercepted at several places on the road linking Kashmir's state capital

Srinagar with Leh district in Ladakh, threatening the logistical supply line to the Indian troops deployed in the Siachen Glacier. The ensuing military conflict—known as the Kargil War and lasting from May to July 1999—erupted exactly a year after India and Pakistan conducted their nuclear tests. The conflict remained geographically confined to the area and did not escalate horizontally along the LoC or along the international border. Vajpayee could have escalated the conflict into a wider war in Kashmir, but he chose instead to restrict military operations to the Kargil sector and to escalate it vertically using airpower.[124] Vajpayee's strategic restraint and controlled use of force won many global accolades, praising him as a true statesman who understood the potential of nuclear instability. More importantly for India, it made Pakistan look like a "reckless ... risk-acceptant, untrustworthy state" in the nuclear environment.[125]

Two years later, in the summer of 2001, in yet another bold initiative, Vajpayee invited President General Pervez Musharraf—the architect of the intrusion into Kargil—to a summit meeting in Agra, hoping to restart the stalled peace process of Lahore in 1999. Although the Agra summit failed to reach a formal agreement, Vajpayee's desire to change the nature of India-Pakistan relations displayed the extended spirit of the Gujral Doctrine. Yet, for all his political sagacity and strength as a leader, Vajpayee faced the same obstacles within the bureaucracy as his predecessor Gujral, particularly the deeply embedded resistance to engagement with Pakistan.

September 11, 2001, saw the terror attacks in New York and Washington, DC, and just a few months later, five militants of Pakistani origin attacked the Indian parliament and killed nine security personnel.[126] In the post-9/11 security environment, such an attack on India's parliament—the symbol of Indian democracy—shocked the world and radically changed international perceptions of the nature of India-Pakistan relations and the Kashmir dispute. The uprising in Kashmir was now conflated with terrorism. Prime Minister Vajpayee described the attack as an "act of war" and ordered the mobilization of over 500,000 Indian troops to the border with Pakistan. By April 2002, Pakistan had counter-mobilized, deploying 300,000 troops and bracing to meet an Indian offensive; it also made subtle nuclear signaling through missile tests. This was by far the biggest coercive military deployment on the Subcontinent's history.[127]

For 10 months, the military standoff between the two nuclear-armed neighbors loomed over the Subcontinent; meanwhile, American forces were conducting major military operations (Operation Enduring Freedom and Operation Anaconda) in Afghanistan.[128] Just before the Indian elections in 2004, Vajpayee reached out to Islamabad for a third time to kick-start the peace process. Both sides agreed to begin talks, but just a few weeks later the BJP lost the elections and Vajpayee left office. With Vajpayee's departure from the political scene, the Subcontinent lost an astute and determined leader who truly held out the promise of establishing a peace and security architecture.

The incoming government under Prime Minister Manmohan Singh (2004–2013) continued efforts to reach détente with Pakistan.[129] As long as President Pervez Musharraf was in office, an optimal window for India-Pakistan rapprochement remained alive, and both sides used back-door diplomacy to discuss a possible end to the conflicts, including a solution to Kashmir, the Siachen Glacier, and Sir Creek. Musharraf's downfall in 2007–2008 closed this rare window of opportunity. Since then, Pakistan has struggled with intense domestic problems, and the promise of peace has retreated.

In November 2008, as the United States commemorated Thanksgiving weekend, India's commercial capital Mumbai came under fierce attack. The target was Mumbai's prestigious Taj Hotel, its railway station, and a synagogue; it was a calamitous attack that killed 174 people. Foreign Secretary Shivshankar Menon stated he had "never seen levels of anger like this" amongst the Indian people following the attack.[130] Mayhem and confusion temporarily reigned until Indian security forces eventually restored order, killing all but one of the terrorists. The survivor was traced to a Pakistan-based organization called Lashkar-e-Tayyaba (LeT).

Just as in 1999, when the Kargil crisis dashed all hopes of building peace on the back of the Lahore Agreement, the 2008 Mumbai attack quashed similar hopes arising from the efforts of President Musharraf and Prime Minister Manmohan Singh. The liberal Gujral Doctrine was now dead in the water, and India's domestic situation meant that all peace overtures to Pakistan were henceforth politically impossible.

STILL SEARCHING

In sum, both the Indira Doctrine and the Gujral Doctrine provided two separate pathways to the same end at critical junctures in India's history. The moderate approach of Gujral, Vajpayee, and Singh failed to resolve India's "Pakistan problem," primarily due to resistance amongst the strategic enclaves. The hardline approach only compounded India's internal security and eventually provided greater space for the hyper-realists and extreme right-wing hardliners to come to power. Since the election of the BJP in 2014, India has adopted a radically different approach that has changed India's secular character and pushed minorities—especially Indian Muslims—farther out of the political arena.[131] The implications of India's new doctrine will be discussed in full detail in chapter 6.

India currently wishes to dominate the Indian Ocean region through naval expansion and power projection capabilities.[132] It is developing ties with the West—particularly the United States, which has begun buttressing India as a bulwark against the rise of China. However, for India to maintain regional influence, it must first gain the confidence of its South Asian neighbors. At the same time, critics argue that unless India develops a self-sufficient, indigenous defense-industrial base, boosts domestic production of its military materials, and relies less on external powers, it will continue to face challenges in applying its version of the Monroe Doctrine on the Subcontinent and in the wider neighborhood.[133]

As we move into the third decade of the twenty-first century, India's quest for a viable grand strategy continues. Indian leaders desire their nation to brandish its prowess as a global power, but they are unable to devise a clear strategy to achieve that objective. At the system level, India's most pressing strategic concern is competition from China, which is expanding its influence and economic interests across Asia and moving into India's neighborhood. The incentives being offered by China are very attractive to India's neighbors, who are far more concerned with coming out of the shadow of their "big brother" India than the probability of distant partners seeking a geopolitical foothold in South Asia.[134]

Notes

1. Jawaharlal Nehru, "Not Forgotten: The 'Tryst with Destiny' Speech that Divided India and Pakistan," *New York Times*, August 14, 2016, https://www.nytimes.com/interactive/projects/cp/obituaries/archives/india-pakistan.

2. Suzelle Thomas, "India's Grand Strategy: Ambitions and Capacity" (Master's thesis, Naval Postgraduate School, 2019).

3. Shivshankar Menon, *Choices: Inside the Making of India's Foreign Policy* (Washington, DC: Brookings Institution Press, 2016), 132.

4. C. Raja Mohan, *Crossing the Rubicon: The Shaping of India's New Foreign Policy,* (New Delhi: Penguin/Viking, 2003), 204. See also C. Christine Fair, "Waiting for Lord Curzon: India's Grand Strategy in the Long Shadow of Nehru," *SSRN Electronic Journal* (January 2018), https://www.doi.org/10.2139/ssrn.3271245.

5. Rajesh Rajagopalan, "Neorealist Theory and the India-Pakistan Conflict," *Strategic Analysis* 22, no. 9 (December 2008): 1261–1272, https://www.tandfonline.com/doi/abs/10.1080/09700169808458882.

6. Feroz Hassan Khan, *Eating Grass: The Making of the Pakistani Bomb* (Palo Alto, CA: Stanford University Press, 2012), 4–5.

7. George Tanham, *Indian Strategic Thought: An Interpretive Essay*, R-4207-USDP (Santa Monica, CA: RAND Corporation, 1992), v, https://www.rand.org/pubs/reports/R4207.html.

8. Tanham, *Indian Strategic Thought*, 1–22; Cohen, *India: Emerging Power* (Washington, DC: Brookings Institution Press, 1978), 10.

9. Tanham, *Indian Strategic Thought*, 23–24.

10. Cohen, *India: Emerging Power*, 10–13.

11. Tanham, *Indian Strategic Thought*, 6.

12. Cohen, *India: Emerging Power*, 7–8.

13. Cohen, *India: Emerging Power*, 10; Tanham, *Indian Strategic Thought*, 24, 29.

14. Tanham, *Indian Strategic Thought*, 12.

15. M. S. Rajan, "The Impact of British Rule in India," *Journal of Contemporary History* 4, no. 1 (January 1969): 90, https://doi.org/10.1177/002200946900400106.

16. The term used by a retired Indian navy participant in a bilateral US-India Track II naval dialogue held in Sydney, Australia, in April 2019.

17. John H. Gill, "Challenges for India's Military Strategy: Matching Capabilities to Ambitions?" in *Strategic Asia 2017–18: Power, Ideas, and Military Strategy in the Asia-Pacific*, ed. Ashley Tellis, Alison Szalwinski, and Michael Wills (Washington, DC: National Bureau of Research, 2017), 148.

18. Cohen, *India: Emerging Power*, 8.

19. Stephen P. Cohen and Sunil Dasgupta, *Arming without Aiming: India's Military Modernization* (Washington, DC: Brookings Institute Press, 2010).

20. Kanti Bajpai, Saira Basit, and V. Krishnappa, *India's Grand Strategy: History, Theory, Cases* (New Delhi: Routledge, 2014), 1–10.

21. See V. D. Savarkar, "Essentials of Hindutva," BJP Central Library, http://library.bjp.org/jspui/bitstream/123456789/284/3/essentials_of_hindutva.v001.pdf. See also Lala Lajpat Rai, *Young India: An Interpretation and a History of the Nationalist Movement from Within* (New York: B. W. Huebsch, 1916). Lala Lajpat Rai was a staunch Hindu nationalist.

22. See, for example, Bharat Karnad, *Nuclear Weapons and Indian Security: The Realist Foundations of Strategy*, (New Delhi: MacMillan, 2002).

23. Ian Hall, "Narendra Modi's New Religious Diplomacy," *International Studies Perspectives*, 2019 (20), pages 11-14.

24. Kanti Bajpai, "India Does Do Grand Strategy," *Global Brief*, Winter, 2013, https://globalbrief.ca/2013/03/india-does-go-grand-strategy/.

25. C. Raja Mohan, *Modi's World: Expanding India's Sphere of Influence*, (New York: HarperCollins Publishers, 2015), 113.

26. Shantanu Bhagwat, "The Nonsense about the 'Hindu Rate of Growth,'" *Times of India*, February 8, 2013, https://timesofindia.indiatimes.com/blogs/reclaiming-india/the-nonsense-about-the-hindu-rate-of-growth/.

27. Selig S. Harrison, *India: The Most Dangerous Decades* (Princeton, NJ: Princeton University Press, 1960).

28. Harrison, *India*, 3.

29. Maya Chadda, *Ethnicity, Security, and Separatism in India* (New York: Columbia University Press, 1997), 1–8.

30. Srinath Raghavan, *War and Peace in Modern India* (Bangalore: Orient Black Swan, 2010), 18.

31. Cohen and Dasgupta, *Arming without Aiming*, 29.

32. K. Subrahmanyam, "India's Grand Strategy: Knowledge, Not Weapons, Will be the Currency of Power in This Century," *Indian Express*, February 3, 2012, https://indianexpress.com/article/opinion/columns/indias-grand-strategy/.

33. Subrahmanyam, "India's Grand Strategy."

34. Ashley J. Tellis, *Nonalignment Redux: The Perils of Old Wine in New Skins* (Washington, DC: Carnegie Endowment for International Peace, 2012), http://carnegieendowment.org/2012/07/10/nonalignment-redux-perils-of-old-wine-in-new-skins-pub-48675.

35. Gill, "Challenges," 140–172.

36. Menon, *Choices*, 134.

37. Happymon Jacob, "The 'Delhi Dogma' Fallacy of the Right," *The Hindu*, December 24, 2019, https://www.thehindu.com/opinion/lead/the-delhi-dogma-fallacy-of-the-right/article30279716.ece.

38. Mohan, *Crossing the Rubicon*, 1–12.

39. Shyam Saran, *How India Sees the World: From Kautilya to Modi* (New Delhi: Juggernaut Books, 2017), 42; Mohan, *Crossing the Rubicon*, 38.

40. Saran, *How India Sees the World*, 33; Ramesh Thakur, "India and the Soviet Union: Conjunctions and Disjunctions of Interests," *Asian Survey* 31, no. 9 (September 1991): 826–830, https://doi.org/10.2307/2645298.

41. Rajesh Rajagopalan, *India's Strategic Choices: China and the Balance of Power in Asia* (Washington, DC: Carnegie India, 2017), 10–13. https://carnegieendowment.org/files/CP_312_Rajesh_Strategic_Choices_FNL.pdf.

42. Mohan, *Crossing the Rubicon*, 260.

43. Mohan, *Crossing the Rubicon*, 37–38; C. Raja Mohan, "India and the Balance of Power," *Foreign Affairs* (July/August 2006), https://www.foreignaffairs.com/articles/asia/2006-07-01/india-and-balance-power. 18–21; Cohen, *India: Emerging Power*, 25–34.

44. Jean-Alphonse Bernard and Michel Pochoy, *L'ambition de l'Inde* [The Ambition of India] (Paris: Fondation pour les études de défense nationale, 1988), 32.

45. Jaswant Singh, *Defending India* (London: Macmillan Press, 1999), 195–200.

46. Richard Sisson and Leo F. Rose, *War and Secession: Pakistan, India, and the Creation of Bangladesh* (Berkeley: University of California Press, 1990), 208.

47. Singh, *Defending India*, 144.

48. Ashley J. Tellis, *Nonalignment Redux: The Perils of Old Wine in New Skins* (Washington, DC: Carnegie Endowment for International Peace, 2012), https://carnegieendowment.org/2012/03/12/nonalignment-2.0-foreign-and-strategic-policy-for-india-in-twenty-first-century-event-3587.

49. Mohan, *Crossing the Rubicon*, xvii–xx.

50. Saran, *How India Sees the World*, 45–51.

51. Mohan, *Crossing the Rubicon*, 12.
52. Strobe Talbott, *Engaging India: Diplomacy. Democracy, and the Bomb* (Washington, DC: Brookings Institution Press, 2004), 5.
53. Mohan, *Crossing the Rubicon*; Mohan, "India and the Balance of Power."
54. Verghese Koithara, *Managing India's Nuclear Forces* (Washington, DC: The Brookings Institution, 2012), 2.
55. Strobe Talbott, *Engaging India*, 6, 86.
56. For more information, see Mark Rosen and Douglas Jackson, *The US-India Defense Relationship: Putting the Foundational Agreements in Perspective* (Arlington, VA: Center for Naval Analyses, 2017), https://www.cna.org/CNA_files/PDF/DRM-2016-U-013926-Final2.pdf.
57. Yogesh Joshi and Frank O'Donnell, *India and Nuclear Asia: Forces, Doctrine, and Dangers* (Washington, DC: Georgetown University Press, 2018), 1.
58. Tellis, *Nonalignment Redux.*
59. Thomas, "India's Grand Strategy."
60. Surjit Mansingh, *India's Search for Power: Indira Gandhi's Foreign Policy 1966–1982* (New Delhi: Sage Publications, 1984), 34.
61. Sisson and Rose, *War and Secession*, 208.
62. Madhuparna Gupta, "Indira Gandhi: Elections and Domestic Policy," in *Women, Power, and Leadership: Case Studies of Indira Gandhi, Margaret Thatcher, and Golda Meir* (Bloomington, IL: Partridge Publishing India, 2015), 37–118, http://shodhganga.inflibnet.ac.in/bitstream/10603/13308 7/7/07_chapter%202.pdf.
63. "Indira Gandhi Convicted of Election Fraud," *History*, https://www.history.com/this-day-in-history/indira-gandhi-convicted-of-election-fraud.
64. Rajat Ganguly, "India's Military: Evolution, Modernisation and Transformation," *India Quarterly* 71, no. 3 (August 2015), https://journals.sagepub.com/doi/10.1177/0974928415584021.
65. Balraj Puri, "Era of Indira Gandhi," *Economic and Political Weekly* 20, no. 4 (January 1985): 148.
66. Daniel P. Marston, "The Indian Army, Partition, and the Punjab Boundary Force," *War in History* 16, no. 4 (November 2009): 469–505.
67. Fred Burton and Ben West, "A Closer Look at India's Naxalite Threat," Stratfor Worldview, July 8, 2010, https://worldview.stratfor.com/article/closer-look-indias-naxalite-threat.
68. Ayush Manandhar, "The Rise, Fall, and Triumph of South Asian Insurgencies: Part III—India," *Georgetown Public Policy Review*, March 21,

2019, http://gppreview.com/2019/03/21/rise-fall-triumph-south-asian-insurgencies-part-iii-india/.

69. "Naxalism Greatest Threat to Internal Security: PM," *India Today*, February 7, 2010, https://www.indiatoday.in/india/story/naxalism-greatest-threat-to-internal-security-pm-66750-2010-02-06.

70. "Akali Sikh Movement," *Encyclopedia Britannica*, March 13, 2020, https://www.britannica.com/topic/Akali.

71. Puri, "Era of Indira Gandhi," 150.

72. "Indira Gandhi," *History*, August 21, 2008, https://www.history.com/topics/india/indira-gandhi.

73. Mark Tully and Satish Jacob, *Amritsar: Mrs. Gandhi's Last Battle* (London: Jonathan Cape, 1985), 2.

74. Chadda, *Ethnicity, Security, and Separatism*, 75.

75. "India State Calm after Take Over," *New York Times*, February, 8, 1976, https://www.nytimes.com/1976/02/08/archives/india-state-calm-after-takeover-tamil-nadu-accepting-rule-by-the.html.

76. Chadda, *Ethnicity, Security, and Separatism*, 76.

77. Ganguly, "India's Military."

78. Tanham, *Indian Strategic Thought*, 31–35

79. Ganguly, "India's Military."

80. Navine Murshid, "India's Role in Bangladesh's War of Independence: Humanitarianism or Self-interest?" *Economic and Political Weekly* 46, no. 52 (2011), 53–60, http://www.jstor.org/stable/41719989.

81. India claims that the Simla Agreement supersedes UN resolutions because the international dispute remains a bilateral issue, whereas Pakistan rejects this interpretation. However, it is widely believed that at the time both leaders informally agreed to put the issue of Kashmir on the backburner.

82. Chadda, *Ethnicity, Security, and Separatism*, 100. Many Kashmiri leaders would later deny that Sheikh Abdullah gave any commitment to forgo Kashmiris' right to self-determination.

83. Sten Widmalm, "The Rise and Fall of Democracy in Jammu and Kashmir", *Asian Survey* 37, no. 11 (November 1997): 1005–1030, https://www.jstor.org/stable/2645738.

84. Paven Nair, "The Siachen War: Twenty-Five Years On," *Economic and Political Weekly* 44, no. 11 (March 2009): 35–40, https://www.jstor.org/stable/pdf/40278612.pdf?refreqid=excelsior%3A3b85be63f22dd370b8f39560850e8202.

85. "Factbox: India's Role in Sri Lanka's Civil War," Reuters, October 17, 2008, https://uk.reuters.com/article/idUKCOL223047.
86. Reuters, "Factbox."
87. Devin T. Hagerty, "India's Regional Security Doctrine," *Asian Survey* 31, no. 4 (April 1991): 351–363, https://doi.org/10.2307/2645389.
88. James R. Holmes and Toshi Yoshihara, "India's 'Monroe Doctrine' and Asia's Maritime Future," *Strategic Analysis* 32, no. 6 (2018): 1000, https://doi.org/10.1080/09700160802404539.
89. Sandra Destradi, "India and the Civil War in Sri Lanka: On the Failures of Regional Conflict Management in South Asia," German Institute for Global and Area Studies (GIGA), 2010, http://www.jstor.org/stable/resrep07570.
90. "Rajiv Gandhi," *Encyclopedia Britannica*, May 17, 2019, https://www.britannica.com/biography/Rajiv-Gandhi.
91. Niranjan Koirala, "Nepal in 1989: A Very Difficult Year," *Asian Survey* 30, no. 2 (1990): 136–143, https://doi.org/10.2307/2644891.
92. David Brewster, "Operation Cactus: India's 1988 Intervention in the Maldives," in *India's Ocean: The Story of India's Bid for Regional Leadership* (New York: Routledge, 2014Error! Hyperlink reference not valid.).
93. Arafat Kabir, "The Maldives Crisis: Will India Intervene?", *The Diplomat*, February 27, 2018, https://thediplomat.com/2018/02/the-maldives-crisis-will-india-intervene/.
94. Brewster, "Operation Cactus."
95. Mansingh, *India's Search for Power*, 5.
96. Holmes and Yoshihara, "India's 'Monroe Doctrine,'" 999; see also Mansingh, *India's Search for Power*, 34.
97. Walker K. Andersen, "The Domestic Roots of Indian Foreign Policy," *Asian Affairs* 6, no. 3 (1983): 51, https://doi.org/10.1080/00927678.1983.10553720.
98. Thomas, "India's Grand Strategy," 14.
99. "Inder Kumar Gujral: Prime Minister of India," *Encyclopedia Britannica*, January 3, 2020, https://www.britannica.com/biography/Inder-Kumar-Gujral.
100. Rajiv Kumar Sharma, "Diplomat Prime Minister I. K. Gujral: His Foreign Policy and Gujral Doctrine," *Remarking* 3, no. 1 (June 2016): 63, http://www.socialresearchfoundation.com/upoadreserchpapers/5/106/16080 10943211st%20rajiv%20kumar%20sharma.pdf.
101. Sharma, "Diplomat Prime Minister," 63.

102. Padmaja Murthy, "The Gujral Doctrine and Beyond," *Strategic Analysis* 23, no. 4, (1999): 639, https://doi.org/10.1080/09700169908455072.

103. Murthy, "The Gujral Doctrine," 640.

104. Ashok Kumar Behuria, "Anil Kumar Reddy Asked: What is Gujral Doctrine?," Manohar Parrikar Institute for Defense Studies and Analyses, https://idsa.in/askanexpert/GujralDoctrine%3F

105. For examples, see Mohan, *Crossing the Rubicon*, 260–263.

106. Murthy, "The Gujral Doctrine," 641.

107. "The Gujral Doctrine," Henry L. Stimson Center, January 21, 1997, https://www.stimson.org/the-gujral-doctrine.

108. Jabin T. Jacob, "Book Review of Does South Asia Exist? Prospects for Regional Integration," *Journal of South Asian Development* 7, no. 1 (2012): 65–79, https://doi.org/10.1177/097317411200700105.

109. Feroz Hassan Khan, "Security Impediments to Regionalism in South Asia," in *Does South Asia Exist? Prospects for Regional Integration*, ed. Rafiq Dossani, Daniel C. Sneider, and Vikram Sood (Washington, DC: Brookings Institution, 2010), 227–247. See also "South Asian Association for Regional Co-operation," *Encyclopedia Britannica*, https://www.britannica.com/topic/South-Asian-Association-for-Regional-Co-operation.

110. Sandy Gordon, *India's Rise As An Asian Power: Nation, Neighborhood, and Region* (Washington, DC: Georgetown University Press, 2014), xxiv.

111. Bhabani Sen Gupta, "India in the Twenty-first Century," *International Affairs* 73, no. 2 (April 1997): 297–310, https://doi.org/10.2307/2623830.

112. Murthy, "The Gujral Doctrine," 647.

113. "Gujral Doctrine Notes," BYJU's, https://byjus.com/free-ias-prep/gujral-doctrine/.

114. Sajad Padder, "The Composite Dialogue between India and Pakistan: Structure, Process, and Agency," (Working Paper, South Asia Institute, 2012), 1, http://archiv.ub.uni-heidelberg.de/volltextserver/13143/1/Heidelberg_Papers_65_Padder.pdf.

115. Padder, "The Composite Dialogue," 1.

116. Murthy, "The Gujral Doctrine," 647.

117. BYJU's, "Gujral Doctrine Notes."

118. Gupta, "India in the Twenty-first Century," 310.

119. See, for example, Tom Kirk, "South Asia: How Regional Cooperation Could Bring Stability to the Region," *Global Policy* (online blog), October

1, 2018, https://www.globalpolicyjournal.com/blog/01/10/2018/south-asia-how-regional-cooperation-could-bring-stability-region.

120. Abdul Ghafoor Majee Noorani, "The Truth about the Lahore Summit," *Frontline* 19, no. 4 (February 2002), https://frontline.thehindu.com/other/article30244030.ece, 1.

121. Mansingh, "*India's Search for Power*," 8.

122. "Lahore Declaration," NTI, October 26, 2011, https://www.nti.org/learn/treaties-and-regimes/lahore-declaration/.

123. Murthy, "The Gujral Doctrine," 651.

124. "Kargil War," *New World Encyclopedia*, April 12, 2018, https://www.newworldencyclopedia.org/entry/Kargil_War.

125. Ashley J. Tellis, C. Christine Fair, and Jamison Jo Medby, *Limited Conflicts under the Nuclear Umbrella: Indian and Pakistani Lessons from the Kargil Crisis*, MR-1450 (Santa Monica, CA: RAND Corporation, 2001), https://www.rand.org/pubs/monograph_reports/MR1450.html.

126. Prakhar Gupta, "To the Brink: 2001–02 India-Pakistan Standoff," *Indian Defense Review*, June 22, 2016, http://www.indiandefencereview.com/spotlights/to-the-brink-2001-02-india-pakistan-standoff/.

127. Gupta, "To the Brink."

128. Gupta, "To the Brink."

129. Murthy, "The Gujral Doctrine," 647.

130. "Revisiting India's Restraint in Response to Mumbai," Belfer Center, December 4, 2013, https://www.belfercenter.org/node/89264.

131. Isaac Chotiner, "An Indian Political Theorist on the Triumph of Narendra Modi's Hindu Nationalism," *The New Yorker*, May 24, 2019, https://www.newyorker.com/news/q-and-a/an-indian-political-theorist-on-the-triumph-of-narendra-modis-hindu-nationalism; Mujib Mashal, "In a Region in Strife, India's Moral High Ground Erodes," *New York Times*, November 6, 2021.

132. Holmes and Yoshihara, "India's 'Monroe Doctrine,'" 1004.

133. Holmes and Yoshihara, "India's 'Monroe Doctrine,'" 1005.

134. T. V. Paul, "When Balance of Power meets Globalization: China, India, and the Small States of South Asia", *Politics* 39, no. 1, 50–63.

CHAPTER 4

ASSESSING PAKISTAN'S GRAND STRATEGY

> We have a psychological problem ... irrespective of our resources or strength, our thinking is that if India can do it, we can do it; if India won't do it, we won't do it; and if India gets away with, we will get away with it as well.
>
> —Anonymous former Pakistan military official[1]

Few nations in the world face a security predicament comparable to that of Pakistan. The country's history is essentially a story of national survival and a search for identity. Almost every nation-state has a litany of historical grievances, but some states internalize them to the point where past grievances become the basis of national identity, frame all threat perceptions, and drive strategic policy. Like India, Pakistan struggles to find a viable grand strategy suitable for the strategic conundrum it faces.[2] However, while Nehru determined India's national direction after independence, Pakistan was hampered by an absence of leadership in the early years and failed to determine a national course. In addition, while India followed a path of secular democracy, non-alignment, and autarky, Pakistan experienced military rule, strategic alliances with major powers, and an open, free-market economy. These divergent pathways and opposing strategies help to explain the intensity of the rivalry between the two countries and the Subcontinent's drift.

India looms as a permanent existential threat to Pakistan. Mired in conflicts and excessively reliant on its military and external alliances, Pakistan has been unable to harness its full national potential. Like India, which aspires to be a global power but expends its energies isolating Pakistan and dominating its neighbors, so too Pakistan has abandoned its national aspirations because it is preoccupied with competing with India. The net result of these obsessive pursuits is that the region fails to integrate and both countries are continually pushed into conflict. While India despises the meddling of external powers in South Asia, Pakistan embraces them as strategic partners and willingly rents itself to others (imperiling its own sovereignty in the process) in order to protect itself against India. Pakistan's security thinking and threat perceptions are framed within an enduring sense of grievance and a pivotal geostrategic position that it leverages to its best advantage.

A Perpetual Sense of Victimhood

The birth of Pakistan was accompanied by religious violence and the mass migration of different populations. After independence, the almost-stillborn nation found itself surrounded by larger, hostile neighbors— some of whom were unprepared to accept its existence as a new state carved out of British India. Embedded within Pakistan's national psyche, therefore, is an indelible memory that India would rather it didn't exist; and if Pakistan must exist, then it should be preferably as a pliant state subordinate to its "big brother."

Muhammad Ali Jinnah described Pakistan to *LIFE Magazine* in January 1948 as "truncated and moth-eaten," and the world doubted whether the newly born Muslim nation, lacking both the institutions and infrastructure of government, could survive.[3] In his 1967 autobiography, then President

Ayub Khan explains the strategic anxiety underlying Pakistan's grand strategy, which remains unchanged today (emphasis added):

> India's ambition [is] to absorb Pakistan or turn her into a *satellite* ... From the day of Independence, Pakistan struggle[d] for her very existence and *survival* [... the] threat to our security and existence was both real and constant. Indian efforts in the field of foreign policy were all directed toward one aim, the *isolation* of Pakistan and its disintegration ... we have done all that we could to convince India that we wanted to live in peace with her, but India could not accept the existence of a strong and *independent Muslim State* next door.[4]

Ayub Khan's warnings soon became prophesy when India successfully split Pakistan in 1971, and fifty years later, India has become a veritable Hindu state, just as the founding fathers of the Pakistan movement presaged. And now India talks of isolating Pakistan, which reinforces Pakistan's threat hypothesis and assessment of India's intentions and capabilities.

After the 1971 debacle and secession of Bangladesh, the newly defined Pakistan sought peace with India. It signed the 1972 Simla peace accord under duress and in the shadow of defeat, hoping to recover from the trauma of dismemberment and recuperate from the downfall of a proud nation. Both countries focused inward over the next decade, but the peace proved ephemeral, and the crises of the 1980s ended the brief détente. Islamabad's concern deepened when it discovered India's plans for a preventive airstrike to destroy Pakistan's nuclear centrifuge plant at Kahuta. Given the experience of East Pakistan, Pakistan's decision-makers were convinced that India would seize any available opportunity to weaken or further dismember Pakistan. These developments and strategic beliefs contributed to the acceleration of Pakistan's nuclear program.[5]

The Kashmir uprising in 1989 and India's continued forward-leaning policy along the Line of Control has once again placed the Kashmir dispute center-stage in the India-Pakistan relationship—not only is it responsible for generating a series of military crises, but it remains the flashpoint for a potential nuclear war on the Subcontinent. Especially because, with the passage of each decade since independence, India's aggressive pursuit of the Indira Doctrine against Pakistan exacerbates Pakistan's sense of injustice and victimhood.

By the mid-1960s, Jinnah's "truncated and moth-eaten" Pakistan had transformed into a "model developing country," politically allied to the West, with a blossoming economy (6% growth in annual GDP), a professional military armed with the most modern weapons, and a prosperous scientific and technological cadre researching peaceful applications of nuclear energy under the Atoms for Peace Initiative.[6] To all intents and purposes, Pakistan was on the way to becoming a successful, modern Muslim state and a middle power in the international system.

However, Pakistan then became embroiled in a series of internal and external regional crises and wars with India—losing half its territory in the process—and mismanaged its economy. Decades of poor governance, corruption, and the rise of retrograde religious elements once again took Pakistan on a search for national identity and purpose. The late General Khalid Mahmood Arif—a scholar and astute observer of regional politics, security, and Pakistan's strategic culture—expressed his anguish with the following lament:

> Pakistan is a wounded nation, hurt by both friends and foes. Her national body is riddled with injuries of insult, neglect and arrogance inflicted by dictators and democracy; judges and generals; the bureaucrats and media. None ... are blame-free.[7]

Arif's observation pertains to the internal incoherence that prevented Pakistan from achieving its national aspirations or realizing its immense potential. However, Pakistan's unremitting resolve to match India's military power and relentlessly compete with its larger neighbor has also contributed to the dismal situation. The primacy of military strategy over all other instruments of national power has resulted in the military's dominant role within national security—an imbalance that has both contributed to internal discord and complicated Pakistan's external problems.

The growth of India's conventional forces, its demonstrated nuclear capability, and the widening gap in economic resources between the two countries have incentivized Islamabad to rely on nuclear weapons as an independent variable and a means for strategic balancing. And yet, more than two decades after developing a sizeable nuclear capability, Pakistan continues to be perplexed about its identity and confounded by the continuing security crises, cleaving to a consistent narrative of victimhood that—in the words of former Pakistani ambassador Maleeha Lodhi—is "self-denigrating," "disempowering," and "does nothing for national self-confidence."[8] Consequently, an endless competition with India will only be to the detriment of Pakistan. If Pakistan wants to balance the existential threat from India, then it must carefully assess its own strengths and weaknesses.

Strategic Geography: Leverage or Curse?

Lord George Curzon's optimistic predictions about the Subcontinent's geopolitical future at the beginning of the twentieth century exemplified the fascination felt by many British officials of the period, particularly in relation to the northwestern region of modern Pakistan and Afghanistan. He reportedly described this gateway to and from Central Asia and beyond as the "cockpit of Asia."[9] While the Indian strategic thinker K. Subrahmanyam visualized India as the "swing state" for Asian power balancing, geography had placed Pakistan at the crossroads of global and regional power politics. It was a frontline state during the Cold War, has played a central role in the US global "war on terror," and is a potential *pivotal state* in the evolving great power competition of the twenty-first century.[10] Against the backdrop of Pakistan's geostrategic roles past and present, its search for security and a grand strategy has important implications for the world.

Pakistan's strategic geography produces both positive and negative consequences. As C. Raja Mohan observes, the partition of the Subcontinent provided Pakistan with geopolitical leverage that has attracted global powers in search of an alliance.[11] Its geographical location provides a natural corridor to the landlocked nations of Afghanistan and Central Asia, giving the latter access to the Arabian Sea and enabling Pakistan to block India's physical connectivity with West and Central Asia. Pakistan's geography makes it a potential conduit for energy routes and a strategic space connecting the western rim of Asia with the Persian Gulf and the vast Muslim nations beyond.

At the same time, Pakistan's geography has brought it what Canadian scholar T. V. Paul describes as a "geostrategic curse."[12] Dwarfed by its giant neighbors—China, India, and the Soviet Union/Russia—Pakistan found itself in a security-intensive environment that encouraged its elites to leverage with the major powers and the Islamic world for "geopolitical renting," rather than exploiting Pakistan's geographical advantage for national development.[13] From the very beginning, Pakistan's geography has produced major external threats to its security on three fronts: first, because it was divided into two wings (until 1971) with a hostile India in between; later, because of threats on its northwestern border due to the wars and crises in Afghanistan that commenced in the 1970s, intensified with the Soviet invasion in the 1980s, and continued after the US invasion in 2001; and today, Pakistan faces a forward-leaning India militarily poised on its eastern border.

Pakistan's elongated shape with a narrow waistline where it lacks strategic depth makes it vulnerable to multiple military thrusts from India.[14] The Pakistani military cannot afford to lose any territory and must therefore operate a forward-leaning defense that is tactically offensive and strategically defensive. These are the principal reasons for Pakistan's military force posture and its land-centric military strategy; this in turn affects its nuclear force posture and doctrine, which will be analyzed in chapters 5 and 6.[15]

Internally, Pakistan faces serious ethnic divisions and questions about the proper role of religion in the public sphere. Domestic militants (including extremist organizations) now pose a threat to internal security, having grown significantly over the past 15–20 years and indicating that Pakistan's strategy of supporting jihadi proxies in Kashmir and Afghanistan has become its own internal security challenge. These external and internal threats often interact in ways that have exacerbated Pakistan's insecurity. Above all, they form the basis of Pakistani threat perceptions and have aided its evolution as a security state at the cost of being a welfare state for its people.

STRATEGY FOR SURVIVAL: BANDWAGON OR BALANCE

Pakistan's grand strategy is centered around ensuring the viability of the state of Pakistan against numerous threat vectors, with the primary external threat coming from India and the secondary threat from Afghanistan. Pakistani security policies stem from the basic notion of surviving with dignity and maintaining sovereignty and independence at all costs—epitomized by the centrality of "separate entity" and "existential threat" across all segments of the Pakistani security establishment. Pakistan's choice of grand strategy therefore presents it with the greatest dilemma: whether to resist India's hegemonic pressure or give up the fight and become a vassal state of India.

Realist theory suggests that states in an anarchic international system are forced by "self-logic to do whatever they can to protect their security and other national interests."[16] Structural theories—such as neorealism—expect small or weak states confronting threats from stronger states to choose between bandwagoning and balancing. They can "bandwagon" by accepting the dominance of the stronger state, or they can "balance" against the emerging threat.[17] The option to bandwagon is a feasible one, but often—especially if there is a history of acrimony—acquiescence puts the weaker nation on a slippery slope of relentless concessions, which can gradually erode its independence. In the case of Pakistan, such fears dominate security thinking, and Islamabad not only resists India, but also steadfastly refuses the perceived slow evolution toward becoming a pliant state, a kind of "West Bangladesh." The balancing option, on the other hand, involves developing arms and military capabilities (internal balancing) and/or entering into countervailing alliances with major powers (external balancing).[18] While Pakistan preferred the option of internal balancing, it lacked the resources and inherent strength to alleviate its security concerns. It also attempted external balancing, but this again proved insufficient to address its national security requirements. This explains Pakistan's motivation to develop nuclear weapons.[19]

Bandwagoning: Acquiescence or Accommodation

Pakistan faced a similar dilemma to that faced by India in the early years of independence. When China annexed Tibet, India vacillated between accommodating and confronting China, resulting in the 1962 war. China similarly knocked on Pakistan's borders in 1949 and claimed territory that was under Pakistani control at the time. Seeing how India fared in the 1962 war, Pakistan decided to resolve its border problem with China and handed over the Shaksam Valley that China claimed. In essence, Pakistan decided to accept China's claim and embrace China in a friendship (bandwagon) that turned into a lasting strategic partnership and power balance against India. Similarly, the acrimony and conflict with India from the very outset pushed weaker Pakistan into an alliance with the United States to bolster its military strength against India.[20]

One argument often heard is that Pakistan views India exclusively through the lens of narrow military interests, but this is only partly true.[21] Such opinions are generally the expression of parochial interests regarding the perennial civil-military divide in Pakistan's domestic polity and are principally directed against military rule in Pakistan.[22] One of the prime reasons for the dominance of Pakistan's military over other facets of national security (such as economic security) and development is the perception of India's openly challenging political position and threatening military posture. Pakistan's national threat perception concludes that

India is an existential military threat, based on a systematic collation and professional assessment of its adversary's intentions and capabilities. Perceptions of political rhetoric, threatening statements by civil and military officials, and continual media propaganda reinforce public perceptions of the "enemy" in the domestic political discourse of both countries. This, in turn, traps both leaderships into hardening positions, making any form of rapprochement or conflict settlement even more difficult.

Western scholars offer different perspectives on how the situation could be resolved. For example, C. Christine Fair posits, "the longer Pakistan defers the inevitable acquiescence, the more costly the eventual concession will be."[23] Whereas Ashley Tellis suggests that Pakistan's best grand strategy is to find the "best possible accommodation with India," because it cannot match India, and "no matter what stratagem it chooses—it is bound to fail." He further suggests that Pakistan should "shift gears toward a grand strategy centered on economic integration in South Asia."[24]

There is a distinction between a posture of acquiescence and one of accommodation. The former implies Pakistan's one-sided capitulation and subservience to India, whereas the latter suggests a pragmatic settlement on the best possible terms for "two to tango." Several scholars of Pakistani origin directly or indirectly endorse the idea of Pakistan's acquiescence to India.[25] Nonetheless, neither the advocates of acquiescence nor accommodation suggest what "grand strategy" India should adopt for seeking détente with Pakistan and forging regional integration.

What would Pakistan's acquiescence to India involve? Judging from New Delhi's publicly stated maximalist demands, India would require Pakistan to make the following key concessions:

- compromise its sovereignty and only conduct relations with foreign powers in accordance with New Delhi's terms;

- accept India's annexation of Kashmir and hand over Pakistan-administered Kashmir, which includes Gilgit-Baltistan on the border with China;

- proscribe and physically eliminate all religious militant infrastructure to India's satisfaction;

- revoke all defense and economic agreements with China, including opting out of the BRI and CPEC (which would in any case come to an end if Pakistan were to hand over its portion of Kashmir);

- reduce the size of the Pakistani armed forces (including the elimination of existing nuclear weapons and dismantling of all strategic weapons organization);

- accept India's terms and conditions for trade and economic integration;

- permit India's involvement in domestic politics by supporting political parties favorable to India (as was the case with the Awami League in Bangladesh).

Short of state collapse or a complete surrender in war, India's hope for the "inevitable acquiescence" of nuclear-armed Pakistan on these terms is simply an illusion and a dangerous proposition. Conversely, an accommodation or modus vivendi with India could herald feasible options for a negotiated settlement. Such a scenario would place the following conditions on both Pakistan and India:

- maintain their sovereign status with an explicit assurance that none of their external relations would be detrimental to the other's national security interest;

- resolve the Kashmir conflict according to the status quo, convert the existing LoC into a formal border, reduce military deployments, and regulate cross-border contacts for culture, trade, and communications to normalize the situation;

- disarm, eliminate, and legally proscribe all violent extremist organizations with a past record of militancy, communal violence, and/or religious or sectarian hatred;

- reduce their military and nuclear positions to the level of a mutually balanced force;
- normalize trade and economic relations, including improved land connectivity for all countries in the region, and resume religious tourism and cultural exchanges, including sports, arts, and cinema;
- mutually agree not to interfere in the other's domestic politics.

It is obvious that an approach aimed at accommodation on a reciprocal basis opens up far greater possibilities for détente and a positive strategic future. The final chapters of this book will analyze these aspects in greater detail. However, based on these countries' history of animosity and ever-deepening distrust, there seems little prospect of Pakistan either acquiescing to India or accepting accommodation with it any time soon. As long as the Modi regime holds power in New Delhi and political stability in Pakistan remains as shaky as it is at the time of this writing, the most likely scenario is that Pakistan will choose to balance against what it perceives as the ever-increasing Indian threat.

External Balancing

External balancing became a necessary imperative for Pakistan, primarily because of its intrinsic military insecurities and because it lacked the strength to balance against India on its own. The onset of the Cold War and exigencies for "containment" of the communist threat in Eurasia brought Pakistan to the attention of Western powers. Pakistan's geographical proximity to communist China and the Soviet Union heightened its geopolitical significance, presenting a window of opportunity for economic succor and national survival. As a new nation-state, Pakistan depended on the support of the West, and this required forging alliances with major powers and building and modernizing its armed forces.[26]

Pakistan's alliance with the United States, especially the decade under the regime of President Ayub Khan (1958–1968), propelled Pakistan forward as a model developing country in Asia. Although overall Pakistan developed rapidly, this was never evenly balanced between East and West

Pakistan. Pakistan's internal policy of discrimination and deprivation of East Pakistani citizens became the basis of Bengali disenchantment that led to Pakistan's eventual dismemberment. Pakistan's decision in 1965 to liberate Kashmir from Indian control resulted in a major war between the two countries and was ultimately unsuccessful. This strategic failure did not just stall Pakistan's economic prosperity; it exposed the domestic fissures, ethnic centrifugal movements, retrogressive religious forces, and geostrategic vulnerabilities that India was then able to exploit and turn against its nemesis.

The United States rebuffed Pakistani threat perceptions vis-à-vis India and placed an embargo on its ally during the 1965 war. Further, the United States was unable to save Pakistan from dismemberment in its war with India in 1971, despite the US presidential directive to "tilt" in Pakistan's favor.[27] Later, in the 1990s, the US abandoned Pakistan, leaving it to cope by itself with the socioeconomic fallout of an asymmetric war against the Soviet Union in Afghanistan, only to return to the region after 9/11. By this point, Pakistan had concluded that external balancing was necessary but not sufficient for its full security. Stephen Cohen captured Pakistan's policy dilemma incisively:

> Like Israel, Pakistan was founded by a people who felt persecuted when living as a minority, and even though they possess their own states (which are based on religious identity), both remain under threat from powerful enemies. In both cases, an original partition demonstrated the hostility of neighbors, and subsequent wars showed that these neighbors remained hostile. Pakistan and Israel have also followed parallel strategic policies. Both sought an entangling alliance with various outside powers (at various times, Britain, France, China, and the United States), both ultimately concluded that outsiders could not be trusted in a moment of extreme crisis, and this led them to develop nuclear weapons.[28]

T. V. Paul observes that South Asian states have generally avoided "bandwagoning and balancing in the classic sense" and notes that even weak states are able to maintain a degree of strategic autonomy. Small powers can play off major powers by offering them "room to maneuver" and so achieve "upwards mobility," which he describes as the "power of the weak."[29] Although geopolitical renting has been an unpleasant experience for Pakistan, external alliances will continue to be important, so long as it can maintain a degree of strategic autonomy while receiving the political, military, and economic succor it needs. External allies are not necessarily expected to be sympathetic to Pakistan's sense of insecurity vis-à-vis India, but as long as Pakistan remains a relevant piece on the geopolitical chessboard, it retains the "power of the weak" and can bolster its defense through arms purchases and supplies, which in turn fosters its self-help and self-reliance.

Finding the United States to be fickle, Pakistan made the Machiavellian choice of seeking a strategic alliance with India's rival, China.[30] While India's other smaller neighbors are keen to attract both China and India for economic investment, Pakistan has deftly used this "umbrella strategy" to incorporate the strategic interests of other major powers in balancing against India.[31]

Internal Balancing: A Three-tiered Strategy

Although the external balancing strategy is necessary, it is insufficient to alleviate Pakistan's national security concerns or to meet its regional threats. Pakistan has therefore been compelled to implement a strategy of internal balancing because of the changing nature of its security threats and gaps in the relative power differential with India.

S. Paul Kapur outlines three instruments for internal balancing available to Pakistan in its strategic toolbox: conventional forces, nuclear weapons, and militant proxies.[32] The first of these is necessary to protect Pakistan's territorial integrity, defend its eastern and western borders, and maintain internal security. The second provides a full-spectrum deterrence against India at the tactical, operational, and strategic levels. The third strategy is to support sub-conventional forces involved in insurgencies (particularly in Kashmir), which serves both political and military purposes.

Conventional Forces Capability

From the outset, Pakistan's armed forces have had to face India's large conventional forces while lacking geographical strategic depth. Indian and Pakistani forces have been deployed along the LoC in the disputed territories of Jammu and Kashmir since 1948. Nearly two-thirds of India's army and air force bases are organized, structured, and pre-disposed toward major cities and communication lines (roads and railways) in Pakistan within striking distance of India.

The Indian army comprises 12 corps under five regional commands. Of these 12 corps, nine are deployed on India's western front against Pakistan. The three-strike corps are built around armored divisions, mechanized divisions, and the Reorganized Army Plains Infantry Divisions—divisions that are ideally suited and organized to launch an offensive across the plains and deserts of Pakistan. India could move forces quickly from its eastern and southern commands to the western front against Pakistan within the space of one or two weeks.[33] As the Indian air force's capability improves, the likelihood increases—according to Pakistan's calculus—of India inflicting disabling strikes at the start of a conventional war. Furthermore, India could not only threaten and jeopardize Pakistan's infrastructure, major industries, and command centers; unless defended up front, the terrain could easily be dominated with a simple thrust of mechanized forces. Meanwhile, the Indian navy could blockade the Pakistani coastline in the north Arabian Sea. India could also divert the rivers flowing from Indian-administered Kashmir away from Pakistan. Such a naval blockade and river diversion would strangle Pakistan's economy.

On its western border with Afghanistan, Pakistan's military has been involved in deep counterterrorist and stabilization operations for almost two decades. The forces involved in these operations are drawn from forces that were previously deployed on the eastern border with India. As Pakistan's western border stabilizes, its defenses against India weaken, which incites the Indian military to contemplate a new operational military doctrine, colloquially called "Cold Start"—a concept of waging a swift conventional war against Pakistan.[34] Hence the Pakistani military is caught balancing contingencies on two fronts.

These strategic anxieties lie at the heart of Pakistan's compulsion to have a standing armed force of substantial size and quality. The drive to build up its military sector overshadows all other civil national institutions and, consequently, causes significant internal resentment concerning the sharing of national resources. Furthermore, the dynamic nature of any potential conflict means it is imperative for Pakistan to maintain constant vigilance and keep its professionally trained armed forces in a near-ready state to respond to any sudden emergency or military buildup. However, because of its geographical vulnerability and the need for quick reactions and unity of command in the event of a crisis, Pakistan lacks the assurance that its conventional deterrence will be sufficient. For this reason, Pakistan's grand strategy relies on a combination of conventional and nuclear deterrence that should, in its estimate, dissuade India from initiating a conflict.[35]

Nuclear Deterrence

The structural asymmetry inherent to Pakistan's security environment is a permanent feature of its coexistence with India. It has been compounded by the development of India's Pakistan-centric military doctrines that began in the 1980s and have been evolving ever since. The implications of these opposing military doctrines will be analyzed in the next chapter, but the important point here is how India's conventional thinking has affected Pakistan's own grand strategy and convictions.

Pakistan's leaders believe that nuclear weapons will deter India from starting a war in the first place. Should the deterrence fail and India decides to attack, the Pakistani strategy is to deny India victory by making the cost of war unacceptably high. Consequently, over the past two decades Pakistan has worked to integrate its nuclear forces into its conventional forces war plans and thus created a credible deterrent force against India.[36] At the same time, at the highest level, Pakistan's command system believes that the "conventional hand" should not know what the "nuclear hand" is doing. In this way, Pakistan keeps its policy for nuclear weapons use deliberately ambiguous and its so-called strategic red lines—loss of space, significant destruction, economic strangulation, and threat to internal stability—intentionally vague.[37] For now, the risk of tipping Pakistan over its nuclear threshold holds India back from attempting to translate its numerical military superiority into an outright victory.[38] Meanwhile, Pakistan closely watches India's growing strategic partnership with the United States, particularly the implications of this for India's military modernization and the region's current deterrence stability.

Even though Pakistan has not articulated a formal nuclear declaratory doctrine, there is a wealth of official decisions and statements that provide important clues to Pakistan's stance as a nuclear state.[39] As Sir Michael Quinlan notes: "Pakistan's rejection of no-first-use seems merely a natural refusal to lighten or simplify a stronger adversary's assessment of risk; it implies the retention of an option, not a positive policy of first use as a preferred course."[40] Pakistan is simply following the advice of US president Dwight Eisenhower to his vice president, Richard Nixon, in 1958: "You should never let the enemy know what you will not do."[41] For policymakers, this deliberate external ambiguity alongside the internal conventional and nuclear integration, provides greater deterrent value, given the precarity of any situation in which a prospective conflict could arise.

In sum, nuclear capability has given Islamabad an internal balancing instrument without compromising its core strategic interests; it has allowed it to withstand Indian coercion and offset the conventional forces imbalance with India while increasing military deployments elsewhere. Nonetheless, while nuclear deterrence can offset the imbalance in conventional forces, it is not a remedy for national security, as the next chapters will show.

Sub-conventional Forces

The third instrument in Pakistan's strategic toolbox—using sub-conventional forces to complement its conventional force asymmetry—has provided ever-decreasing returns and has even been counterproductive.[42] As new global norms and rules became established in the post-9/11 international order, Pakistan realized it was in its national interest to abandon such a policy instrument. However, reversing this policy has become an enormous challenge in itself for Pakistan.

Pakistan has engaged in supporting insurgencies in both Kashmir (in 1948, 1965, and from 1989 to the present) and in Afghanistan (from the 1980s through to 2001) as a means of bolstering its own security and as a conduit for American security interests. The Soviet withdrawal from Afghanistan (1988–1989) coincided with the resurgence of indigenous crises in Kashmir. By then, Pakistan already had ten years' experience in waging a successful asymmetric war against the Soviet Union with the full backing, support, and networking of Western powers. In the 1990s, as the Cold War faded, the Soviet Union dissolved, and the United States abandoned the region, the renewed crisis in Kashmir was raging with an unprecedented frenzy. Islamabad saw this as another opportunity to apply the same asymmetric strategy in Kashmir. Hence, while India suppressed the Kashmiris, Pakistan began supporting the "freedom struggle" as they saw it. At the same time, the muddle in Afghanistan morphed into an intra-tribal civil war throughout the 1990s and beyond.

During this period, Islamabad sensed it had a favorable wind to turn the tables on India using its asymmetric strategy in Kashmir and to resolve its problem with Afghanistan. After the catastrophic 9/11 events in the United States, however, the tide turned dramatically in India's favor. With terrorism now being universally condemned, India conflated the Kashmir problem and applied military pressure to force Islamabad to give up the proxy war in Kashmir. Additionally, as US forces in Afghanistan toppled the Taliban regime and installed a new dispensation in Kabul, India regained its foothold there. Once again, Afghanistan became a hub of proxies—and not just between India and Pakistan. The Afghan factor is closely connected with Pakistan's deeper geographical, historical, and cultural compulsions, which explain the latter's curious relationship with Afghanistan's sub-conventional elements. Essentially, Pakistan's Afghanistan problem represents its quest for "strategic depth."

Strategic Depth in Afghanistan

Pakistan-Afghanistan relations have never been cordial since India and Pakistan achieved independence from Britain. Pakistan's litany of grievances against Afghanistan includes the following charges:

- Afghanistan was the only country to vote against Pakistan's membership of the United Nations;
- Afghanistan refuses to accept the border with Pakistan as drawn by Great Britain in 1893;
- Afghanistan fomented discord among the Pashtun and Baluchistan tribes, leading to sub-nationalist revolt for independence from Pakistan;
- Afghanistan has provided sanctuary to the Soviet Union and India for their sub-conventional proxy wars against Pakistan, including close intelligence networking between Afghan and Indian intelligence.

Most critical of all for Pakistan's national security has been Afghanistan's strategic partnership with India, which potentially creates a two-front situation for Pakistan in the event of a war or other crisis with India. Geographically, Afghanistan is a landlocked country that is dependent on Pakistan's ports and harbors for external trade. There is a significant strategic imperative for Pakistan to desire a friendly government in Kabul, stability in Afghanistan, and—most importantly—for Afghanistan to stop doing India's bidding by conducting clandestine activities against Pakistan.[43] With these objectives in mind and having invested in Afghanistan's security in the 1980s, Pakistan has followed a forward policy in Afghanistan by supporting Afghan tribal warlords to ensure its strategic depth.[44]

Pakistani strategy in Afghanistan did briefly succeed in creating a friendly space and temporary strategic depth when the Taliban took power in Kabul in the 1990s. However, Pakistan soon discovered that the Afghan Taliban was made up of uncontrollable extremists who were not about to become puppets of Islamabad. After the 9/11 attack and the launch of the "war on terror," it became clear that such an asymmetric strategy could only be sustained for a short while. It was counterproductive as a security policy and in the long run would only lead to violence and anarchy.

While Pakistan's three-tiered strategy against its much larger and better-resourced adversary has succeeded in frustrating India, it has failed to resolve Pakistan's India problem. It has taken a high premium in terms of economic and opportunity costs, and as the following chapters will show, modern India has been adept at shifting policies and exploiting the internal fault lines and weaknesses Pakistan's grand strategy has exposed.

Surviving—Not Thriving

There are two lenses through which we can assess the efficacy of Pakistan's grand strategy. Few would disagree that Pakistan has survived as a nation-state, but the country we see today matches neither the vision of its founders nor the physical shape at its birth. It continues to define its identity in hard ideological terms and remains focused on internal and external security issues. Its governance alternates between presidential and parliamentary systems and the dominant role of the military.

From an alternative standpoint, Pakistan could claim that its three-tiered strategy has been reasonably successful in achieving its objectives. The combined Pakistani conventional and nuclear deterrence has prevented a major war with India, while its sub-conventional strategy has kept the Kashmir issue alive and its strategic interests in Afghanistan intact. Pakistan has maintained its sovereignty, steadfastly defied India, and learnt to leverage its geopolitical location to its own advantage; in the past, Pakistan allowed external powers to use its soil for their geostrategic interests, but now it is leveraging its location to develop economic connectivity with China and restore regional balance.

In the final analysis, Pakistan has exhausted itself in surviving and cannot be said to be thriving. Its internal balancing strategy has checked Indian ambitions, but at enormous political, economic, and social costs. While the next chapter will analyze in detail Pakistan's conventional and nuclear doctrines and their implications for deterrence stability, I will now discuss how the use of militant proxies as an instrument of strategic policy became counterproductive and perhaps represents an even greater existential threat to Pakistan.

Jihad Unleashed

Pakistan's strategy of working indirectly through sub-conventional forces in Kashmir was veritably buried under the twin towers of the World Trade Center in 2001. Pakistan made an about-face with its former militant proxies by allying itself with the US in its "war on terror." Since then, Pakistan's western borderlands have deteriorated into a war zone riven by tribal guerrilla wars. Tens of thousands of Pakistani soldiers and civilians have been casualties of the conflict in the 20-year war in Afghanistan. Religious extremist organizations inside Pakistan are now directing their aggression internally, carrying out suicide attacks against civilians, soldiers, and military leaders.[45] This included an attempt on President Pervez Musharraf's life in 2003 and a suicide attack in December 2014, when terrorists crossed the border from Afghanistan and massacred around 140 children and their teachers at the Army Public School in Peshawar. These attacks have not only wrecked Pakistan's internal stability but its economy as well.

Meanwhile, Pakistan's alliance with the United States also began to sour, especially after the spectacular raid that killed Osama bin Laden in the Pakistani city of Abbottabad in 2011, shocking the world and placing an embarrassed Pakistani security establishment between a rock and a hard place. Analysts wondered if the Pakistani security establishment was incompetent, or whether some elements within it were complicit in hiding the world's most wanted terrorist in the Abbottabad compound. These questions were never satisfactorily answered. What was clear, however, was that jihadi forces were wreaking havoc across the region while the United States, India, Pakistan, and Afghanistan were engaged in a mutual blame game.

The United States accused Pakistan of double-dealing by providing safe havens for the Afghan Taliban and began to forge closer strategic relations with India instead, including signing a nuclear deal in 2008. From Pakistan's perspective, the United States was once again proving to be a fickle and unreliable ally,[46] just like when it abandoned Pakistan in 1990 and applied nuclear sanctions. Barely twenty years later, the United States provided nuclear legitimacy to Pakistan's archrival India and slammed its former ally for nuclear proliferation—the legacy of A. Q. Khan's black market described in chapter 2. .

With the help of Afghan intelligence agencies, India began supporting insurgents inside Pakistan to foment a covert sub-conventional war in Baluchistan and tribal Pashtun areas.[47] Baluchistan has been in a state of sporadic insurgency against Pakistan ever since, and Pakistani security forces have been engaged in fighting separatist forces in Baluchistan and cross-border terrorists using safe havens in the tribal borderlands with Afghanistan and Iran. As a consequence of India and Pakistan's asymmetric strategies against each other, nearly half a million Indian security forces are deployed in Kashmir, while half that number of Pakistani forces are entangled in counterinsurgencies and other internal crises.

TO BALANCE OR NOT TO BALANCE

Time and again, Pakistan has been forced to reconsider its security choices: whether to bandwagon with India or continue balancing against it. And even if Pakistan were inclined to consider some form of *modus vivendi*, it does not seem possible without a third party in the equation. For Pakistan to continue balancing, it will need to make significant adjustments to both the external and internal elements of its strategy.

Pakistan believes that despite its past difficulties, it will remain attractive to global powers thanks to its geostrategic location, resilient people, military forces, and nuclear capabilities. Today, its grand strategy involves creating external alliances to counter India's policy of isolating Pakistan internationally and enhancing its internal balancing through a "combination of conventional and nuclear deterrence to obviate [the need for] conventional war."[48]

Modernizing its conventional and nuclear forces together places a huge burden on Pakistan's resources and economy, but Pakistan's national security relies on its nuclear deterrence to offset the strategic asymmetry with India. As long as Pakistan's grand strategy continues to frustrate Indian objectives in the region, and despite the downsides and challenges, Pakistan's sovereignty in determining its future and its destiny is assured.

NOTES

1. Anonymous former Pakistan military official, "Pakistan: A Strategic History" (presentation at a US-Pakistan Track II Strategic Dialogue, Bangkok, December 2016). The dialogue was held under Chatham House rules.

2. Javid Husain, *Pakistan and a World in Disorder: A Grand Strategy for the Twenty-first Century* (New York: Palgrave Macmillan, 2016), 2.

3. "Pakistan Struggles for Survival: Religious Warfare and Economic Chaos Threaten the Newly Born Nation of 70 Million Moslems," *LIFE,* January 5, 1948, 16–26.

4. Mohammad Ayub Khan, *Friends Not Masters: A Political Autobiography* (New York: Oxford University Press, 1967), 134–137.

5. Feroz Hassan Khan, *Eating Grass: The Making of the Pakistani Bomb* (Palo Alto, CA: Stanford University Press, 2012), 203–233.

6. Khan, *Eating Grass,* 32–33.

7. Khalid Mahmud Arif, *Estranged Neighbors: India-Pakistan 1947–2010* (Islamabad: Dost, 2010), 9.

8. Maleeha Lodhi, "Victim Syndrome," *Dawn,* September 27, 2021, https://www.dawn.com/news/1648721.

9. Ahmad Rashid, *Taliban,* (New Haven, CT: Yale University Press, 2001), 7.

10. A 1998 study identified nine countries as "pivotal states," namely: Indonesia, India, Pakistan, Turkey, Egypt, South Africa, Brazil, Algeria, and Mexico. See Robert Chase, Emily Hill, and Paul Kennedy, *The Pivotal States: A New Framework for U.S. Policy in the Developing World* (New York: W. W. Norton & Co., 1998). See also the review by Philip Zelikow in *Foreign Affairs,* May/June 2000, https://www.foreignaffairs.com/reviews/capsule-review/2000-05-01/pivotal-states-new-framework-us-policy-developing-world.

11. C. Raja Mohan, *Modi's World: Expanding India's Sphere of Influence* (New York: HarperCollins Publishers, 2015), 72.

12. T. V. Paul, *The Warrior State: Pakistan in the Contemporary World* (New York: Oxford University Press, 2014).

13. Paul, *The Warrior State*; Mohan, *Modi's World,* 72.

14. Ryan French, "Deterrence Adrift: Mapping Conflict and Escalation in South Asia," *Strategic Studies Quarterly* 10, no. 1 (Spring 2016): 120.

15. Stephen P. Cohen, *Shooting for a Century: The India-Pakistan Conundrum* (Washington, DC: Brookings Institution Press, 2013), 88–92.

16. Scott D. Sagan, "The Origins of Military Doctrine and Command and Control Systems," in *Planning the Unthinkable: How New Powers Will Use Nuclear, Chemical, and Biological Weapons*, ed. Scott D. Sagan, Peter R. Lavoy, and James J. Wirtz (Ithaca, NY: Cornell University Press, 2000), 23.

17. Sagan, "The Origins of Military Doctrine," 23; T. V. Paul, "When Balance of Power meets Globalization: China, India, and the Small States of South Asia," *Politics* 39, no. 1 (2019), 50–63, https://journals.sagepub.com/doi/10.1177/0263395718779930.

18. Kenneth N. Waltz, *Theory of International Politics* (New York: Random House, 1979), 128.

19. Pakistan also pursued a third option of seeking a just and durable resolution of the Kashmir conflict and other disputes through international institutions such as the United Nations and the World Bank, but these institutions proved capricious and ineffective. Khan, *Eating Grass*, 3–5.

20. Waltz, *Theory of International Politics*.

21. John H. Gill, "India and Pakistan: A Shift in the Military Calculus," in *Strategic Asia 2005–06: Military Modernization in an Era of Uncertainty*, ed. Ashley Tellis and Michael Wills (Washington, DC: Carnegie Endowment for International Peace, 2005), 253.

22. For a subjective criticism of the Pakistani military, see Husain Haqqani, *Pakistan: Between Mosque and Military* (Washington, DC: Carnegie Endowment for International Peace, 2005); Hassan Abbas, *Pakistan's Drift into Extremism: Allah, the Army, and America's War on Terror* (New Haven, CT: M. E. Sharpe, Inc., 2005).

23. C. Christine Fair, *Fighting to the End: The Pakistan Army's Way of War* (Oxford: Oxford University Press, 2014), 4.

24. Ashley J. Tellis, Stephen Cohen, Christine Fair, Sumit Ganguly, Shaun Gregory, and Aqil Shah, "What is the Problem with Pakistan?," *Foreign Affairs*, April 2, 2009, https://carnegieendowment.org/2009/04/02/what-s-problem-with-pakistan-pub-22925.

25. See, for example, Ahmad Farooqui, *Rethinking the National Security of Pakistan: The Price of Strategic Myopia* (Farnham: Ashgate, 2003); Aqil Shah, *The Army and Democracy: Military Politics in Pakistan* (Cambridge, MA: Harvard University Press, 2014); Haqqani, *Pakistan: Between Mosque and Military*.

26. Shuja Nawaz, *Crossed Swords: Pakistan, Its Army, and the Wars Within* (New York: Oxford University Press, 2008), 92–121.

27. Dennis Kux, *United States and Pakistan, 1947–2000: Disenchanted Allies* (Baltimore, MD: Johns Hopkins University Press, 2001), 178–214.

28. Stephen P. Cohen, *India: Emerging Power* (Washington, DC: Brookings Institution Press, 2001), 204.

29. Paul, "When Balance of Power meets Globalization."

30. Mooed Yusuf, *Brokering Peace in Nuclear Environments: US Crisis Management in South Asia* (Palo Alto, CA: Stanford University Press, 2018).

31. Paul, "When Balance of Power meets Globalization."

32. S. Paul Kapur, *Jihad as Grand Strategy: Islamist Militancy, National Security, and the Pakistani State* (New York: Oxford University Press, 2017), 8.

33. IISS, *The Military Balance for 2002–2003* (London: Oxford University Press, 2002), 129.

34. Walter C. Ladwig III, "Indian Military Modernization and Conventional Deterrence in South Asia," *Journal of Strategic Studies* 38, no. 5 (2015): 729–772, http://dx.doi.org/10.1080/01402390.2015.1014473; IISS, *The Military Balance 2020: The Annual Assessment of Global Military Capabilities and Defence Economics* (London: International Institute of Strategic Studies, 2020), 269–275, 299–303.

35. Agha Shahi, Zulfiqar Ali Khan, and Abdul Sattar, "Securing Nuclear Peace," *News International* (Pakistan), October 4, 1999.

36. Feroz Hassan Khan, "Pakistan's Nuclear Force Posture and the 2001–2002 Military Standoff," in Zachary S. Davis, ed., *The India-Pakistan Military Standoff: Crisis and Escalation in South Asia* (Palgrave Macmillan, 2011), 127–142.

37. Khan, *Eating Grass*, 351–352; Gill, "India and Pakistan." Error! Hyperlink reference not valid.

38. Feroz Hassan Khan, *Going Tactical: Pakistan's Nuclear Posture and Implications for Stability*, Proliferation Papers no. 53 (Paris: IFRI Security Studies Center, 2015), 28–35.

39. Khan, *Eating Grass*, 393–397; Paolo Cotta-Ramusino and Maurizio Martellini, "Nuclear Safety, Nuclear Stability and Nuclear Strategy in Pakistan," interview with Khalid Kidwai (Como, Italy: Landau Network-Centro Volat, 2002), https://pugwash.org/2002/01/14/report-on-nuclear-safety-nuclear-stability-and-nuclear-strategy-in-pakistan/.

40. Michael Quinlan, "How Robust is India-Pakistan Deterrence?," *Survival* 42, no. 4 (Winter 2000/2001): 149–150, https://doi.org/10.1080/0039633 0500248045.

41. McGeorge Bundy, "The Unimpressive Record of Atomic Diplomacy," in *The Use of Force: Military Power and International Politics*, 6th edition,

ed. Robert Art and Kenneth Waltz (Lanham, MD: Rowman & Littlefield, 2004), 89.

42. Kapur, *Jihad as Grand Strategy*. Kapur identifies four explanatory strands in the literature.

43. Pervez Musharraf, *In the Line of Fire: A Memoir* (New York: Simon & Schuster, 2006), 3.

44. For a detailed analysis of Pakistan's quest for strategic depth, see Fair, *Fighting to the End*, 103–135.

45. Peter R. Lavoy, "Pakistan's Kashmir Policy after Bush Visit to South Asia," *Strategic Insights* 5, no. 4 (April 2006), https://calhoun.nps.edu/handle/10945/11260.

46. Ayesha Jalal, "The Past is Present," in *Pakistan: Beyond the Crisis State*, ed. Maleeha Lodhi (New York: Columbia University Press, 2011), 7.

47. In March 2016, Pakistani security forces in Baluchistan arrested a serving Indian naval officer, Commander Kulbhushan Jadhav, as an Indian spy; Jadhav belonged to the Indian intelligence agency known as the Research and Analysis Wing. See Evangeline Elsa, "The Case of Kulbhushan Jadhav in Pakistan: Everything You Need to Know," *World Asia*, September 2, 2019, https://gulfnews.com/world/asia/pakistan/the-case-of-kulbushan-jadhav-in-pakistan-everything-you-need-to-know-1.66160866.

48. Pakistan Army, *Pakistan Army Doctrine 2011: Comprehensive Response*, AP 1001 E (Rawalpindi: Pakistan Army, 2011), 1.

CHAPTER 5

MILITARY DOCTRINES AND DETERRENCE STABILITY

Classical strategists of the twentieth century such as British historian B. H. Liddell Hart and French strategist André Beaufre were both proponents of the concept of "indirect strategy,"[1] and in their similar definitions of "strategy," both emphasize the use of military force as a common element. Hart defines strategy as "the art of distributing and applying military means to fulfill policy ends,"[2] and Beaufre describes it as "the art of the dialectic of two opposing wills using force to resolve disputes."[3] With the advent of nuclear capabilities, however, the application of military force as a strategic means was put into question. The grand strategies of India and Pakistan are typical cases of opposing wills clashing to subdue the resolve of the other—not just to resolve structural disputes on their own terms but also to undermine the ideological basis of the other's existence.

At various times, both India and Pakistan have strategically applied other instruments of power apart from the military, such as subversion through proxies, economic pressure, propaganda, and diplomacy. Nonetheless, reliance on military force remains central to the grand strategy of each.[4] The predominance of the military in national security—

especially with the growth of nuclear capabilities—has exacerbated the cycle of violence and perpetuated the politics of revenge, resulting in a fragile stability.

India and Pakistan emerged as independent nations barely two years after the first ever use of nuclear weapons that ended one of the greatest conventional wars in history. The devastating nature of atomic weapons revolutionized military affairs and transformed the character of war, especially the strategic role of military force. In 1946, renowned scholar Bernard Brodie famously observed: "Thus far, the chief purpose of our military establishment has been to win wars. From now on, its chief purpose must be to avert them. It can have almost no other purpose."[5] Decades later in 1989, Robert Jervis, another famed scholar, noted that nations take time to understand the impact of the "nuclear revolution" on their policies.[6]

Brodie's and Jervis's caution seems to have largely escaped South Asia. In the two decades following the advent of nuclear weapons on the Subcontinent, both nuclear-armed states have resisted changing their respective national objectives or security policies. India continues to envisage using military force to defeat or subdue Pakistan, and Pakistan relies on an integrated strategy of conventional forces with nuclear deterrence to ensure that any Indian victory would come at enormous cost.[7] Rather than reconciling themselves to the fact that the security objectives set in the pre-nuclear era can no longer be achieved through military means, India and Pakistan continue to test each other's resolve and refine their strategic doctrines in order to achieve these same ends. While both have signed up to the nuclear precept, the true meaning of the "nuclear revolution" is yet to dawn on either.[8]

Building on the assessment of India and Pakistan's grand strategies in chapters 3 and 4, this chapter analyzes the challenges to deterrence stability and explains how the two countries' military doctrines are dangerously mismatched. Military doctrines present an approved set of principles and methods that foster a common outlook and a uniform basis for action across all sectors and branches of the armed forces.[9] A state's military doctrine is therefore understood as its formal policy regarding the use of its military forces and weapons to achieve its political, military, or other objectives. The dialectic of opposing military and nuclear strategies, which is affecting the dynamics and risks of conflict escalation, is leading to crisis instability in the region and accentuating the Subcontinent's drift.

The first section of this chapter evaluates the gradual genesis of India's military doctrine known as "Cold Start." This is followed by an examination of the Pakistan army's "Comprehensive Response," including its "Full-Spectrum Deterrence." The third section analyzes the dynamics of escalation and its effect on crisis stability. It explains how doctrinal dissonance, false assumptions, and the tussle for regional control could escalate into a limited war between the two nuclear-armed neighbors, creating a regional inferno with no clear off-ramps for de-escalation or pathways to war termination.

Pakistan's internal and external security problems were already worsening when its traditional ally, the United States, began to distance itself from Pakistan in favor of India. On the one hand, Pakistan's investment in a sub-conventional strategy through jihadi proxies was providing diminishing returns in the changed security landscape after September 2001. On the other, the war-fighting potential of its conventional forces was being systematically depleted due to continuous operations in Swat, Baluchistan, Khyber Pakhtunkhwa, and the tribal borderlands with Afghanistan, as well as the increasing ceasefire violations on the Line of Control (LoC) with India. Meanwhile, India's frustration with the situation in Kashmir was increasing. By 2010, the two opposing militaries armed with nuclear weapons were reevaluating their military and nuclear doctrines that had been evolving over the previous four decades.

STRIKING FAST AND HARD: FROM THE SUNDERJI DOCTRINE TO COLD START

General Krishnaswamy Sundararajan (commonly referred to as K. Sunderji and described as the "flamboyant, most fiercely disputed general") left a legacy of controversy and bold initiatives that is unmatched by any other in Indian military history.[10] Stephen Cohen once remarked: "Of all the generals I have met in South Asia and elsewhere, Sunderji stands out for his professional and intellectual ability to apply modern science to the art of warfare."[11] General Sunderji veritably applied his military muscle to the doctrine of Indira Gandhi during the 1980s, both within India and in its neighborhood. In 1983, during the Dig Vijay military exercise, Prime Minister Indira Gandhi observed Sunderji's aggressive maneuver of increasing the operational advance of armored and mechanized tanks from the traditional speed of 15 kilometers per day to a new record of 90 kilometers in one day.[12]

A year later, Sunderji was the Indian army's western command leader (on the border with Pakistan) when the Sikh insurgency peaked in Punjab. Sunderji planned Operation Blue Star to subdue the Khalistan movement by storming the Golden Temple in Amritsar, using tanks and heavy firepower against the Sikh militants holed up inside. He was later severely criticized for the heavy-handed operation, not least because Operation Blue Star heightened Sikh anger, which eventually led to Indira Gandhi's assassination. In February 1986, her son Rajiv appointed the General Sunderji as the Indian army chief, and he remained in office till May 1988. Under his leadership the Indian army made significant shifts in its military doctrine alongside far-reaching modernization programs, including the development of integrated concepts for ground-to-air battles.

Sunderji was the architect of a decisive strategy aimed at severing Pakistan with a deep mechanized military offensive, which would significantly reduce Pakistan's military offensive power and destroy its nascent nuclear weapons program in the process. Under his watch, the Indian army restructured its infantry formations into Reorganized Army Plains

Infantry Divisions (RAPID), specifically designed for operations against Pakistan. He also oversaw the development of air assault divisions and set out a 15-year perspective plan for future operational contingencies.

Sunderji's most controversial move was the organization of one of India's biggest ever military exercises in the winter of 1986–1987. Known as "Brass Tacks," it was to be an exhibition of "dissuasive posture, deterrent capability, and coercive diplomacy to signal to Pakistan that India had the muscle and the willpower to launch an offensive in India's national interest."[13] The Brass Tacks military exercise was to be conducted using live ammunition and full logistical arrangements, and it seemed deliberately designed to provoke a military crisis with Pakistan and provide an opportunity for launching a counter-proliferation strike to destroy Pakistan's nuclear centrifuge facility at Kahuta near Islamabad. India also firmly believed that Pakistan was supporting the Khalistan movement raging in Indian Punjab at the time.

The military exercise created a diplomatic crisis that was eventually diffused at the political level, but what is less well-known is how potentially catastrophic the Brass Tacks Crisis could have been for the region: had the military exercise turned into a preventive war—as Sunderji purportedly planned[14]—it could have resulted in a full-scale nuclear war because unbeknownst to India, Pakistan had already produced enough fissile material and developed the capability to assemble and deliver a Hiroshima-sized bomb.[15] During his two-and half-year tenure, the general also planned and conducted several other exercises and operations, including Operation Pawan in Sri Lanka and Operations Checkerboard and Falcon against China. For the latter, he planned to airlift logistics beyond the disputed border areas with China in the North-East Frontier Agency (NEFA, which later became the Indian state of Arunachal Pradesh). In sum, General Sunderji's aggressive moves created several military crises simultaneously with Pakistan, China, and Sri Lanka at a time when India was also experiencing severe internal crises.

Since the mid-1980s, India's peacetime military disposition has been heavily oriented toward Pakistan. Under the Sunderji Doctrine, seven holding corps were tasked for a defensive role against Pakistan, with three offensive strike corps located in central India (I Corps at Mathura, II Corps at Ambala, and XXI Corps at Bhopal). These strike corps take time to mobilize and reach the western borders with Pakistan.[16] While the offensive corps mobilize, the defensive corps, which have a limited offensive capability, would undertake tactical offensive operations against the Pakistani defenses to secure limited space for the follow-on strike corps to exploit. Indian incursions or bridgeheads across rivers or irrigation defense canals would threaten Pakistan's strategic communications, which generally lie within just 100 kilometers of the Indian border. This threatening incursion across the border would draw the Pakistani army's strategic reserves onto the battlefield in a counterattack, while the Indian strike corps (comprising armored and RAPID divisions) could invade, cutting Pakistan in half and destroying the bulk of Pakistan's offensive capabilities.[17]

With the advent of Pakistan's nuclear capability, however, such plans had become extremely risky. Given the possibility that a deep penetration through the middle of Pakistan and destruction of Pakistan's strategic reserves could trigger a nuclear response from Pakistan, India had to seriously rethink its military strategy.[18]

LIMITED WAR UNDER THE NUCLEAR UMBRELLA

Early in 1999, Pakistani forces secretly crossed the Line of Control and threatened the Srinagar-Leh highway at Kargil. India did not discover the incursion until the spring, but by the summer of 1999, this had led to a short war lasting two months. For India, a successful Pakistani interdiction of the critical highway through Kashmir would cut off supplies to Indian forces in the Siachen Glacier, which they had been occupying since 1983. In May and June 1999, the Indian army launched sustained attacks (including airpower) to destroy Pakistani outposts across the LoC. On July

4, President Bill Clinton met Prime Minister Nawaz Sharif in Washington, DC, and with his intervention the crisis was diffused.

The Kargil crisis had all the potential to escalate into a major war, like in 1965, but it remained contained within the geographically limited mountainous terrain of Kashmir where the incursions had taken place. India and Pakistan each drew different lessons from the outcome of the conflict. India's military success gave birth to a new concept of limited war under the nuclear umbrella: India believed that a conventional war against Pakistan was possible *despite* the latter's nuclear capabilities, and that the international community would be sympathetic to India in any future crisis with Pakistan. In Pakistan, civil-military relations fell apart in the aftermath of the conflict, leading to a military takeover in the country in October 1999. At the same time, the belief in nuclear deterrence was further reinforced: Pakistani strategists concluded that the Kargil War remained contained and did not expand horizontally precisely *because* of its nuclear deterrent. These opposite lessons—India seeking space for a conventional war and Pakistan relying on its nuclear deterrence as a critical variable to deny India that space—set South Asia on a dangerous path.

Indian defense minister George Fernandez and army chief General V. P. Malik—who led the Indian army in the Kargil War but has since retired —became key proponents of the limited war concept. Since Kargil, Indian proponents of a limited war have been convinced there is sufficient space for a limited conventional war between sub-conventional forces and/ or proxies at the lower end of the spectrum, with the nuclear threshold lying well toward the higher end. In line with this view, India believes that Pakistan holds an advantage in terms of sub-conventional forces at the lower end, but that there would be nuclear parity at the higher end of the conflict. India's conventional military might could therefore take full advantage of the space between the two ends of the conflict spectrum. Accordingly, India could wage a short, swift war against Pakistan that would be "limited in scope, in time, and in geography" and terminate operations before the conflict could reach the nuclear threshold.[19]

India's limited war doctrine is based on two potentially dangerous assumptions. First, Indian planners would have to calibrate their military operations by calculating and based on the assumptions of the Pakistani nuclear threshold, which is ambiguous. Second, India assumes that at every rung of the military operation it could maintain escalation control. These two assumptions and Pakistani reactions to them (discussed in the next section) hold the region's precarious strategic stability in the balance.

India's Cold Start Doctrine (2004–2014)

In 2001, terrorists with links to Kashmiri militants attacked the Indian parliament building in New Delhi. In response, India launched Operation Parakram to force Pakistan to stop supporting the Kashmiri militants. It took several weeks for India's large formations to mobilize—far longer than the planners had anticipated—by which time India had lost the element of surprise.[20] Taking advantage of its shorter distances and internal lines of communication, Pakistan counter-mobilized and moved its forces into defensive positions, ready for the Indian forces. The military standoff lasted 10 months and was only de-escalated through political maneuverings.. However, in reviewing the botched mobilization, India's planners realized it was time to rethink the Sunderji Doctrine and overhaul the limited war doctrine as propounded by Fernandez and Malik.

The review process immediately revealed that the capacity of India's holding corps was too limited to carry out a cross-border offensive and that the offensive options were entirely dependent on the arrival of the strike corps located some distance away. Hence, increasing the tactical offensive capacity of the holding corps and reducing the need for a prolonged mobilization of the strike corps would enable India to begin offensive operations while retaining an element of surprise.

This new military doctrine, dubbed "Cold Start," was made public in April 2004. Under this doctrine, the plan was for India to strike quickly after any provocative incident while the political temperature was still heated, domestic anger and the desire for revenge still high, and the likelihood of international intervention still distant. More importantly, the swift military action would present the Indian political leadership with a *fait accompli*, offering little or no time to procrastinate or backtrack from decisions. In other words, military exigencies would determine political decisions rather than the other way around.

The Indian army's concept envisages shallow penetration using 8–10 division-sized combined infantry, armor, and artillery forces known as "integrated battle groups." These would maneuver along multiple broad axes to bite and hold enough territory to threaten Pakistan's key rail and road routes at several locations until reinforcements or the strike corps could arrive for further operations. India's holding corps were redesignated as "pivot corps," and there would be additional mechanized forces and firepower to undertake tactically offensive operations.[21]

Calling for multiple thrusts by Indian forces into Pakistan, the Cold Start doctrine was designed to paralyze Pakistani military planners with uncertainty as to the direction of the main thrust of the mobilizing Indian strike corps.[22] Indian planners assured themselves that India's declared nuclear doctrine of assured massive retaliation against any nuclear use would dissuade Pakistan from using nuclear weapons. India would therefore be able to terminate its military operations on its own terms after causing significant damage to Pakistan's armed forces and also having discredited the military's prestige and position within Pakistani society. Subsequently, India could use the captured territory as a "bargaining chip for post-war diktat or negotiations."[23]

Under Cold Start, the Indian air force and navy would support Indian ground forces with firepower, counter air operations, and other actions. The Indian navy would simultaneously undertake actions against the Pakistani coastline, ports, and harbors to harass the maritime forces and enforce a maritime exclusion zone or naval blockade to strangulate Pakistan's economy, which is almost entirely dependent on maritime supplies.[24] India's limited war strategy was designed as a proactive solution to the operational problems experienced in the 2001–2002 standoff. In the years since its launch, it has been repeatedly revised and refined through annual military exercises, which Pakistan has closely observed from across the border.

From Beg to Kayani: A New Playbook for Pakistan

For a decade after the 1971 war, Pakistan's perception of the threat from India reduced perceptibly. Under the leadership of Prime Minister Zulfiqar Ali Bhutto, Pakistan slowly recovered from the shock of defeat and dismemberment, although it faced a multitude of internal problems. Militarily, following the creation of independent Bangladesh, the new Pakistan was geographically contiguous along a single hostile front with India. After the 1973 coup in Afghanistan that overthrew King Mohammed Zahir Shah, however, another potentially hostile front developed when the Afghan army reinforced its garrisons along the border with Pakistan; Afghanistan's new president Sardar Dawood refused to accept the Afghanistan-Pakistan border established by the British in 1893 (the Durand Line) and wanted to bring together all Pashtun areas— including those in Pakistan's western provinces—in a new Pashtunistan. In addition, a renewed separatist insurgency flared up in Baluchistan in the 1970s, and in May 1974 India carried out its first nuclear test, presenting Pakistan with a qualitatively new security threat that went beyond the conventional forces imbalance.

Pakistan found itself in a completely novel position of having to defend two military fronts while simultaneously dealing with internal threats and cross-border tensions in the wider Baluchistan region (bordering Afghanistan and Iran) as well as a nuclear threat from its principal adversary, India. These security factors were weighing heavily on the Pakistani threat perceptions matrix when the Soviet Union invaded Afghanistan in 1979. Furthermore, while Pakistan focused on the war in Afghanistan on its western front, Indira Gandhi returned to power in India, exacerbating the security threat from that quarter.

Beginning with India's occupation of the Siachen Glacier and the Sunderji Doctrine's muscular manifestation in the region, Pakistani threat perceptions altered significantly to include the risk of a preemptive Indian strike against Pakistan's nuclear installations or strategic assets. These multiple threat perceptions developed at a time when, in addition to the Soviet Union's occupation of Afghanistan, shockwaves from the Iranian revolution were being felt across the border in Pakistan. Under these circumstances, and especially after India's Brass Tacks exercise, the Pakistani military contemplated its first plans for modernization, reviewing its combat potential through the conduct of exercises and re-organizing its forces to meet India's RAPID and mechanized forces as well as its air and artillery firepower.

Zarb-e-Momin: A Strategic Riposte

President General Muhammad Zia-ul-Haq ruled Pakistan from 1977 until he died in a plane crash in August 1988. After the crash, General Mirza Aslam Beg took over as army chief. Many in South Asia compared General Beg with General Sunderji because both were regarded as thinking generals—both conceived the military modernization plans for their respective armies, and both demonstrated nonconformist tendencies.

In 1989, General Beg conceived a large military exercise called Zarb-e-Momin (Strike of the Faithful), in which he wanted to test out new operational concepts, purportedly in response to India's Brass Tacks exercise. Beg introduced the concept of a strategic riposte, which would take the battle into India rather than allowing the Indian strike corps to penetrate Pakistan and exploit its lack of strategic depth. Under this strategy, Pakistan's defense corps would hold back the initial Indian attack and "stabilize threatened sectors" with counterattacks and a counteroffensive comprising infantry and armored divisions launched at India.[25] This riposte would have two advantages. The immediate advantage would be to divert India's strike forces toward Pakistan's tactical offense, and any captured territory could later be used as a bargaining tool in the postwar negotiations. Beg argued that this offensive-defense strategy he introduced "made a radical departure from stereotyped maneuvers and the self-defeating concept of holding formations." He believed his concept provided for an effective deterrence "even in an environment where they [Pakistani offensive forces] may be outnumbered"[26] and that the deterrent effect of nuclear weapons made the risks of a strategic riposte acceptable.[27]

For several decades, the strategies conceived by Sunderji and Beg remained the core war-fighting concepts in their respective militaries, even after each nation had begun developing nuclear capabilities. It was not until the 2001–2002 military standoff with its full-scale mobilization of both armies that India's limited war doctrine was really put to the test, leading to new thinking and its refinement into the Cold Start concept. It also took many years for Islamabad to take the Cold Start threat seriously before finally developing a response of its own.

Pakistan's Muted Reaction to Cold Start

Adversaries are often accused of exaggerating the threats they perceive, and in the case of Pakistan it certainly appears that its military is fixated with the Indian threat to the extent of influencing all aspects of public rhetoric and diplomacy. Yet, between 2004 and 2008, at the height of President General Pervez Musharraf's rule, Pakistan was uncharacteristically indifferent to India's doctrinal changes and even downplayed the implications of Cold Start. For example, when asked about the Cold Start doctrine in June 2004, Major General Shaukat Sultan, Director General of the Pakistan army's Inter-Services public relations bureau, stated: "We cannot outrightly ignore the Cold Start doctrine, but we strongly believe that it is not a viable proposition in the case of Pakistan. This could perhaps work for a banana republic or for that matter a small state," but as far as he was concerned, Pakistan's case was "altogether different."[28]

As Moeed Yusuf observed, many Pakistani analysts at the time viewed Cold Start as "highly futuristic" and "unlikely to be operationalized for the foreseeable future."[29] Various reasons were cited for Pakistani officials' initially muted response. These included the beliefs that India lacked adequate capability for the operation, that it would be impossible to launch the operation with any degree of surprise; that the Pakistani defense forces would be well prepared (as in 2001–2002), and that such an operation would be too risky against a nuclear-armed adversary. In addition to considerations of operational infeasibility, from 2004 to 2008 President Musharraf and Prime Minister Manmohan Singh were heavily engaged in back-door diplomacy to resolve the conflict. Relations between Pakistan and the United States were also still close at the time, to the extent that Pakistan was relatively indifferent to the evolution of a nuclear deal between its ally and India in the early years.

In 2008, after the US-India nuclear deal was passed under the US Hyde Act and significant improvements and refinements to India's military capability had become visible, Pakistan grew more concerned about the implications of Cold Start. India-Pakistan relations deteriorated sharply after the Mumbai terror attack, by which time relations with the US had also begun a downward trend. Even more importantly, President Musharraf had resigned, handing political power to a civilian government and military command to the new Chief of the Army Staff (COAS), General Ashfaq Parvez Kayani.

The Pakistan Army Doctrine (2011)

General Kayani served as COAS for six years from November 2007 to November 2013. In this period, he led the army through a critical phase in Pakistan's recent history of transitioning—once again—from military to civilian rule. His first step was "a course correction" to reform the Pakistan army's image; to "get [it] out of politics and return it to its professional duties."[30] Kayani brought the army's focus back to national security policy. He cautiously engaged with the United States on Afghan policy and selectively employed his forces in counterinsurgency operations; all the while keeping the India-centric threat in focus in view of the renewed tensions after the 2008 Mumbai crisis and India's continual improvements to its Cold Start program.[31]

Under Kayani's watch, Pakistan carried out a series of military exercises, code-named Azm-e-Nau (A New Age), from 2009 to 2013, which involved 40,000–50,000 troops. The Pakistan military also conducted a significant counterinsurgency and counterterrorism operation in the Swat valley, the Federally Administered Tribal Areas, and Baluchistan.[32] The Azm-e-Nau exercises emphasized rapid mobilization to meet India's Cold Start incursions and reinforced the riposte or counteroffensive into enemy territory. Reflecting the 1989 Zarb-e-Momin exercises, which had been Pakistan's response to India's Brass Tacks strategy, Azm-e-Nau refined the army's operational concepts to respond to the changes presented by India's Cold Start.

Pakistan had to calibrate its counterinsurgency and counterterrorism operations carefully since they were depleting its military forces while needing to preserve their resources for a potential war with India. These were extremely challenging objectives, given the increasing number of military commitments and the progression of India's Cold Start program, prompting a comprehensive review of Pakistan's military plans. According to one senior retired officer involved in strategic planning at the time, the most important priority for Pakistan was to maintain the "viability of military force" while retaining "strategic balance" in tackling the Indian and Afghan fronts simultaneously and stabilizing internal security.[33]

Kayani initiated a review of the Pakistani military doctrine that included an appraisal of all threats across the whole spectrum: sub-conventional, conventional, and nuclear. The General Headquarters (GHQ) of the Pakistani army took on responsibility for assessing the conventional aspect, while the Strategic Plans Division (SPD), under the Joint Services Headquarters (JSHQ), assessed the nuclear response strategy. This full-scale review was completed with the public release of the *Pakistan Army Doctrine 2011: Comprehensive Response* in December that year. This was an important document that meticulously examined the full spectrum of threats arising from India's Cold Start and other strategies—the document was apparently redacted by the army after its release.[34]

The *Pakistan Army Doctrine 2011* derives from its national security policy and articulates the role of the army in the tri-service defense strategy. It is a fusion of doctrine and strategy and represents more than just the army perspective.[35] Most significantly, it challenges India's limited war doctrine by promising not just an aggressive defense against incursions, but a guaranteed escalation and expansion of the conflict into India, thereby undermining India's fundamental assumptions about escalation control and expectations that Pakistan would play by India's limited war playbook. The *Pakistan Army Doctrine 2011* describes the strategic environment as "volatile, uncertain, complex, and frequently ambiguous" and replete with economic competition, resource manipulation, insurgencies, regional instability, and conventional "disparity"—all now under the shadow of nuclear weapons.[36] Pakistan's internal problems are a by-product of its external security challenges; therefore, the army believes that it must handle the external security challenges first.

The *Pakistan Army Doctrine 2011* broadly defines sub-conventional warfare as "conflict between ... violent sub-state actors and ... the state."[37] It is at this level that Pakistan's insurgencies—or "domestic security challenges"—tend to "flow [from] external threats," being the "direct fallout of regional and extra-regional powers' pursuit of options other than war in realizing or furthering regional and global policies."[38] Although the doctrine does not explicitly state as much, it implies that a regional power—India—supports insurgent groups within Pakistan and that a global power—the United States—has destabilized Afghanistan through the pursuit of its global "war on terror," which in turn has destabilized Pakistan. The *Pakistan Army Doctrine 2011* obliquely refers to India's Cold Start doctrine as the "traditional adversary's" coercive strategy, which emphasizes the use of firepower to undermine nuclear deterrence and seeks to create "space for war."[39]

On the conventional plane, the advent of India's Cold Start and the *Pakistan Army Doctrine 2011* places both the Indian and the Pakistani armed forces on a perpetual war footing against each other. Because "wars may occur at short notice," all of Pakistan's forces must be prepared to respond immediately to an external threat.[40] From corps to squad levels, the army must be ready for war within two days. Furthermore, commanders must anticipate fighting on their own with the resources at hand and take charge of civil infrastructure as needed.[41] Although the Pakistani air force would support missions, commanders are cautioned against relying on this "very potent but scarce resource" in their planning.[42] Even in peacetime, army logisticians must "disperse" their forces against enemy air attack, provide staff with estimated "on hold resources only," and establish "permanent ammunition storage facilities well forward within formation areas of responsibility."[43] At all levels, fires and effects planners are directed to "update their target lists in peacetime" for prompt execution in the event of war.[44]

From an initially lackluster and even dismissive response to Cold Start during the Musharraf years, Kayani took cognizance of the emerging threat and demanded full readiness and preparation from the army. The revised army doctrine shows that the Pakistan army is not just preparing to face an anticipated threat; it is psychologically preparing its soldiers to fight Indian forces and to rely on their strong morale and "Islamic faith" to defeat the threat of "Hindu aggression."[45] For Pakistan, India's limited war doctrine is just another manifestation of the presence of its eternal enemy; India has never reconciled itself to the existence of a sovereign Pakistan and it is therefore incumbent on all Pakistan's armed forces to remain constantly vigilant against this highest priority threat.

As stated in the *Pakistan Army Doctrine 2011*: "The emergence of two nuclear powers in South Asia has ... added new variables in the extant strategic military equation," and "any future war will invoke disproportionate responses."[46] Furthermore, a "key enabler" of Pakistan's conventional forces is the national "will to upscale the scope of violence [to] create retrospective politico-military dis-incentives for the aggressor."[47]

According to the late General Khalid Shamim Wynne, former Chair of the Joint Chiefs of Staff Committee, after initially ignoring India's Cold Start, the Pakistani side gradually began to believe it was an "achievable military doctrine, especially if India continues to improve its capabilities, reduces its mobilization times and acquires more state-of-the-art arsenals."[48] The Pakistani military inferred that India's Cold Start was designed to operate with speed to preempt any counter-mobilization and terminate operations before Pakistan's strategic planners could contemplate using their nuclear capability. According to General Wynne's assessment, Cold Start sought to negate any advantage that Pakistan had gained through its nuclear deterrent.[49] Consequently, from the Pakistani perspective, nothing short of a "forward presence, rapid deployment, and [a] prompt, flexible, and aggressive response" could hope to deter India from commencing operations.[50]

There was no certainty, however, that Pakistan's comprehensive conventional forces response would be sufficient to deter India. The most obvious concern related to the depletion of border defenses with India as Pakistani forces were pulled away to address other contingencies, particularly on the Afghan border, which Pakistan viewed as a deliberate Indian ploy. Further, Indian official statements were adamant about continuing to conduct military operations—regardless of Pakistan's nuclear capability—with some either dismissing it or even threatening to call out Pakistan's nuclear bluff. Pakistani strategic planners then began to think innovatively and decided to close the space and "pour cold water on Cold Start."[51]

Full-Spectrum Deterrence

As explained in the previous chapter, the objective of Pakistan's strategy is to maintain sufficient conventional and nuclear forces to deter India from attacking Pakistan.[52] If this deterrence fails, Pakistan intends to hold off an Indian conventional attack long enough for the international community to intervene to stop the war from escalating further. If that fails, however, and Pakistan's nuclear threshold is crossed, then the use of nuclear weapons would become inevitable.

In April 2011, before the release of the *Pakistan Army Doctrine 2011*, Pakistan's Strategic Plans Division (SPD)— the secretariat of the National Command Authority (NCA)—announced the successful testing of the Nasr/Hatf-IX short-range ballistic missile to be deployed as a battlefield nuclear weapon or a tactical nuclear weapon (TNW) against Indian forces at a range of only 60 kilometers. Pakistan does not formally publish details about its nuclear doctrine, keeping it purposefully ambiguous for the sake of deterrence. However, explanations from the SPD as well as commentaries from academics and military experts illuminate that TNWs are intended to deter a conventional Indian attack by creating multiple uncertainties and challenges for India's military planners.[53] The Nasr missile's short range means that in the event of hostilities, it must be deployed near the front lines, where the invading Indian military would meet nuclear weapons on the battlefield—this would place the onus of risk calculations on Indian field commanders.

Within Pakistan's new military doctrine, nuclear weapons play a role in hostilities right from the outset and "extend their cover to conventional forces across the continuum from deterrence to war" by their added presence on the battlefield.[54] The *Pakistan Army Doctrine 2011* acknowledges the escalation ladder by explicitly stating: "Nuclear exchanges, even if localized and limited, register on the highest pedestal of violence."[55] Pakistani planners understand that in this context the term "tactical" or "battlefield" is really a misnomer.[56] In a 2020 keynote address in London, former SPD Director General, retired Lieutenant General Khalid Kidwai, explained:

> Pakistan's nuclear capability operationalized under the well-articulated policy of *full-spectrum deterrence* comprises of a large variety of strategic, operational and tactical nuclear weapons,

on land, air, and sea, which are designed to comprehensively deter large-scale aggression against mainland Pakistan. [emphasis added][57]

Pakistan's response to India's Cold Start presents an automatic glide path to strategic nuclear escalation and mutually assured destruction.[58] The country's strategic planners are applying the same reasoning that led Cold War weapons developers in the United States and the Soviet Union to deter conflict through the deployment of TNWs; namely, the concern with escalation. If those great powers were fearful enough of TNWs to reject them completely in the final years of the Cold War—so Pakistan's planners reason—then surely India would likewise fear the consequences of TNW use sufficiently to refrain from attacking Pakistan.[59]

Mutual Non-Assurance: Escalation Dynamics and Crisis Instability

The doctrinal dissonance between India and Pakistan is fraught with the risk of escalation from a limited conventional war to a nuclear exchange. Pakistan's geographical vulnerability to any cross-border incursions from India, its doctrine of assured expansion of a conflict into Indian territory, and the addition of TNWs into the mix have all created a complex and dangerous security milieu.

From New Delhi's perspective, stable peace in the region is only possible if Pakistan eliminates its terrorist infrastructure to India's satisfaction. However, given how terrorism has metastasized across the region, no regional state can assure that it is safe from the terrorists, much less another state. In any case, Pakistan doubts that anything it does would be sufficient to allay India's concerns. Yet, as long as India believes the Pakistani government is complicit in terrorist incidents in India, it will reserve the right to use military force against Pakistan if a terror attack is traced back to any entity operating in or from Pakistan. In turn, Pakistan reserves the right to use nuclear weapons in response to any form of conventional aggression by India. This cyclical framework of non-assurance contains all the ingredients for conflict escalation to the point of a nuclear exchange.

The history of warfare tells us that no sooner do military operations commence on the battlefield than conditions change due to enemy actions and the fog of war. Unless tightly controlled, political objectives also shift with the exigencies and momentum of military operations. India's prewar assumptions of controlling the extent of military operations and correctly interpreting Pakistan's nuclear threshold would be out of the window as soon as the taper was lit, which makes crisis de-escalation and termination of a potential war extremely difficult.

India's limited conventional war could quickly deepen and broaden within just a few days. Consequently, the moment Pakistan sees India shifting gears from peace to war and India's offensive corps mobilizing, the entire Pakistani armed forces would brace for total war. The nuclear weapons would shift to varying levels of alertness, either remaining in their peacetime storage silos or moving to deployment areas where they can mate up with delivery vehicles and their respective military units.[60] For effective deterrence posturing in the battlefield areas, Pakistan would deploy short-range nuclear weapons either prior to the commencement of hostilities or shortly thereafter, depending on operational contingencies.[61] In sum, following any Indian mobilization and simultaneous cross-border attack, Pakistan would respond with a complete mobilization for defense, including a possible riposte into Indian territory. By the time India's offensive strike corps reached the battlefields, its limited war would likely have turned into a total war, and Pakistan's nuclear threshold would likely have been crossed many times over.[62]

Threat perceptions on the Subcontinent are so deeply entrenched that both India and Pakistan assume the worst of the other's intentions in a crisis. Their enduring rivalry, chronic mistrust, and entrenched frustrations with each other have resulted in an accumulation of grievances which encourages excessive military actions whenever the opportunity arises. Even during peacetime, whenever there are ceasefire violations on the LoC in Kashmir, tit-for-tat tactical exchanges from both sides often escalate disproportionately. Thus, every cross-border skirmish heightens bilateral tensions, and local infringements are logged in the memory, to be avenged whenever the next military action takes place. These enduring enmities undermine crisis stability at the national level and exacerbate the security dilemma between India and Pakistan.

Limited versus Total War

Since 2015, India has reacted rapidly and forcefully to the military crises stemming from terror attacks on its soil. The Indian political leadership has given the armed forces a certain amount of leeway for initiating a punitive military response to perceived Pakistani provocation, and so Indian military planners are predisposed to use maximum force within these limited windows. However, unless political oversight is vigilant in a so-called "limited war," there is a real danger that inter-service competition among the Indian services will lead each to attempt to inflict the heaviest blow against their joint nemesis. Believing that India could overcome Pakistan with its conventional forces advantage, India's military doctrine invites the use of maximal tactics so as to achieve a quick and impressive victory—or stalemate—before international intervention forces a cessation of hostilities.

Although aware of the potential risk of an escalation spiral, the Indian military believes it can halt operations before Pakistan's nuclear threshold is crossed. India certainly expects to terminate any war on its own terms. However, Pakistan has its own ideas about how it would respond if India were to initiate a so-called limited response, and tit-for-tat reciprocity cannot be ruled out—as evidenced in February 2019 over the Pulwama-Balakot crisis in Kashmir (discussed further in chapter 6). Indeed, Pakistani officials have pledged to initiate their own *quid pro quo plus* response, which implies Pakistan could escalate to the next rung on the ladder if it deemed it necessary.[63]

India and Pakistan are each convinced that they have a legitimate grievance against the other as well as the right of retribution. Each also assumes that the other side is aware of the self-imposed restrictions in their respective operational plans. Hence, the Indian strategic community is dismissive of the suggestion that a future military conflict might lead to a nuclear exchange because, first, India's intention would be only to wage a limited conventional war, and second, India's threat of a massive retaliation as delineated in its declared doctrines would deter Pakistan from using nuclear weapons. In contrast, Pakistan not only dismisses any notion of no-first-use but also threatens to respond using its full-spectrum deterrence with a mix of conventional and nuclear weapons at the tactical, operational, and strategic levels. As far as India is concerned, Pakistan's declared response of a conventional escalation and potential nuclear deployment are nothing more than bluster. In sum, both sides are prepared to act on their *perceptions* of what the other side will or will not do, rather than accept at face value what the other side has *actually* articulated or set down in its doctrine.

Alongside the acute doctrinal dissonance between India and Pakistan, they also operate within a strategic framework where neither side has any form of assurance. Consequently, both typically respond according to their worst-case scenarios. Limited war for India means a full-scale war for Pakistan. India's growing conventional forces advantage represents an existential threat for Pakistan that keeps "all options" open for its defense. Considering the crisis in Kashmir in February 2019, one could surmise that one-off air strikes and tit-for-tat responses fall below Pakistan's threshold for war.[64] However, the Pulwama-Balakot crisis managed to find an off-ramp when Pakistan shot down an Indian aircraft, captured the pilot, and returned said pilot as a peace gesture. Will the region be so lucky the second time around?

Pressure to Lower the Nuclear Threshold
Were a war on the Subcontinent to escalate horizontally and vertically, pressure on Pakistan to lower its nuclear threshold would be high. At

such a moment, if Pakistan chose to signal its resolve and showcase its nuclear capability, this could inadvertently lead to escalation and may even culminate in a nuclear exchange. The greatest challenge for both sides—apart from ceasing hostilities—would be how to reestablish deterrence after such an outbreak.[65] India perceives that its deterrence is failing because Pakistan—shielding behind its nuclear capability—continues to bleed India through proxies without fear of India's military response. Furthermore, Pakistan has stated its preparedness to expand the conventional conflict and risk a nuclear escalation. At the same time, India seems to dismiss Pakistan's nuclear threat and is prepared to call Islamabad's nuclear bluff by continuing to escalate its conventional operations, regardless of Pakistani tactical weapons in the battlefield.

Essentially, Pakistan is signaling to India that should India plan to use war as an instrument of policy, escalation of the conflict is guaranteed, and Islamabad would never offer any assurance that intensification of military operations would not lead to a nuclear employment. For its part, India has made it clear that it would consider a tactical nuclear strike as equivalent to a strategic strike, which would give India grounds to launch a retaliatory strategic nuclear response. Pakistan challenges this logic, however, by suggesting that it may launch TNWs strictly in defense within its own territory, which would make an Indian strategic retaliation extremely provocative and possibly no longer justifiable. In any event, an Indian second strike would be met with a Pakistani third strike—and on and on it would go.[66]

Deterrence Stability: Threat Manipulation with TNWs

India's Cold Start has produced two interrelated strategic effects by placing integrated, mobile, and flexible military forces on Pakistan's border and increasing its range of military options from punitive strikes to full-scale conventional war. Going forward, as it integrates new and emerging technologies into its armed forces, India will continue to enhance its mobility and firepower capabilities, enabling an ever more flexible response. In sum, India aims to neutralize Pakistan's forward military posture and speed up its strategic forces mobilization through shorter interior lines.

India's conventional innovation has pushed Pakistan to revise its war-fighting concept, as expressed in the *Pakistan Army Doctrine 2011*, and to restructure and reposition its conventional forces. By introducing TNWs into the equation, Pakistan's strategy is designed to complicate Indian decision-making when it comes to initiating conventional operations, even on a limited scale. In the Pakistani strategic planning assessment, TNWs place stringent limitations on India's options to begin a conventional conflict in the first place, since the danger and risk associated with deploying TNWs is precisely the uncertainty that is intended to ensure stability through deterrence at the conventional forces level.

Pakistani officials and experts have insisted that the deployment of short-range weapons is not war-fighting per se but a tactic to deter a conventional attack by India; however, it is a tactic that places Pakistani nuclear weapons on the battlefield in the midst of its own conventional defenses. Such a tactic also complicates the articulation of command and control between conventional and nuclear command channels and creates a complex set of field security concerns. In the fog of war, these downsides pose a significant risk of general deterrence breakdown.

The informal deterrence relationship between India and Pakistan transformed into a structured deterrence framework after the 2001–2002 military standoff. The Indian military strategy has shifted because of three factors: (1) a belief that Pakistan is aggressively engaged in a sub-conventional war against India, (2) India's insistence that nuclear weapons have not made conventional war irrelevant, and (3) the knowledge that India's conventional war strategy was too cumbersome to fight a limited conventional war with Pakistan.

Based on this assessment, India developed its innovative Cold Start strategy. In turn, Pakistan revised its war-fighting capabilities by reviewing its own doctrine and developing TNWs to undercut India's continued reliance on conventional war as a policy instrument. In short, both militaries are indulging in brinkmanship and risk manipulation, while engaging in an arms race based on military modernization and the growth of strategic arsenals.[67]

NOTES

1. Michael Howard, "The Classical Strategists," *Adelphi Papers* 9, no 54 (London: Institute of Strategic Studies, 1969): 18–32, https://doi.org/10.1080/05679326908448125.
2. B. H. Liddell Hart, *Strategy: The Indirect Approach* (London: Faber, 1967), 335.
3. André Beaufre, *An Introduction to Strategy: With Particular Reference to Problems of Defense, Politics, Economics, and Diplomacy in the Nuclear Age* (London: Faber, 1965), 22.
4. Howard, "The Classical Strategists."
5. Bernard Brodie, *The Absolute Weapon: Atomic Power and World Order* (New York: Harcourt Brace, 1946), 76.
6. Robert Jervis, *The Meaning of the Nuclear Revolution: Statecraft and the Prospect of Armageddon* (Ithaca, NY: Cornell University Press, 1989).
7. Jervis, *The Meaning of the Nuclear Revolution*, ix.
8. Jervis, *The Meaning of the Nuclear Revolution*.
9. See Peter R. Lavoy, Scott D. Sagan, and James J. Wirtz, eds., *Planning the Unthinkable: How New Nuclear Powers Will Use Nuclear, Biological and Chemical Weapons* (Ithaca, NY: Cornell University Press, 2000), 8.
10. Inderjit Badhwar and Dilip Bobb, "General Sundarji Leaves behind a Legacy Most Fiercely Disputed in the History of the Army," *India Today*, May 15, 1988, https://www.indiatoday.in/magazine/cover-story/story/19880515-general-sundarji-leaves-behind-a-legacy-most-fiercely-disputed-in-the-history-of-the-army-797243-1988-05-15.
11. Stephen P. Cohen, cited in Zorawar, The National Identity XI: India's Most Ambitious Hawk, *The National Identity*, November 28, 2016: https://medium.com/the-national-identity/the-national-identity-xi-the-story-of-indias-most-ambitious-hawk-c85affbdecc1.
12. Badhwar and Bobb, "General Sunderji."
13. Badhwar and Bobb, "General Sunderji."
14. Scott D. Sagan and Kennth Waltz, *The Spread of Nuclear Weapons: A Debate Renewed* (New York: WW Norton and Company, 2002), 91.
15. Feroz Hassan Khan, *Eating Grass: The Making of the Pakistani Bomb* (Palo Alto, CA: Stanford University Press, 2012), 159–160, 221–222.

16. IISS, *The Military Balance 2020: The Annual Assessment of Global Military Capabilities and Defence Economics* (London: International Institute of Strategic Studies, 2020), 269–275, 299–303.

17. Walter C. Ladwig III, "A Cold Start for Hot Wars? The Indian Army's New Limited War Doctrine," *International Security* 32, no. 3 (Winter 2007/2008): 160, https://doi.org/10.1162/isec.2008.32.3.158.

18. In the late 1990s, Sunderji reportedly said that with the advent of Pakistan's nuclear capabilities, gone were the days when the Indian army could think of undertaking deep strikes. This was told to me in discussions with retired Indian military officers during the many Track II dialogues that I organized over the years.

19. V. P. Malik, "Limited War Concept in South Asia" (presented at the Conference on Strategic Stability in South Asia, Monterey, California, July 2005).

20. Peter Lavoy, "Pakistan's Nuclear Posture: Security and Survivability," Nonproliferation Policy Education Center, January 21, 2007, http://npolicy.org/article.php?aid=291&tid=30.

21. Ladwig, "A Cold Start for Hot Wars?" See also Ryan French, "Deterrence Adrift: Mapping Conflict and Escalation in South Asia," *Strategic Studies Quarterly* 10, no. 1 (2016): 108–137, https://www.jstor.org/stable/2627 1089.

22. Ladwig "A Cold Start for Hot Wars?"

23. French, "Deterrence Adrift," 108.

24. This scenario is drawn from several Track II crisis simulation exercises organized by the US Naval Postgraduate School since 2013.

25. Khan, *Eating Grass*, 220–229.

26. Mirza Aslam Beg, "Deterrence, Defence, and Development," *Defence Journal* 3, no. 6 (July 1999), http://www.defencejournal.com/jul99/deterrence.htm.

27. Beg, "Deterrence, Defence, and Development," 1–2.

28. Moeed Yusuf, "India's Cold Start: Explaining Pakistan's Silence" (presented at Cold Start: India's New Strategic Doctrine and Its Implications, Monterey, California, May 29–30, 2008). See also "Cold Start Doctrine Being Closely Studied: ISPR," *Dawn*, June 13, 2004, https://www.dawn.com/news/394812/cold-start-doctrine-being-closely-studied-ispr. The military held several internal briefings as well as a press conference in May 2005, but the response remained low-key even on these occasions.

29. Yusuf, "India's Cold Start."

30. "Resolving the Mystery That Is Ashfaq Kayani," *Kashmir Monitor*, December 2, 2013, https://defence.pk/pdf/threads/general-impressions-resolving-the-mystery-that-is-ashfaq-parvez-kayani.298309/.

31. Praveen Swami, "General Kayani's Quiet Coup," *The Hindu*, August 3, 2010, https://www.thehindu.com/opinion/lead/General-Kayanis-quiet-coup/article16120868.ece.

32. Arif Jamal, "Pakistan's Ongoing Azm-e-Nau-3 Military Exercises Define Strategic Priorities," *Terrorism Monitor* 8, no. 18, May 7, 2010, https://jamestown.org/program/pakistans-ongoing-azm-e-nau-3-military-exercises-define-strategic-priorities/.

33. Discussions with General Khalid Shamim Wynne on the sidelines of the Track II dialogue in Garmisch-Partenkirchen, Germany, October 2015.

34. Pakistan Army, *Pakistan Army Doctrine 2011: Comprehensive Response* (Rawalpindi: Pakistan Army, 2011), xi.

35. Pakistan Army, *Pakistan Army Doctrine 2011*, 2, 123.

36. Pakistan Army, *Pakistan Army Doctrine 2011*, 2–9.

37. Pakistan Army, *Pakistan Army Doctrine 2011*, 25.

38. Pakistan Army, *Pakistan Army Doctrine 2011*, 30, 85.

39. Pakistan Army, *Pakistan Army Doctrine 2011*, 12, 13, 27, 55.

40. Pakistan Army, *Pakistan Army Doctrine 2011*, 27.

41. Pakistan Army, *Pakistan Army Doctrine 2011*, 43–45, 72.

42. Pakistan Army, *Pakistan Army Doctrine 2011*, 76.

43. Pakistan Army, *Pakistan Army Doctrine 2011*, 69–71.

44. Pakistan Army, *Pakistan Army Doctrine 2011*, 54.

45. Pakistan Army, *Pakistan Army Doctrine 2011*, 19, 38.

46. Pakistan Army, *Pakistan Army Doctrine 2011*, 27.

47. Pakistan Army, *Pakistan Army Doctrine 2011*, 42.

48. Discussions with General Khalid Shamim Wynne, Garmisch-Partenkirchen, Germany, October 2015.

49. Discussions with General Khalid Shamim Wynne; Ladwig, "A Cold Start," 158–163.

50. Pakistan Army, *Pakistan Army Doctrine 2011*, 24.

51. Khan, *Eating Grass*, 396.

52. Pakistan Army, *Pakistan Army Doctrine 2011*, AP 1001 E.

53. Christopher Clary, "The Future of Pakistan's Nuclear Weapons Program," in *Strategic Asia 2013–2014: Asia in the Second Nuclear Age*, ed. Ashley Tellis, Abraham M. Denmark, and Travis Tanner (Washington, DC: National Bureau of Asian Research, 2013), 153.

54. Clary, "Pakistan's Nuclear Weapons Program," 12. See also Khalid Kidwai, "Deterrence Stability" (presented at the South Asian Strategic Stability: Deterrence, Nuclear Weapons and Arms Control Workshop, London, February 7, 2020), https://www.iiss.org/events/2020/02/7th-iiss-and-ciss-south-asian-strategic-stability-workshop.

55. Pakistan Army, *Pakistan Army Doctrine 2011*, 10.

56. Khan, *Eating Grass*, 395–396.

57. Kidwai, "Deterrence Stability."

58. Jamal Hussain, "Impact of the Induction of Tactical Nuclear Weapons by Pakistan on Overall Deterrence," *Defence Journal* 17, no. 7 (February 2014): 24.

59. Hussain, "Impact of the Induction of TNW," 23–25.

60. Feroz Hassan Khan, "Challenges to Nuclear Stability in South Asia," *Nonproliferation Review* 10, no. 1 (Spring 2003): 68, http://cns.miis.edu/npr/pdfs/101khan.pdf.

61. Feroz Hassan Khan and Ryan W. French, *US-Pakistani Nuclear Relations: A Strategic Survey*, PASCC Report 2014-005 (Monterey, CA: Naval Postgraduate School, 2014), 27, http://www.hsdl.org/?view&did=754217.

62. Feroz Hassan Khan, *Going Tactical: Pakistan's Nuclear Posture and Implications for Stability*, Proliferation Paper No. 53 (Paris: IFRI Security Studies Center, 2015).

63. Kidwai, "Deterrence Stability."

64. Kidwai, "Deterrence Stability."

65. Khan, "Challenges to Nuclear Stability," 59–73.

66. Clary, "Pakistan's Nuclear Weapons Program," 145.

67. Feroz Hassan Khan, "The Independence-Dependence Paradox: Stability Dilemmas in South Asia," *Arms Control Today* (October 2003), https://www.armscontrol.org/act/2003-10/features/independence-dependence-paradox-stability-dilemmas-south.

Chapter 6

Gray-Zone Warfare and Arms Race Instability

You may do one Mumbai; you may lose Baluchistan.

–Ajit Doval[1]

American scholars Glenn Snyder and Robert Jervis explain how nuclear deterrence induces stability by preventing full-scale wars, even as it —paradoxically—creates space for violence at the lower end of the conflict spectrum. This is known as the "stability-instability paradox."[2] South Asian policymakers are often skeptical about applying Cold War experiences to regional security in South Asia, even though—as the previous chapters illustrate—the advent of nuclear capabilities did not prevent India and Pakistan from stumbling into a military crisis.[3] While some scholars described the Kargil War and the 2001–2002 military standoff as typifying the stability-instability paradox, most attributed these crises to the inexperience of two nuclear powers unaccustomed to the statecraft needed after acquiring such powerful weapons.[4] In the two decades since, although India and Pakistan have experienced multiple military crises, they have desisted from high-intensity battles and costly mobilizations, indulging instead in limited cross-border ventures and localized tactical operations. In some ways, therefore, India and Pakistan have perfected the "stability-instability paradox" as an acceptable security paradigm for South Asia.

Nuclear optimists might attribute this restraint to the stabilizing effect of the nuclear deterrent or to apparent progress on the nuclear learning curve. India's strategic enclave may have concluded that its assumptions around escalation control in a limited conventional war—as envisaged within Cold Start—were not only too ambitious but could also lead to a dangerous miscalculation. Similarly, there may have been a realization in Islamabad that the risks associated with deploying and/or using tactical nuclear weapons (TNWs) were much greater than the potential deterrent value of such a strategy.

By 2021, India's Cold Start doctrine and Pakistan's embrace of TNWs already appeared obsolete as both sides apparently realized that the risks were greater than any potential benefits. Any cross-border war that India might start with Pakistan—no matter how limited—would be certain to escalate and come up against TNWs on the battlefield. At the same time, even though Pakistan's policymakers seemed confident they could deploy integrated forces safely and maintain control of TNWs, balancing the tradeoffs between authority and security would be fraught with challenges. These challenges include articulation of command and control between conventional and nuclear forces operating within the same space, deciding on the choice of target-sets between forward invading forces and follow-on forces, and balancing the operational efficacy of conventional forces against the vulnerability of TNWs to Indian counterforce strikes.[5]

India has nuanced its military doctrine by conducting lower-level military operations involving hit-and-run/punish tactics. Known as "surgical strikes," such operations provide less potential for escalation and greater domestic political returns. For its part, Pakistan has implemented its *quid pro quo plus* response to any Indian cross-border operations (discussed later), while keeping its threat to deploy battlefield nuclear weapons ambiguous. Although neither India nor Pakistan have publicly denounced the old doctrines, their behavior in recent crises indicates that both sides are seemingly content to restrict military operations to a lower level of intensity.[6]

It is not only pragmatic and practical considerations that have pushed the Indian and Pakistani military doctrines in the direction of restraint; political transformations and technological innovations have also had a revolutionary impact on national policies and military strategies. The political transformation in India since 2014 and the speed of India's military and strategic modernization have significant implications for arms race (in)stability. With its modern weapons, information technology revolution, and induction of emerging technologies into its arsenal, India now has innovative new tools at its disposal to conduct both overt and covert low-level operations and even threaten Pakistan's nuclear forces and command systems.[7] This combination of hardline politics and military/technological advances is radically altering the region's stability-instability paradigm and sending the Subcontinent further adrift.

THE RISE OF HINDUTVA

Narendra Modi's rise to power was viewed with both hope and trepidation. For the hopeful, he was a strong leader who would realize India's full potential by expanding its influence in the world. More pessimistic observers within India and across the region worried about the country's secular future, given the empowerment of Hindu extremist groups.

The central vision of India's founding fathers was the notion of communal harmony—especially harmony between Hindus and Muslims within a pluralist state—which laid the foundations for a secular India. This vision was not uniformly shared across India, however. The Rashtriya Swayamsevak Sangh (RSS) organization (formed in 1925) was committed to the idea of a Hindu India, wherein all minorities would submit to the supremacy of "Hindutva." Consequently, fearing Hindu domination in the run-up to independence from Britain, the All-India Muslim League demanded a two-nation solution, eventually leading to the creation of Pakistan. Muslims and other minorities who remained in India were given constitutional guarantees against persecution by Hindu extremists. Furthermore, following the brutal assassination of India's revered leader Mahatma Mohandas Gandhi in January 1948 at the hands of RSS activist Nathuram Godse, the RSS was proscribed and marginalized for nearly four decades.

The idea of Hindu supremacy gained new momentum in the 1990s when the RSS started a movement against a sixteenth-century mosque in Ayodhya (the Babri Masjid), which they claimed was built on the site of a former Hindu temple, which was purportedly also the birthplace of the Hindu god Ram. The Hindu extremists demanded that the mosque be demolished, and the temple rebuilt in its place. In 1992, a procession led by the RSS turned into a assault on the mosque, which resulted in its demolition. The delicate harmony that had existed between Hindus and Muslims in India up to that point immediately dissolved into violent sectarian riots. Although the riots were eventually brought under control, these events gave birth to the populist Hindu right-wing movement in India and propelled its political arm, the Bharatiya Janata Party (BJP), to mainstream power.[8]

Born in Gujarat in 1950, Narendra Modi was recruited into the RSS at an early age and has remained a member of the movement throughout his life. At the time of the Hindu-Muslim riots in the early 1990s, he was an unknown figure, but he soon rose to become chief minister in the state of Gujarat, where he ruled for 13 years. In 2014 Modi led the BJP to victory in India's national elections, becoming the country's 14th prime minister.

Across the border in Pakistan, a new civilian government led by Nawaz Sharif in his third term as prime minister came to power. That same year saw the installation of Xi Jinping as China's president, adopting an overtly outward-focused policy agenda that would make Xi "the most powerful leader since Mao Zedong."[9] This shifting political environment understandably affected the strategic approaches adopted by India and Pakistan, and Modi and Sharif briefly flirted with rapprochement to address the hostility and issues between the two nations. However, a combination of the deepening crisis in Kashmir, the aggressive policies of Hindu right-wing hardliners in India, and the perennial civil-military discord in Pakistan effectively derailed any prospects for peace and détente in South Asia.[10]

THE MODI-DOVAL DOCTRINE

Modi's arrival as prime minister led to a radical departure from the previous approaches of Atal Bihari Vajpayee and Manmohan Singh. India's strategic policy approach was aggressive in all three of the mandala circles through which India views the world (as described in chapter 3). Modi moved with unprecedented speed on the diplomatic front: in his first year in office, he met with some 50 world leaders, actively participated in global and regional multilateral forums, and worked unceasingly to draw international attention and interest toward India and its new leadership. On China, Modi's public position during the elections was that of an aggressive adversary; once in office, however, Modi was eager to engage with China and develop mutual economic interests, although he remained apprehensive of China's Belt and Road Initiative (BRI) and its agenda of expanding connectivity with India's neighborhood. Once again, the dichotomy between ideals and pragmatism surfaced in Indian policy. [11]

Modi adopted a clever approach regarding Pakistan by working to establish good personal relations with his counterpart Nawaz Sharif, while conspicuously avoiding any form of official dialogue. This was a deliberate strategy designed to (1) send a message to the world that democratic India preferred to negotiate with elected civilian leaders; (2) massage Sharif's ego, whose past run-ins with the military were well-known; and (3) more importantly, annoy the military establishment in Pakistan. Modi knew well that this approach was bound to fail, but to the world, it would underscore his sincerity and ultimately ensure that the blame for failure lay with the Pakistani military. Meanwhile, Modi continued with his policy of suppressing Kashmir, while Pakistan continued to support the Kashmiri leaders fighting for self-determination. The net outcome of Modi's overtures to Sharif was to create even more fissures between the civilian and military leadership in Pakistan and sow suspicions about Sharif's private motivations for such informal and private interactions.

India began to reevaluate its policy of responding to perceived provocation by Pakistan's proxies. India began to contemplate innovative means of directing its sub-conventional, conventional, and nuclear instruments against Pakistan. At the same time, Sharif began to consider reversing the course of jihad and setting the country back on track toward economic development; a pathway for which rapprochement with India and Afghanistan was essential. By this point, however, the Modi regime and his team already had their own ideas about how to pressure Pakistan using a combination of aggressive diplomacy, coercion, and sub-conventional warfare.[12]

The Gray-Zone Approach

Immediately after his inaugural ceremony in May 2014, Modi appointed Ajit Doval as his national security advisor (NSA). Doval, a former police officer known for his hawkish views on national security, had an illustrious career in Indian intelligence (including, allegedly, a five-year stint undercover in Pakistan), and at the time of his retirement in 2005 he was director of the Intelligence Bureau. A few months before his appointment as NSA, Doval articulated his views on Indian national security in a hard-hitting lecture at SASTRA University in Tamil Nadu, in which he was critical of Manmohan Singh's policy toward Pakistan and China. Doval used the lecture to advocate his own doctrine—apparently an offshoot of the Indira Doctrine—concerning relations with India's archrivals. Doval advanced three approaches for dealing with India's adversaries: defensive, offensive, and defensive-offensive. With regards to Pakistan, he prescribed the hybrid defensive-offensive approach, which involves a "range of subversive instruments, many of which are non-military" (also commonly known as Russian hybrid warfare or the gray-zone doctrine).[13]

Doval surmised that India's approach to Pakistan had either been too defensive, like a *chowkidar* (guard), or too offensive, implying war—and with it, the potential escalation to nuclear war. India's "fifth-generation" doctrine, as represented by Doval's strategy of defensive-offense, involves utilizing the "gray zone" of a coercion campaign that would lead the offense from inside Pakistan itself. For Doval, India should respond to Pakistan's use of proxies in places like Kashmir by using the same tactic, taking it back into Pakistan from whence it came:[14]

> We start working on the vulnerabilities of Pakistan. It can be economic. It can be internal security, it can be political, it can be their isolation internationally ... exposing their terrorist activities ... it can be anything. It can be defeating their policies in Afghanistan, making it difficult for them to manage internal political balance or internal security ... there is no nuclear war involved in [defensive offense]; there is no engagement of troops.[15]

The Modi-Doval Doctrine represents an implicit acceptance of the risks posed by India's Cold Start, including the possibility of a nuclear exchange—especially since the introduction of tactical nuclear weapons and cruise missiles, along with increases in the range of Pakistani ballistic missiles. Being a proponent of the limited war concept, India's Ministry of Defense has fully embraced the new doctrine—as illustrated in May 2015, when Defense Minister Manohar Parrikar endorsed the hybrid concept of using terrorism in Pakistan. He famously used a Hindi phrase, "*kaante to kaante se nikalna*" ("use a thorn to extract a thorn"), explaining: "We have to use terrorists to neutralize terrorists. Why can't we do it? We should do it. Why does my soldier have to do it?"[16]

Covert Operations

While the Indian government unveiled its new approach in 2014, the Indian military and intelligence agencies had been working on sub-conventional strategies for some time, even as the Indian army was refining its Cold Start concept and proactive conventional operations. A dedicated covert operations cell—the Technical Support Division (TSD)—had long been established within the Indian military intelligence directorate, working in concert with the Research and Analysis Wing (RAW). George Perkovich and Toby Dalton explain that the purpose of the cell was to "enable the military intelligence directorate to provide a quick response to any act of state-sponsored terrorism with a high degree of deniability."[17] The idea behind the cell was to develop capability inside Pakistan to "respond quickly, secretly, and more or less symmetrically to another Mumbai-like attack."[18]

In the 1990s, Prime Minister Gujral had "ordered [RAW] to cease covert operations in Pakistan and to demobilize the assets that had been developed to pursue them."[19] Gujral's successor as prime minister, Atal Bihari Vajpayee, did not change Gujral's policy, despite persistent urging by India's intelligence community.[20] Under Modi, however, the policy of covert actions against Pakistan reached an altogether new level.

In a two-pronged move, Indian intelligence stepped up its covert activities to support separatist or aggrieved sub-nationalist movements in Pakistan, in particular the separatist movement in Baluchistan, whose leadership was in exile in Europe and Afghanistan. The first prong operated from Afghanistan in partnership with the Afghan state intelligence agency, Khadamat-e-Aetela'-e-Dawlati (KAD). RAW sponsored the Tehrik-i-Taliban Pakistan (TTP) organization based in eastern Afghanistan to carry out a series of espionage and terror attacks across the border with Pakistan into Khyber Pakhtunkhwa and Baluchistan. The second prong operated from eastern Iran, abetting espionage in Baluchistan and Sindh (including the port of Karachi). The Indian consulate in Zahedan, Iran, served as the hub of this operation.[21] These

Indian intelligence operations generated a spate of terror right across Pakistan, which prompted a fierce counterintelligence response from Pakistan's Inter-Services Intelligence (ISI).

In March 2016, Pakistani security forces in Baluchistan arrested an Indian spy—an Indian naval officer, Commander Kulbhushan Jadhav, who was a member of RAW. Jadhav publicly admitted abetting insurgents and engaging in a series of espionage, sabotage, and terror activities inside Pakistan. Jadhav's confession was widely telecast in Pakistan.[22] One year later in April 2017, a Pakistani military court sentenced him to death, although the sentence is currently in abeyance following referral to the International Court of Justice (ICJ) in The Hague and its directive for a re-trial. Jadhav currently remains in Pakistani custody, awaiting execution. The exposure of Jadhav as an Indian spy in Baluchistan in March 2016 created an explosive atmosphere which ignited a series of crises across the region, particularly in Kashmir.

The Surgical Strike Stratagem
During his election campaign in 2014, Modi had mocked the policies of his predecessor, Manmohan Singh, as being "defensive" toward Pakistan.[23] Now however, India had a hawkish national security team led by NSA Doval, who began implementing his no-nonsense "defensive-offensive" strategy against Pakistan. Besides the launch of covert operations, India's new security policy included cross-border hot pursuits of militants, surgical strikes, and aggressive coercive military posturing vis-à-vis its neighbors—not just Pakistan. Indeed, throughout the Modi regime, the Indian military has been fighting pitched battles with separatists in Kashmir and in the northeastern states bordering Myanmar against the Naxalites, and India continues to experience border tensions with China in the disputed Himalayan borderlands.[24]

Following the unmasking of Jadhav in spring 2016, India adopted a hard-hitting policy in Indian-administered Kashmir, including the use of pellet guns by soldiers that blinded protesters and the assassination of the Kashmiri militant leader Burhan Wani in July. This triggered a new wave of insurgency that engulfed the Kashmir Valley. On September 18, four militants attacked Indian brigade headquarters in the town of Uri and killed 19 Indian soldiers.[25] Ten days later, the Indian army's director general of military operations, Lieutenant General Ranbir Singh, stated at a press conference held jointly with the Ministry of External Affairs that "some terrorist teams had positioned themselves at launch-pads along the Line of Control [LoC]. The Indian army conducted surgical strikes last night."[26] Despite the fact that these claims were never verified or pursued, the new term "surgical strike" became the buzzword of choice within India's strategic community, media and even in the Indian movie industry, which released the Bollywood blockbuster *Uri: The Surgical Strike* in 2019.

The Pakistan army's press release in response dismissed the suggestion that India had undertaken any cross-border operations. It downplayed the "alleged" surgical strike as an Indian "illusion to create false effects," although it did acknowledge heavy exchanges of fire along the LoC, which had been ongoing every day for several months during the summer.[27] Throughout the crisis, however, the air forces of both countries were on full alert, indicating that Pakistan was prepared to intercept any further cross-border adventures.[28]

The Joint Military Doctrine and the Land Warfare Doctrine

Although Pakistan may have dismissed India's surgical strikes as an impossibility, India formally adopted the strategy in two publicly released documents: the *Joint Doctrine of Indian Armed Forces 2017* and the *Land Warfare Doctrine 2018*.[29] The *Joint Doctrine* formalized the practice of surgical strikes, which it suggests are undertaken purely in "response to terror provocations."[30] The *Land Warfare* publication emphasizes the role of the Indian army as the "primary instrument of the overall deterrence capability of the nation," and it includes a refinement to the Cold Start strategy by reforming the integrated battle groups and breaking down the strike corps into smaller combat commands for faster mobility.[31]

This document explicitly incorporates *surgical strikes* to pursue military objectives along the LoC in Kashmir and the expansion of "special forces and reliance on Intelligence, Surveillance, and Reconnaissance [ISR] inputs."[32]

What constitutes a "surgical strike" remains a matter for debate in both countries. In theory, surgical strikes keep violence at a relatively low level, somewhere in the gray zone between the sub-conventional and conventional domains. Although the possibility of escalation cannot be ruled out, the assumption is that surgical strikes are not on the same scale as Cold Start or proactive operations, which could provoke an escalation. This compromise between high-intensity operations and spectacular low-intensity ones producing greater political dividends has become established as the innovative South Asian gray-zone strategy.

Surgical Strikes and Quid Pro Quo Plus

In February 2019, in response to a terror attack in the city of Pulwama in the Indian-administered Kashmir, India carried out another surgical strike in Pakistan, this time using the Indian air force to hit Balakot in Khyber Pakhtunkhwa Province in what India's foreign secretary described as a "non-military preemptive action."[33] In a tit-for-tat response, the Pakistani air force retaliated across the LoC, targeting areas around the Indian army bases while declaring that the bases themselves had been intentionally avoided. This was a message of deterrence delivered through an assured response, exemplifying Pakistan's policy of *quid pro quo plus*. During this operation, the Pakistani air force claimed to have shot down two Indian aircraft—with the wreckage from one of them falling on the Pakistani side of the LoC—and captured an Indian pilot. This operation marked a new departure in South Asian relations; it made it clear that the Indian government would not balk at applying a military instrument to bolster their political fortunes, especially with an eye on the approaching elections.[34]

Although the military operation ended in an embarrassing misadventure, there was no negative fallout among Modi's Hindu supporters. On the contrary—the Modi-Doval Doctrine set a new norm in South Asia, whereby victory or defeat in the Pulwama-Balakot crisis was not contingent on the battlefield setbacks of February but on the electoral results announced in May 2019.[35] Modi's security policy is designed mainly to impress in the domestic political arena. It is predicated on seeking political victory with minimal use of military force and little to no casualties, accompanied with loud propaganda and a disinformation campaign to create the dramatic effect of a leader who is tough, especially where Pakistan is concerned. Modi's spectacular victory in 2019 is testimony to his successful political campaign in an era of twenty-first-century strongman politics.

As with previous standoffs, both India and Pakistan drew completely opposite lessons from the crisis, with dangerous implications. Pakistan's retaliation bolstered the Pakistani military's confidence by redeeming itself against conventionally superior India. Likewise, India claimed that it had jettisoned its self-imposed strategic restraint by undertaking operations deep inside Pakistani territory (beyond Kashmir) without evoking any form of international condemnation.[36] India's policymakers concluded that the threat of surgical strikes would persuade Pakistan to rein in the terrorist elements operating within its borders, while their Pakistani counterparts similarly believed that the assurance of a *quid pro quo plus* response would deter India from further military adventures on Pakistani soil.

Modi blamed the poor performance at Balakot in February 2019 on the Indian air force's lack of a modern aircraft such as the French-built Dassault Rafale, which was under negotiation at the time. Speaking at a gathering after the two Indian aircraft had been shot down, he pointedly remarked: "The country is feeling the absence of Rafale. If there was Rafale with us, the result probably would have been different."[37] India has since doubled down on its military purchases, and Pakistan stretches its resources in response; the two archrivals—engaged in a constantly shifting duel between offense and defense—have added another ingredient to the precarious mix of crisis and arms race instability.

PAKISTAN'S NEW SECURITY STRATEGY

S. Paul Kapur surmises that Pakistan's use of militant proxies yielded several strategic benefits—forging domestic political cohesion, compensating for Pakistan's military and material imbalances with India, challenging India's control of Kashmir, and protecting Pakistan's interests in Afghanistan—and that this is why jihad became "a central component of Pakistani grand strategy."[38] In reality, this asymmetric strategy, although successful in the 1980s, has been producing diminishing returns for many years now, especially after September 2001. The jihadi networks that Pakistan was once able to manipulate have metastasized and, as Kapur notes, are not just threatening the entire region, they are "endangering Pakistan as a whole."[39]

Pakistani policymakers have incurred a huge reputational cost for their proxy wars, which directly affects Pakistan's diplomatic and economic standing in the world. For nearly two decades, US forces operated in Afghanistan, but although the "war on terror" crippled the perpetrators of the September 2001 terror attacks, it was unable to resolve the Afghan conflict. For Pakistan, alongside losing thousands of its citizens and soldiers, the war has cost it billions in terms of economic losses and fractured its alliance with the United States. These changed circumstances have forced Pakistan to reevaluate its policies and undertake military operations against those same jihadi forces it once thought to utilize, which have become Pakistan's proverbial hydra.

The Sharif-Aziz Strategic Vision

After winning the Pakistani general elections in 2013, Prime Minister Nawaz Sharif personally retained the portfolio of minister of foreign affairs, and he appointed Sartaj Aziz as his national security advisor.[40] Aziz is a Pakistani economist with experience as a bureaucrat, politician, diplomat, writer, and academic.[41] In a speech to the senate in June 2014 entitled "Strategic Vision of Pakistan's Foreign Policy," Aziz set out Pakistan's national security strategy and the Sharif administration's accomplishments.[42] Aziz's speech represented a rare instance in which a comprehensive political vision of a civilian government was presented. Aziz first identified the threats to Pakistan, then outlined strategies to counter those threats, and finished by providing an assessment of the indicators of success or failure. The opening remarks of the speech expressed the dire situation of this nuclear-armed country:

> Pakistan today is at war within, while isolated abroad. Its independence and sovereignty stand compromised; its economic weaknesses are forcing [Pakistan] to go begging, bowl in hand, while foreign states undertake unilateral strikes on its territory and nonstate actors use it as a sanctuary to pursue their own agendas, oblivious to Pakistan's national interests.[43]

Aziz's reference to "unilateral strikes" pertained to the US drone operations being conducted in the tribal areas on Pakistan's western border, which had been going on for almost a decade. The US raid that killed Osama Bin Laden in May 2011 managed simultaneously to embarrass the Pakistani government and its military, anger the general population, and generate concerns that similar operations could be used to target Pakistani nuclear weapons.[44] Dependent on aid and loans from the international banking system, Pakistan remained a "begging" nation, beholden to external powers, which regularly compromised its "sovereignty," as indicated in Aziz's speech.

Aziz proposed a four-step strategy to combat these threats: (1) defeat militant violence at home and end the militants' ability to project violence abroad, (2) build upon domestic tranquility with economic development, (3) enhance economic growth by achieving stable relations with

Afghanistan and India, and (4) leverage regional peace to attract investment for geo-economic priorities, such as pipelines and trade corridors.[45]

Aziz established these new criteria as the way forward for Pakistan. He
advocated replacing "radicalization" with a "grand national narrative,"
calling for Pakistan to maintain "balanced relationships" with other
nations, particularly the United States as well as India, and to establish
security through "economic cooperation" with regional partners like
India and Afghanistan.[46] Aziz placed Pakistan's security on a par with
fighting the insurgents and above achieving regional peace with Pakistan's
traditional enemies. He reaffirmed the military's leadership not just in
defense but also in "safeguarding national security."[47] Aziz re-emphasized
the role of nuclear weapons in Pakistan's security and directed the
military to take the lead in combating militants. He pledged to "build
a new grand national narrative" that transcended religious extremism,
although "solidarity with the Islamic world" would continue to guide
Pakistan's foreign policy.[48] Nonetheless, modern counterinsurgency
theory suggests that an effective strategy needs to combine military,
political, and economic efforts rather than arrange them sequentially,
and critics have noted the absence of a political direction in Aziz's vision
here.[49]

Long before Aziz set out this agenda, the military had initiated its
operational strategy for combating internal militant threats. Thus, while
the conventional forces were establishing their priorities as directed under
the *Pakistan Army Doctrine 2011* (see chapter 5), the nuclear divisions
were operationalizing their tactical nuclear weapons and developing
nuclear delivery capabilities across all three services. Despite the poor
record of friction between Pakistan's army and its elected government,
each time that Nawaz Sharif became prime minister, the military adapted
its priorities to match the government's strategic policy. Under the
watch of two successive army chiefs, the Pakistan army chalked out
major counterterror and internal security operations while continuing
to counter Modi and Doval's gray-zone strategy against Pakistan.

Operation Zarb-e-Azb

In June 2014, the same month that Aziz set out his "Strategic Vision of Pakistan's Foreign Policy," General Raheel Sharif (army chief since November 2013) launched the Pakistan army's counterinsurgency campaign—Operation Zarb-e-Azb (Sharp and Cutting Strike)—in the tribal areas of North Waziristan. Zarb-e-Azb was a response to the storming of Karachi Airport by Pakistani Taliban terrorists disguised as soldiers,[50] and by September 2014, the army claimed to have eliminated at least 1,000 insurgents. However, the scale of the military operation and its continuation in the tribal areas resulted in one million internally displaced persons whose return to their homes has become a long, slow process; this has brought new disenchantment and suffering to the Pashtun populations and made them susceptible to radicalization by terrorists.[51]

On December 16, 2014, seven heavily armed fighters stormed an army-run primary and secondary school in Peshawar, Pakistan, and killed 150 people, of whom at least 134 were students. In this ghastly attack, the terrorists—wearing suicide jackets—began to shoot indiscriminately, using automatic rifles, hand grenades, and explosives to kill teachers before murdering the children. The fight lasted about eight hours before all the terrorists were killed. The attackers were traced to the TTP in Afghanistan, who claimed that the massacre was in retribution for Operation Zarb-e-Azb, underway in North Waziristan.[52]

Never before in Pakistan had there been such a horrific terrorist attack, and it evoked unprecedented and widespread public anger. Within 10 days of the event, Prime Minister Nawaz Sharif had presented a 20-point national action plan outlining a "comprehensive, consolidated list of steps needed to be taken by the state and law enforcement institutions to curb terrorism and extremism in the country."[53] The National Counter Terrorism Authority was established, tasked with the responsibility for improving the overall security situation by setting specific goals for the counterterrorism force. By 2016, the army had succeeded in eradicating several terrorist enclaves in the tribal areas and had conducted many other internal security operations, significantly reducing the level of internal violence in Pakistan.

Operation Radd-ul-Fasaad

In November 2016, General Qamar Javed Bajwa took over command of the army and ordered a comprehensive review of Pakistan's counterinsurgency strategy, including counter-radicalization. A new policy—Operation Radd-ul-Fasaad (Elimination of Discord)—was announced in February 2017 with the explicit aim of rooting out violent extremist organizations in the borderlands and stabilizing the border with Afghanistan. Bajwa also decided to erect a physical fence along the Afghanistan-Pakistan border and regulate cross-border movement.[54] The tribal areas that straddle the border have been a bane for the security forces for well over a century. The British Indian army constantly struggled to quash rebellions and bring the tribal forces to heel, and this legacy has been passed on to its heir the Pakistan army and its various paramilitary subsidiaries.

Initially, and not unusually, the army's counterinsurgency strategy was "enemy-centric," relying on force to bring the insurgents to the negotiating table without paying much attention to addressing popular grievances. Gradually, however, the Pakistani military learned to calibrate its use of force and balance security exigencies with public sympathy—in full accordance with the *Pakistan Army Doctrine 2011*, which set the goal of "re-establishing the writ of the government" through "rehabilitation" when possible and "defeating militants" when necessary.[55] Announcing the completion of three years of Operation Radd-ul-Fasaad and reflecting on more than a decade of continual military operations against terrorists and extremism, army chief General Bajwa stated that "the operation had consolidated gains of previous operations, indiscriminately eliminating [the] residual and latent threat of terrorism and ensuring security of Pakistan's borders."[56]

An Upsurge in Violence in Kashmir

The western borderlands were not the only area of concern for Bajwa. Immediately on taking command of the army in 2016, he was confronted with an enflamed situation on Pakistan's eastern front along the Line of Control and an upsurge in violence in Kashmir. In a related chain of events, from the Indian forces' killing of Kashmiri rebel leader Burhan Wani in July to the September attack by militants on the Indian army base at Uri and India's response in the form of a surgical strike and continuing cross-border operations, the inevitable outcome was that the Indian and Pakistani militaries would exchange heavy fire.

The gray-zone policy was starting to backfire, and some Indian analysts were concerned that the Kashmiri insurgency was returning to levels not seen since the early 1990s.[57] According to Indian scholar Happymon Jacob, "2017 was the bloodiest year in Kashmir," and by the spring of 2018, India and Pakistan reported an average of 2,500 ceasefire violations across the LOC.[58] Nonetheless, Modi remained defiant. Addressing a political rally in Bhatinda, he said: "Pakistan is not far from here; look at the valor of our army *jawans* [young soldiers] when they conducted the surgical strike, it created havoc across the border."[59] While Prime Minister Modi was eliciting domestic support for India's offense-defense strategy, across the border in Pakistan, Ajit Doval's nuanced military doctrine—built around covert terrorism, support for sub-national insurgencies, and strategy of "surgical strikes" and hot pursuits—was keeping the Pakistani army fully occupied as it searched for a suitable countervailing response.

By the end of 2020, the character of conflict and crisis in the region had changed significantly. India and Pakistan were once again set on divergent paths with no prospect of peace or dialogue in sight. Meanwhile, Hindutva-inspired extremists in India were being unleashed just as New Delhi was pressuring Islamabad to crush the Muslim extremists in Pakistan. In sum, the forces challenging crisis stability are not necessarily proliferating, but they are becoming institutionalized and modernized. At the same time, the second component of strategic stability—arms race stability—is under threat due to the acquisition of modern conventional arms, strategic weapons modernization, and a plethora of new technologies that are blurring the lines around deterrence stability.

MILITARY MODERNIZATION ON THE SUBCONTINENT

In the previous chapter, I analyzed how doctrinal dissonance between the two militaries created the conditions for crisis instability. At the same time, both countries continue to increase their arsenals, as India competes with China and Pakistan aims to restore the offense-defense balance with India. Such arms competition in the mix of regional and global complexities presents significant challenges to overall strategic stability in South Asia

Modi's hyperrealist approach has been applied in all spheres of Indian policymaking at the global, regional, and domestic level. At the global level, for example, his diplomatic offensive has three main objectives: (1) to convince Western powers that India faces a double threat from China and Pakistan, (2) to attract economic investment in India's vast market, and (3) to develop defensive and strategic ties with other major powers so as to mitigate India's military modernization challenges and boost its strategic arsenals.

India has already been successful in persuading the West to transfer its focus in the Asia Pacific theater to the Indo-Pacific.[60] This repositioning places India right in the center of great power competition, making it the quintessential "swing power" that K. Subramanyam had prophesied a decade before. The Indian Ocean Region (IOR) is viewed as the potential arena of a twenty-first-century strategic contest between China and India, and the latter has positioned itself to leverage its military and strategic prowess as a critical variable in the US-led strategic balancing against China. India's strategic modernization and outreach complements Western interests—if they are prepared to overlook India's regional and domestic policies. For these reasons, US Secretary of Defense Leon Panetta identified India as the linchpin to counter China in the Asia Pacific.[61] Yet, as we have seen in previous chapters, India is reluctant to enter into any military alliances and doggedly clings to its strategic autonomy.

From a regional standpoint, India's military buildup evokes a direct response from Pakistan, which seeks to counter India's capabilities by increasing its own nuclear production and delivery mechanisms. Pakistan's balancing strategy is to heighten the potential cost to India of any conflict—especially by maintaining complete ambiguity over its possible use of nuclear weapons—and to avoid becoming entrapped in a debilitating arms race with India, which appears to be the latter's intent. In Pakistan's eyes, India is rationalizing its military buildup based on the China threat, but its military posture is aggressively tilted against Pakistan. In the final analysis, both sides' military forces and nuclear arsenals are growing in terms of number and sophistication, which poses ever greater challenges to crisis stability and arms race stability.

Modernizing India's Conventional Forces

India is increasing the mobility of the mechanized and armored forces that form its RAPID strike corps (see chapter 5) that are ideally suited and organized to fight across the plains and deserts of Pakistan. Similarly, India's pivot corps deployed on the western border against Pakistan are being restructured into integrated battle groups and acquiring limited offensive capacities.[62] With major plans for modernization that include the purchase of aircraft such as the French Dassault Rafale and the F/A Super Hornet, the gap with Pakistan will only increase. In contrast, Pakistan's air force has far more modest plans, with the focus largely on developing a medium-tech fighter base—primarily the Chinese JF-17 (Block III)—complemented by a good ratio of highly technical Western-built fighters.[63]

The Indian navy is operationally divided into the western and eastern fleets. Reports suggest that the western fleet has around the same number of vessels as the eastern fleet, if not more, and that the ratio between the Indian and Pakistani navies is roughly 5:1. The Indian navy has also acquired a P-8I Poseidon maritime patrol aircraft; in combination with its F/A Super Hornet, this gives India two significant assets to help with its air and naval domination over Pakistan.[64]

Modernizing India's Strategic Forces

India's modernization of its strategic forces demonstrates ambitions for power projection capabilities to match the country's strategic goals.[65] Since 2012, India has conducted six flight tests of the Agni-V intercontinental ballistic missile (ICBM). According to the US Center for Strategic and International Studies (CSIS), the "Agni 5 is a three-stage, solid-fueled missile with full operational range as far as 7,500 km."[66] India claims the Agni-V will be equipped with multiple independent re-entry vehicle (MIRV) nuclear warheads, designed to penetrate and defeat enemy missile defenses.[67] To date, India has demonstrated five types of the Agni series of nuclear-capable ballistic missiles. Whereas the Agni-I, Agni-II, and Agni-III have most likely been developed to target Pakistan, the longer-ranged Agni-IV and Agni-V are primarily designed to target China and for other contingencies. India's Defense Research and Development Organization is also reported to be working on the next generation ICBM—the Agni-VI—which is a four-stage ICBM with both MIRV and Maneuverable Re-entry Vehicle (MaRV) capabilities, with an estimated range of over 10,000 km. India claims that both the Agni-V and Agni-VI will feature increased accuracy and a reduced launch time.[68]

Some of India's long-range missile tests involved "a hermetically sealed canister mounted on a mobile transporter erector launcher which is labeled as a 'deliverable configuration.'"[69] This canister-based warhead capability implies that some of India's arsenal is in a ready-to-launch posture, which is a change from the previously known non-mated or recessed arsenals. From the perspective of China and Pakistan—the two adversaries India is targeting—such a deterrence posture renders India's declared no-first-use nuclear doctrine less credible. Indeed, some Western analysts and retired Indian military officials have observed a discernable shift in Indian doctrinal thinking and an inclination toward a first-strike counterforce capability.[70]

Sea-based Strategic Deterrence

In 2013, India carried out the maiden test of its 400-km range, supersonic submarine-launched cruise missile (SLCM), the BrahMos (PJ-10), which it announced was to be "fully ready for fitment in the Project-75 India submarines ... in vertical launch configuration."[71] By 2019, India's arsenal comprised SLCMs, ground-launched cruise missiles, and air-launched cruise missiles. India has also operationalized a submarine-launched ballistic missile (SLBM) with a 700-km range—the K-15 Sagarika—which is designed to be launched from the Arihant-class submersible ballistic, nuclear (SSBN) submarines and carries a 1,000-kg nuclear warhead. Each Arihant-class submarine will be able to carry twelve K-15 missiles, which will later be replaced by the 3,500-km range K-X missiles. Two additional Arihant-class SSBNs are currently under construction (one at Visakhapatnam and two in Vadodara).[72]

Although India announced on several occasions that its nuclear-powered submarine has been on deterrence patrol—including during the Pulwama-Balakot crisis—it is still only in its nascent stages and will take considerable time and experience to qualify as an effective sea-based strategic deterrence (SBSD). In addition, India has yet to develop a viable concept to deploy its SBSD effectively and securely. It might choose to emulate the American continuous-at-sea concept, or it might prefer the bastion strategy of the Soviet era. There are advantages and disadvantages with each—the former is dependent on a huge fleet, whereas the latter presents significant risks in terms of vulnerability and safety. The range of operations is also contingent upon the quality and sustaining power of the reactor core in INS Arihant and its successors. The question of sustainability in an era of rapidly developing anti-submarine warfare (ASW) systems and information technologies is another complication. A final concern relates to the command-and-control protocols on board an SSBN, which are entirely different from conventional naval operations.

India's recent track record in relation to safety and security is not very encouraging in this regard.[73]

India's BMD-MIRV Synergy

In tandem with the above offensive delivery systems, India has also been developing a ballistic missile defense (BMD) program, which it formally announced in January 2020. The intention is for it to be deployed within three to four years to "defend India's National Capital Region."[74] India has also signed a deal with Russia to acquire the S-400 surface-to-air missile system. The S-400 is Russia's most advanced long-range air defense missile system that is designed to destroy aircraft and cruise and ballistic missiles and can engage targets at a distance of 400 km and at an altitude of up to 30 km. At the time of this writing, Russia has not yet commenced delivery of the S-400 system. This deal risks sanctions from the United States, even though India seems confident that it would receive a waiver.[75]

Once deployed, the BMD program could allow India's leaders to believe that the country's vital areas are fully defended and hence they will feel sufficiently confident to launch conventional military strikes against Pakistan and challenge Pakistan's nuclear deterrence. As former Indian strategic forces commander Lieutenant General B. S. Nagal put it: "The [BMD] system will provide security to important command and control centres besides protecting value centres. The BMD increases the credibility of the command and control mechanism by protection as well as denial to the adversary."[76] Adding MIRV missiles into the mix greatly expands India's targeting capabilities and increases its ability to engage Pakistani nuclear hard targets and weaken Pakistan's ability to retaliate. Thanks to these technological advances and the induction of bigger and better missiles with nuclear and/or dual-capability delivery systems into its arsenal, India really does appear to be in the process of reconsidering its declared second-strike doctrine and shifting toward a counterforce targeting strategy instead.[77]

All in all, by developing its MaRV, MIRV, BMD, and SBSD capabilities, India has turned the offense-defense equation in its favor against Pakistan at the upper end of the conflict spectrum. India is already bidding to acquire emerging technologies that include cyber systems, unmanned aerial vehicles, artificial intelligence, autonomous weapons systems, precision-guided munitions, and sophisticated intelligence, surveillance, and reconnaissance (ISR) and information technologies. India is set for a revolution in its military affairs, and China and Pakistan are the two countries most directly affected by India's offensive tilt. It is practically guaranteed that both would engage in countervailing strategies to offset India's strategic rise in the crisis-prone Subcontinent.

Modernizing Pakistan's Strategic Forces
India's technological advances clearly threaten the integrity and effectiveness of Pakistan's strategic deterrence—at least in theory—which compels Pakistan to diversify its delivery methods and develop additional aids to penetration.

Pakistan's Mainstay Missile Delivery Systems
In contrast to India's priority for power projection and strategic reach, Pakistan's nuclear-capable arsenals comprise various types of short-range and medium-range ballistic and cruise missiles that can reach the entire Indian mainland as well as Andaman and Nicobar Islands in the Bay of Bengal. This partly explains the doctrinal difference between Pakistan and India as well as Islamabad's deterrence posture. As already mentioned, Pakistan has integrated its conventional and nuclear deterrence much more professionally under the operational command of the Strategic Plans Division at Joint Services Headquarters. Pakistani strategic forces carry out annual field exercises that invariably end with the flight-test demonstration of a ballistic missile, which serves three important purposes: (1) it helps test and refine the military's integrated operational plans, (2) it validates the technical parameters of the missile, and (3) it sends a strong deterrence signal to India as well as boosting public morale.

Pakistan's strategic enclave has repeatedly insisted that its nuclear arsenal is meant for the purpose of deterrence rather than war-fighting, and it is kept under assertive, centralized control at the tactical, operational, and strategic levels (i.e., full spectrum) across all three services. Within this arsenal, the effectiveness of each nuclear warhead determines the role assigned to it. The shortest-range missile is the Nasr (60-km range), which is a designed for tactical deterrence on the battlefield (TNW). Other short-range missiles such as the Abdali (180–200 km), Ghaznavi (290 km), Babur (land cruise missile; 700 km), Raad (air cruise missile; 350 km), and Shaheen I (750 km) can also be deployed with a tactical or operational reach—from the forward battlefield, by follow-on forces, or against counterforce and counter-control targets. Pakistan's strategic categories include medium- to long-range systems such as the Ghauri (liquid fuel; 1,100–1,500-km range), Ababeel (MIRV-equivalent; 2,200 km), Shaheen II (2,000 km), and Shaheen III (2,750 km), which are designed to target high-value hubs, India's heartland, and distant strategic bases.[78]

From the earlier description, the full-spectrum deterrence appears linear and distinct in tactical, operational, and strategic terms. Many of the tri-service delivery systems under development are now moving into operational status, and once combined with the modernization of conventional forces, this nascent triad will likely create a fully effective deterrence.[79]

A Sea-based Nuclear Response
To match India's SBSD, Pakistan introduced its own sea-based delivery systems and inaugurated the Naval Strategic Forces Command in 2012. The sea-based deterrence will most likely comprise Agosta-class submarines armed with nuclear-tipped cruise missiles.[80] In 2017 and 2018, Pakistan flight-tested the Babur III—which has an estimated range of 450 km—from a submerged barge.[81] Pakistan's response of placing a nuclear weapon on a diesel submarine suggests that this is simply an interim measure until it is able to field a nuclear-powered submarine of

its own. It can take decades to build a nuclear-powered submarine with a sufficiently reliable reactor to sustain naval operations, not to mention the operational and technical challenges already being encountered by India. The biggest concern as regards regional instability is the vulnerability of the diesel submarine operating in a limited patrol area (i.e., the northern Arabian Sea), where it is highly likely to encounter its Indian counterpart in any future crisis.

Pakistan's MIRV-BMD Gambit

Pakistan is always carefully watching India's nuclear and technological advances. The natural impulse of Pakistan's decision-makers would be to match each destabilizing offensive technological advance where possible, using all available means. However, because the cost of missile defense deployment is extremely high, they opt instead for increasing the number of warheads and enhancing the effectiveness of existing missile systems. This is already being demonstrated through flight tests of improved versions of ballistic and cruise missiles.[82]

Theoretically, India's MIRV-BMD synergy swings the offense-defense pendulum in its favor, yet the overall effectiveness of the BMD remains debatable. First, the BMD is at most effective for defending a limited area (i.e., New Delhi, and possibly Mumbai to follow), which leaves a wide range of target-sets in India vulnerable to both countervalue and counterforce attacks from Pakistan. Pakistan has multiple active and passive countervailing strategies for penetrating Indian defenses and deflecting incoming missiles, including (1) retaliation with cruise missiles, (2) launching several ballistic missiles of varying ranges simultaneously, (3) launching several missiles with depressed trajectories, especially for shorter-range targets, (4) deploying multiple decoys, and (5) deploying chaffs and balloons to confuse Indian radar.

It is important to emphasize that whereas conventional forces are regarded as an employable instrument in a war situation (war-fighting role), nuclear forces are only intended to be employed *in extremis* and are by implication non-employable (deterrence role). India is pressing Pakistan to engage in a costly strategic competition, a challenge that Pakistan has often responded to in the past. However, for a developing country facing acute economic problems domestically, it is essential to weigh up the potential tradeoff between conventional and strategic forces modernization. Given the fragility of regional crisis stability, the net assessment of national security requirements will always feature as a major strand of Pakistan's security strategy.

THE MOVE INTO SPACE

India's ambitious strategic program necessitates the acquisition of space capabilities to improve the guidance and accuracy of its MIRV missiles and the BMD and to operationalize its SBSD as well as overall command, control, communications, and intelligence functions. India's space program was initially largely civilian in nature, but it shifted toward military application once India's strategic arsenals began to expand and following China's anti-satellite test in 2007.[83] India's military space assets currently consist of its satellite network, BMD equipment, and nuclear missiles—many of which need to travel through space to reach their intended targets.

In cooperation with Israel, India launched Cartosat 2A and Cartosat 2B in 2008 and 2010, respectively—a pair of optical surveillance satellites which serve both civil and military purposes.[84] In 2013, it then launched geostationary satellite (GSAT) 7—its first satellite solely for military use —which India claimed would allow the Indian navy to achieve "full ISR capability by 2017–2018" and "cover an area spread from [the] Persian Gulf to Malacca Strait ... almost 70% of the IOR [Indian Ocean Region]."[85]

As of 2021, India has two satellites (GSAT 6 and GSAT 7) dedicated for military use, in addition to GSAT 7A to provide communications across the military services' bases and platforms.[86] India also wants to break away from its dependence on the American Global Positioning

System (GPS) and has therefore developed the Indian Regional Navigation Satellite System (IRNSS) to allow the Indian armed forces the independent navigational coverage they require across almost the entire Indian Ocean.[87] Additionally, India's space prowess gives it increased accuracy against Pakistan using short-range ballistic missiles such as the Prithvi-II and Prithvi-III (although to be strictly accurate, the Prithvi-III is technically a space weapon due to its re-entry vehicle). The Agni-I and Agni-II both possess re-entry vehicles and utilize guidance systems that operate on C and S band modes—two of the bands on which the transponders of the GSAT 6 and GSAT 7 operate.[88]

On March 27, 2019, a month after India conducted an air strike in Balakot, India tested an anti-satellite weapon and claimed it had joined the elite club of four nations (the others being the US, Russia, and China) that possess the capability to shoot down satellites in space. India's space drive is mainly intended to send a clear message to China, but it has not gone unnoticed in Pakistan. Afterwards, Modi took the opportunity to claim: "Be it land, sky or space, my government has shown courage to conduct a *surgical strike* in all spheres [emphasis added]."[89]

At present, Pakistan is far behind India regarding both space technology and developing MIRV technology, and it will require substantial assistance from external sources, even though it has indigenous experience of compact design with its Nasr/Hatf-IX short-range ballistic missiles. In Pakistan's inventory of missiles, the most likely candidate with the potential to carry MIRVs is the Ababeel. This is an offshoot from the Shaheen missiles and is believed to be in the same league as India's Agni series, although it is probably smaller, with fewer buses (front ends) for carrying MIRVs.[90]

Investing in space technology is clearly a huge technical, engineering, and economic challenge for Pakistan, which would require external support—most likely coming from China. Likewise, just as India has moved away from America's GPS, so Pakistan appears to have transitioned to China's Beidou II satellite navigation system for operating its strategic missiles.[91] China is believed to have completed building its Beidou II constellation in 2020 with 23 satellites initially,[92] which it has since doubled—improving the system's precision by an estimated two meters.[93]

EMERGING TECHNOLOGIES AND CYBER THREATS

Cyberspace is probably the most critical technological revolution that raises major questions when it comes to strategic stability. The rapid growth of the internet and cyberspace has changed the political and national security calculus in significant ways, and the implications for governance and security continue to evolve. Cyber security has not just become an indispensable part of routine management for all aspects of national security, it is also considered a serious security threat to nuclear stability. This is especially true given that command-and-control systems and satellite communications are so vulnerable to cyber-attacks, which could affect the overall reliability of strategic deterrence systems.[94] With both India and Pakistan expanding their land, air, and sea arsenals, there has been a corresponding increase in reliance on assured communications for safety, security, and positive control, alongside the emergence of significant new risks.

Nor does the cyberspace complication appear in isolation; the synergy of emerging technologies complicates the conditions for stability. Advances in artificial intelligence, additive manufacturing, armed and unarmed unmanned air vehicles, underwater unmanned vehicles, autonomous weapons, and precision-strike weapons all provide greater flexibility to policymakers to "make wars less violent" when applying military tools —and to threaten civilian infrastructure instead, particularly through cyber-attacks. These new technological innovations are not just allowing India and Pakistan to institutionalize the stability-instability paradox, they are also inducing change in the respective military doctrines toward more non-kinetic options.

As India and Pakistan move to modernize their conventional forces alongside the introduction of a strategic triad of land, air, and naval delivery platforms and the emergence of innovative technologies, they ought to be in a constant state of engagement and dialogue to forge appropriate architectures of security and stability in the region as well. Unfortunately, at the time of this writing, there appears to be no progress on any constructive engagement between the two security establishments.

What, then, for the strategic future of the region as a whole?

Notes

1. Attributed to Ajit Kumar Doval, who has been national security advisor to India's Prime Minister Narendra Modi since May 2014. See Bindiya Bhatt, "Who is India's NSA Ajit Doval and What is the 'Doval Doctrine?,'" *News Nation*, September 27, 2016, https://english.newsnationtv.com/india/news/who-is-indias-nsa-ajit-doval-and-what-is-doval-doctrine-1 46274.html.

2. Glenn Snyder, *Deterrence and Defense: Toward a Theory of National Security* (Princeton, NJ: Princeton University Press, 1961), 224; Robert Jervis, *The Illogic of American Nuclear Strategy* (Ithaca, NY: Cornell University Press, 1984), 31.

3. For a comprehensive study of these crises, see Peter Lavoy, ed., *Asymmetric War in South Asia: The Causes and Consequences of the Kargil Conflict* (New York: Cambridge University Press, 2009); Zachary Davis, ed., *The India-Pakistan Military Standoff: Crisis and Escalation* (New York: Palgrave Macmillan, 2011).

4. Jeffrey Knopf, "The Concept of Nuclear Learning," *Nonproliferation Review* 19, no. 1 (March 2012): 79–93; see also Joseph Nye Jr., "Nuclear Learning and US-Soviet Security Regimes," *International Organizations* 41, no. 3 (Summer 1987): 378. For a comprehensive analysis see Feroz Hassan Khan, Ryan Jacobs, and Emily Burke, eds., *Nuclear Learning in South Asia: The Next Decade* (Monterey, CA: Naval Postgraduate School, 2014).

5. Feroz Hassan Khan, "Going Tactical: Pakistan's Nuclear Posture and Implications for Stability," *Proliferation Papers*, no. 53 (Paris: IFRI Security Studies Center, 2015), 31–35. See also David O. Smith, "The US Experience with Tactical Nuclear Weapons: Lessons for South Asia," in Michael Krepon and Julia Thompson, eds., *Deterrence and Escalation Control in South Asia* (Washington, DC: Henry L. Stimson Center, 2013), 65–92.

6. Feroz Hassan Khan, "Disputed Narratives Escalate Tensions in Kashmir," *East Asia Forum*, April 18, 2019, https://www.eastasiaforum.org/2019/04/18/disputed-narratives-escalate-tensions-in-kashmir.

7. Lawrence Rubin and Adam N. Stulberg, eds., *The End of Strategic Stability: Nuclear Weapons and the Challenges of Regional Rivalries* (Washington, DC: Georgetown University Press, 2018).

8. In 1984, the BJP had only two seats in the Indian Parliament's Lok Sabha (lower house), and was able to come to power in 1998. See also Christophe Jaffrelot, "Toward a Hindu State," *Journal of Democracy* 28, no. 3 (July 2017): 52–63.

9. John Ruwitch, "Timeline: The Rise of Chinese Leader Xi Jinping," Reuters, March 16, 2018, https://www.reuters.com/article/us-china-parliament-xi-timeline-idUSKCN1GS0ZA.

10. The two prime ministers met personally several times on the sidelines of international meetings, and Modi even paid an unexpected visit to Lahore on December 25, 2015, but they failed to restart any structural dialogue between the two countries. See "The Five Modi-Sharif Meetings," *Times of India*, December 26, 2015, https://timesofindia.indiatimes.com/india/The-five-Modi-Sharif-meetings/listshow/50330022.cms.

11. C. Raja Mohan, *Modi's World*, 108-112.

12. Karthika Sasikumar, "India's Surgical Strikes: Response to Strategic Imperatives," *Roundtable*, 108(2), 159-174.

13. Nithesh S., "Understanding the Doval Doctrine of Defensive Offense," *Opindia*, October 10, 2016, https://www.opindia.com/2016/10/understanding-the-doval-doctrine-of-defensive-offence; "Understanding Russian 'Hybrid Warfare' and What Can Be Done about It." Testimony of Christopher S. Chivvis, RAND Corporation, before the Committee on Armed Services, United States House of Representatives, 115th Congress (2017), https://www.rand.org/content/dam/rand/pubs/testimonies/CT4 00/CT468/RAND_CT468.pdf.

14. Shailaja Neelakantan, "When NSA Ajit Doval Outlined India's New Pak Strategy—Defense Offense—Perfectly," *Times of India*, October 16, 2016, https://timesofindia.indiatimes.com/india/When-NSA-Ajit-Doval-outlined-Indias-new-Pakistan-strategy-defensive-offense-perfectly/articleshow/54670600.cms.

15. Ryan French, "Deterrence Adrift: Mapping Conflict and Escalation in South Asia," *Strategic Studies Quarterly* 10, no. 1 (Spring 2016): 131, https://www.jstor.org/stable/26271089. See also Nitish S, "Understanding the Doval Doctrine of Defensive Offense."

16. George Perkovich and Toby Dalton, *Not War, Not Peace? Motivating Pakistan to Prevent Cross-Border Terrorism* (New Delhi: Oxford University Press, 2016), 136.

17. Perkovich and Dalton, *Not War, Not Peace?*, 148.

18. Perkovich and Dalton, *Not War, Not Peace?*, 148.

19. Perkovich and Dalton, *Not War, Not Peace?*, 144–145.

20. B. Raman, *The Kaoboys of R&AW: Down Memory Lane* (New Delhi: Lancer, 2013), 268.

21. For a detailed overview of India's covert operations in Pakistan, see Perkovich and Dalton, *Not War, Not Peace?*, 133–179.

22. A transcript of his confession can be found at "Transcript of Kulbhushan Jadhav's 'Confession,'" *Wire*, March 29, 2016, https://thewire.in/diplomacy/a-confession-the-indian-government-says-is-tutored.

23. Kabir Taneja, "India and Pakistan Under Prime Minister Manmohan Singh," *New York Times*, April 28, 2018.

24. See Steven Lee Myers, "China and India Move to Defuse Tensions after Clashes in the Himalayas," *New York Times*, June 7, 2020, https://www.nytimes.com/2020/06/07/world/asia/china-india-border-himalayas.html.

25. Mukhtar Ahmad, Rich Phillips, and Joshua Berlinger, "Soldiers Killed in Army Base Attack in Indian-Administered Kashmir," CNN, September 19, 2016, https://www.cnn.com/2016/09/18/asia/india-kashmir-attack/index.html.

26. "India's Surgical Strikes across LoC: Full Statement by DGMO Lt Gen Ranbir Singh," *Hindustan Times*, September 29, 2016, https://www.hindustantimes.com/india-news/india-s-surgical-strikes-across-loc-full-statement-by-dgmo-lt-gen-ranbir-singh/story-Q5yrp0gjvxKPGazDzAnVsM.html.

27. Inter-Services Public Relations, Press Release no. PR-334/2016-ISPR, September 29, 2016, https://ispr.gov.pk/press-release-detail.php?id=3483. See also Atika Rehman, "Was It Really a Surgical Strike?," *Dawn*, September 30, 2016, https://www.dawn.com/news/1287008.

28. "Surgical Strike Aftermath: Indian Army, IAF, BSF on High Alert in Punjab," *Hindustan Times*, September 30, 2016, https://www.hindustantimes.com/punjab/surgical-strike-aftermath-indian-army-iaf-bsf-on-high-alert-in-punjab/story-OIIQowjWMmGbtIIvfUnJ3O.html.

29. Headquarters Integrated Defense Staff Ministry of Defense, *Joint Doctrine: Indian Armed Forces* (New Delhi: Directorate of Doctrines, Headquarters Integrated Defense Staff Ministry of Defense, 2017); Indian Army, *Land Warfare Doctrine 2018* (New Delhi: Indian Army, 2018). There is a note on the cover of *Land Warfare* that it should be read in conjunction with the 2017 *Joint Doctrine*.

30. Headquarters Integrated Defense Staff Ministry of Defense, *Joint Doctrine*, 13–14.

31. Indian Army, *Land Warfare Doctrine*.

32. Zafar Nawaz Jaspal, *India's "Surgical Strike" Stratagem: Brinkmanship and Response* (Islamabad: Khursheed Printers (Pvt) Ltd, 2019), 61.

33. Ashley J. Tellis, "A Smoldering Volcano: Pakistan and Terrorism after Balakot," Carnegie Endowment for International Peace, March 14, 2019, https://carnegieendowment.org/2019/03/14/smoldering-volcano-pakistan-and-terrorism-after-balakot-pub-78593.

34. Tellis, "A Smoldering Volcano."

35. Feroz Hassan Khan, "Disputed Narratives Escalate Tensions in Kashmir," East Asia Forum, April 18, 2019, https://www.eastasiaforum.org/2019/04/18/disputed-narratives-escalate-tensions-in-kashmir.

36. Rahul Roy-Chaudhury, "India's Modi Government 2.0: Foreign and Security Priorities," IISS, June 19, 2019, https://www.iiss.org/events/2019/06/indian-elections.

37. "Country Felt the Absence of Rafale during Balakot Strikes," *News Scroll*, March 2, 2019, https://www.outlookindia.com/newsscroll/country-felt-absence-of-rafale-during-balakot-strikes-modi/1489019.

38. S. Paul Kapur, *Jihad as Grand Strategy: Islamist Militancy, National Security, and the Pakistani State* (New York: Oxford University Press, 2017), 111.

39. Kapur, *Jihad as Grand Strategy*, 112.

40. I am grateful to Major Andrew Giesey, US Army, for his excellent research under my supervision on Pakistan's security strategy for this section.

41. Sartaj Aziz, *Between Dreams and Realities: Some Milestones in Pakistan's History* (New York: Oxford University Press, 2009).

42. Ministry of Foreign Affairs, Government of Pakistan, "Text of the Statement Delivered by Adviser to the Prime Minister on National Security and Foreign Affairs in the Senate of Pakistan on June 25, 2014, http://mofa.gov.pk/text-of-the-statement-delivered-by-adviser-to-the-prime-minister-on-national-security-and-foreign-affairs-in-the-senate-of-pakistan-on-25-june-2014-on-strategic-vision-of-pakistana%C2%A2a/.

43. Ministry of Foreign Affairs, "Text of the Statement Delivered."

44. Ayaz Gul, "Olson: US-Pakistan Relations Still Challenging, Improving," *Asia News Monitor*, February 6, 2014.

45. Ministry of Foreign Affairs, "Text of the Statement Delivered."

46. Ministry of Foreign Affairs, "Text of the Statement Delivered."

47. Ministry of Foreign Affairs, "Text of the Statement Delivered."

48. Ministry of Foreign Affairs, "Text of the Statement Delivered."

49. Ministry of Foreign Affairs, "Text of the Statement Delivered;" Daniel Marston and Carter Malkasian, eds., *Counterinsurgency in Modern Warfare* (Long Island City, NY: Osprey Publishing, 2008), 16.

50. Declan Walsh, "Assault on Pakistan Airport Signals Taliban's Reach and Resilience," *New York Times*, June 9, 2014, https://www.nytimes.com/20 14/06/10/world/asia/karachi-pakistan-airport-attack-taliban.html.

51. "PM, COAS Discuss Operation Zarb-e-Azb," *Financial Post*, September 23, 2014.

52. Robert Lewis, "Peshawar School Massacre," *Encyclopedia Britannica*, https://www.britannica.com/event/Peshawar-school-massacre. See also various articles at "Peshawar School Massacre," BBC News, https://www.bbc.com/news/world-asia-30505448.

53. Zeeshan Salahuddin, "20 Points to Pakistan?," *Foreign Policy*, June 29, 2015, https://foreignpolicy.com/2015/06/29/20-points-to-pakistan/.

54. "Army Capable of Thwarting All Threats Says Bajwa," *Dawn*, February 23, 2020, https://www.dawn.com/news/1536122/army-capable-of-thwarting-all-threats-says-bajwa.

55. Pakistan Army, *Pakistan Army Doctrine 2011: Comprehensive Response* (Rawalpindi: Pakistan Army, 2011), 85.

56. *Dawn*, "Army Capable of Thwarting All Threats."

57. Happymon Jacob, "The Secessionist Movement in Jammu and Kashmir and India-Pakistan Relations," *International Studies*, 51(1-4), 35-55.

58. Happymon Jacob, *The Line of Control: Travelling with the Indian and Pakistani Armies* (Gurgaon, India: Penguin Random House India, 2018), xi–xii; Abhijnan Rej and Shashank Joshi, "India's Joint Doctrine: A Lost Opportunity," ORF Occasional Paper No. 139 (New Delhi: Observer Research Foundation, January 2018).

59. Jaspal, *India's "Surgical Strike" Stratagem*, 6; Karthika Sasikumar, "India's Surgical Strikes."

60. Felix Heiduk and Gudrun Wacker, "From Asia-Pacific to Indo-Pacific: Significance, Implementation and Challenges" SWP Research Paper no. 9, pp. 23–26 (German Institute for International and Security Affairs, July 2020).

61. Gautam Datt, "US Defence Secretary Leon Panetta Identifies India as 'Linchpin' in US Game Plan to Counter China in Asia-Pacific," *India Today*, June 7, 2012.

62. French, "Deterrence Adrift."

63. IISS, *The Military Balance 2020* (London: International Institute for Strategic Studies, October 2020), 301-303.

64. IISS, *The Military Balance 2021* (London: International Institute of Strategic Studies, February 2021), 261–263; 291.

65. IISS, *The Military Balance 2021*, 291-293.

66. Jenevieve Molenda, "India Test Fires Agni-5 Ballistic Missile," https://missilethreat.csis.org/india-test-fires-agni-5-ballistic-missile/.

67. Raja Pandit, "Agni-V, India's First ICBM Test-Fired Successfully," *Times of India*, April 19, 2012, http://articles.timesofindia.indiatimes.com/2012-04-19/india/31367147_1_agni-v-mirv-payload-targetable-re-entry-vehicles.

68. Franz-Stefan Gady, "India Test Fires Most Advanced Nuclear-Capable ICBM," *The Diplomat*, June 4, 2018, https://thediplomat.com/2018/06/india-test-fires-most-advanced-nuclear-capable-icbm/.

69. Franz-Stefan Gady, "India to Test Fire Nuclear Missile Capable of Hitting China," *The Diplomat*, December 15, 2016, https://thediplomat.com/2016/12/india-to-test-fire-nuclear-missile-capable-of-hitting-china/.

70. Christopher Clary and Vipin Narang, "India's Counterforce Temptations: Strategic Dilemmas, Doctrine, and Capabilities," *International Security* 43, no. 3 (Winter 2018/2019), https://doi.org/10.1162/ISEC_a_00340. See also Toby Dalton and George Perkovich, "India's Nuclear Options and Escalation Dominance," Carnegie Endowment for International Peace Paper, May 19, 2016.

71. "India Tests Underwater BrahMos Missile, but Has No Submarine to Fire It," *Times of India*, March 21, 2013, https://timesofindia.indiatimes.com/india/india-tests-underwater-brahmos-missile-but-has-no-submarine-to-fire-it/articleshow/19100380.cms.

72. "Indian Navy's K-15 SLBM Successfully Completes Development Trials," Naval-Technology, January 29, 2013, http://www.naval-technology.com/news/newsindian-navys-k-15-slbm-successfully-completes-development-trials. For more on India's strategic forces modernization, see Hans M. Kristensen and Robert S. Norris, "Nuclear Notebook: Indian Nuclear Forces, 2012," *Bulletin of Atomic Scientists* 68, no. 4 (July/August 2012), http://bos.sagepub.com/content/68/4/96.full.pdf+html.

73. Robert Farley, "INS Arihant Accident Raises Questions about the Sustainability of India's SSBN Force," *The Diplomat*, January 12, 2018, https://thediplomat.com/2018/01/ins-arihant-accident-raises-questions-about-the-sustainability-of-indias-ssbn-force/.

74. Masao Dahlgren, "Official: India Completes Indigenous Ballistic Missile Defense System," *Missile Threat*, Center for Strategic and

International Studies, https://missilethreat.csis.org/official-india-completes-indigenous-ballistic-missile-defense-system/.

75. Under the US Countering America's Adversaries through Sanctions Act, the purchase of defense equipment from Russia can be subject to sanctions. However, the US president can opt to issue a waiver. See: Bilal Kuchay, "Russia S-400 Missile Delivery to India by End 2021: Official," Al Jazeera, February 5, 2020, https://www.aljazeera.com/news/2020/02 /russian-400-missile-delivery-india-2021-official-200205082528342.html; Sriram Lakshman, "Voices on Capitol Hill back CAATSA sanctions waiver for India, *The Hindu*, November 10, 2021.

76. B. S. Nagal, "Perception and Reality: An In-Depth Analysis of India's Credible Minimum Deterrent Doctrine," *Force India*, October 2014, http:// forceindia.net/guest-column/guest-column-b-s-nagal/perception-and-reality/.

77. Clary and Narang, "India's Counterforce Temptations," 7–52.

78. "Missiles of Pakistan," *Missile Threat*, Center for Strategic and International Studies, June 14, 2018, https://missilethreat.csis.org/country/pakistan/.

79. Feroz Hassan Khan, *Eating Grass: The Making of the Pakistani Bomb* (Palo Alto, CA: Stanford University Press, 2012), 250; IISS, *The Military Balance 2021*, 290.

80. For details of Pakistan's strategic forces, see Hans M. Kristensen and Robert S. Norris, "Pakistan's Nuclear Forces, 2011," *Bulletin of the Atomic Scientists* 67, no. 4 (July–August 2011), http://bos.sagepub.com/content/67/4/91.full.pdf+html.

81. Kelsey Davenport, "India Submarine Completes First Patrol," *Arms Control Today*, December 2018, https://www.armscontrol.org/act/2018-12/news/indian-submarine-completes-first-patrol.

82. Feroz Hassan Khan and Mansoor Ahmed, "Pakistan, MIRVs, and Counterforce Targeting," in *The Lure and Pitfalls of MIRVing: From the First to the Second Nuclear Age*, ed. Michael Krepon, Travis Wheeler, and Shane Mason (Washington, DC: Henry L. Stimson Center, 2016), 149–176.

83. "Frequently Asked Questions on Mission Shakti, India's Anti-Satellite Missile Test Conducted on 27 March, 2019," Ministry of External Affairs, March 27, 2019, https://www.mea.gov.in/press-releases.htm?dtl/31179/ Frequently_Asked_Questions_on_Mission_Shakti_Indias_AntiSatellite_ Missile_test_conducted_on_27_March_2019.

84. James Clay Moltz, *Asia's Space Race: National Motivations, Regional Rivalries, and International Risks* (New York: Columbia University Press, 2012), 28.

85. "Navy Gets a Boost with Launch of First Dedicated Defence Satellite," Indian Navy, https://www.indiannavy.nic.in/content/navy-gets-boost-launch-first-dedicated-defence-satellite.

86. Vanilla Sharma, "From Chandrayaan-2 to GSAT-7A, ISRO Set for a Busy Launch Season," *International Business Times* (India edition), April 23, 2018, https://www.ibtimes.co.in/chandrayaan-2-gsat-7a-isro-set-busy-launch-season-767511; "GSAT-7 and 7A (INSAT-4F/Rukmini)," *Janes*, https://janes.ihs.com/Janes/Display/jsd_a415-jsd.

87. "Strategic Weapon Systems," *Janes*, https://janes.ihs.com/Janes/Display/sasa049-sas.

88. "Weapons: Strategic Agni I," *Janes*, https://janes.ihs.com/Janes/Display/jswsa382-jsws; "Agni II," *Janes*, https://janes.ihs.com/Janes/Display/jswsa383-jsws.

89. "My Government Has Shown Courage for Surgical Strikes in All Spheres," *The Hindu*, March 28, 2019, https://www.thehindu.com/elections/lok-sabha-2019/my-government-has-shown-courage-for-surgical-strike-in-all-spheres-says-pm-modi/article26663483.ece.

90. John Dotson, "The Beidou Satellite Network and the 'Space Silk Road' in Eurasia," *China Brief: A Journal of Analysis and Information* 20, no. 12 (July 15, 2020): 2–7.

91. Khan and Ahmed, "Pakistan, MIRVs, and Counterforce Targeting," 159–160.

92. J. Wesley Hutto, "Space Entanglements: The India-Pakistan Rivalry and a US-China Security Dilemma," *Journal of Indo-Pacific Affairs* 4, no. 1 (Winter 2020).

93. Khan and Ahmed, "Pakistan, MIRVs, and Counterforce Targeting," 160.

94. Lu Chuanying, "Forging Stability in Cyberspace," *Survival* 62, no. 2 (April/May 2020): 128–129.

Chapter 7

Strategic Futures

The Good, the Bad, and the Ugly

> Peace cannot be kept by force; it can only be achieved through understanding... There has been a quantum leap technologically in our age, but unless there is another leap in human relations, unless we learn to live in a new way toward one another, there will be a catastrophe.
>
> –Albert Einstein[1]

As the third decade of the century commences, new geopolitical realignments and strategic balances are reshaping the world order. Western powers—especially the United States—are wooing India to come into their orbit as the linchpin in their rebalancing strategy to contain the rise of China. These tectonic shifts in the international system are a huge fillip for India's ambition of becoming a global power, but while India basks in the glory of this global attention, it remains enmeshed in myriad conflicts, both internally and across the region. It has had to stand by and watch as China has lured India's neighbors into its Belt and Road Initiative (BRI) and the Maritime Silk Roads, making inroads into what India regards as its own backyard. It is only a matter of time before the international community becomes apprehensive about India's ability to meet the geopolitical challenge thrown down by China on its own, much less to become an effective global player in the burgeoning great power competition.[2]

Pakistan, for its part, has exhausted itself both economically and strategically in its bid to balance against India. It faces economic difficulties and severe ethno-religious challenges in forging national unity. Much like India, Pakistan also relies on external partners for conventional military and nuclear balance and the acquisition of emerging technologies. However, as America's partnership with India strengthens, it is weakening with Pakistan—not least because of the Taliban's takeover of Afghanistan in August 2021 and the subsequent uncertainty that now prevails. At the same time, China's hand is increasingly discernable in the region— with the expansion of the BRI and development of the China-Pakistan Economic Corridor (CPEC), offering a vital link between landlocked Central Asia and the Arabian Sea. The CPEC is the geopolitical linchpin that enables Islamabad and Beijing to deepen their strategic relationship as China widens its "sphere of influence."[3]

This final chapter aims to assess the possible strategic futures for South Asia, considering the region's complex history and recent past alongside current trajectories. It begins with an appraisal of the repeatedly unsuccessful attempts at peace, highlighting how this cyclical pattern of failed peace initiatives and military crises has contributed to the drift between the two key protagonists. It then evaluates the prospects for a good (better) future, which will only be possible if India and Pakistan's leaders display sufficient sagacity and determination to steer the Subcontinent out of its current gridlock. Failure to take this path would likely perpetuate the ongoing impasse, meaning that India and Pakistan would continue to muddle through intermittent crises in a cycle of hope and despair. The worst scenario would be if the Subcontinent failed to halt its downward trajectory, bringing it to the edge of the nuclear abyss.

One of the profound tragedies of the rivalry between India and Pakistan, as detailed in previous chapters, is that each time one of these two nations sought some form of rapprochement, hawks within the other's conservative strategic enclave effectively derailed any progress toward peace and détente. Each initiative almost always made a promising start, raising peoples' hopes, but then quickly vanished, reverting to the familiar blame-game, threats, and invariably a new military crisis.

PEACE AGREEMENTS AND MILITARY CBMs

The 1949 Karachi Agreement was the first peace agreement between India and Pakistan at the end of the first Kashmir War in 1948, when the United Nations intervened and several resolutions on Kashmir were passed. The Karachi Agreement established the code of conduct for the ceasefire line (CFL) pending full conflict resolution. Several attempts to resolve the Kashmir dispute throughout the 1950s and 1960s went nowhere, except for one major success when the World Bank brokered the Indus Waters Treaty in 1960. This treaty regulates the water distribution between India and Pakistan of the five major rivers emanating from Kashmir and originating in the great mountains in the north.[4]

A second major peace agreement was brokered by the Soviet Union following the second Kashmir War in 1965 and was signed by Pakistani president Ayub Khan and Indian prime minister Lal Bahadur Shastri in Tashkent in January 1966. However, Shastri's sudden death immediately afterwards brought Indira Gandhi to power, and as we have seen, she adopted a hardline policy on regional relations, leading to the 1971 East Pakistan crisis and war with Pakistan that resulted in the creation of Bangladesh. The third major agreement was signed after the Bangladesh War at Simla in 1972 between Zulfiqar Ali Bhutto and Indira Gandhi. This accord changed the CFL in Kashmir into the Line of Control (LoC) and gave the region a decade of peace. The 1980s saw the start of a new series of military crises, leading from one to another in a succession that has continued over the last four decades.

After the tense year of 1984, which saw the Golden Temple (Sikh) crisis and the Siachen Glacier crisis, Pakistan's president General Zia-ul Haq visited New Delhi in December 1985, where he concluded an agreement in principle with Prime Minister Rajiv Gandhi not to attack nuclear installations. The two leaders failed to start a structured process of dialogue, however, and a year later, the Brass Tacks crisis of 1986–1987 once again brought the two countries to the brink of war, which was diffused on the sidelines of the South Asian Association for Regional Cooperation (SAARC) summit in spring 1987. Despite successfully defusing the crisis, both countries still shied away from starting a comprehensive peace process. After Zia's death in 1988, prime ministers Benazir Bhutto and Rajiv Gandhi held summit meetings in December that year which formalized the India-Pakistan Non-attack Agreement and established a hotline between Islamabad and New Delhi to enable the leaders to communicate directly and immediately, particularly in the event of an emergency.[5] Yet, once again, the bonhomie was short-lived, and when the simmering unrest in Kashmir erupted the following year, it created a crisis that came close to full-scale war in 1990.

Although the Kashmiri insurgency has never dissipated, since 1991 India and Pakistan have concluded a series of agreements known as military confidence-building measures (CBMs)[6] and established hotlines between the two militaries called the Director General Military Operations (DGMO) hotlines.[7] Two major military CBMs signed in New Delhi in April 1991 are the Agreement on Advance Notification on Military Exercises, Maneuvers, and Troop Movements and the Agreement on Prevention of Air Space Violation and for Permitting Overflights and Landings by Military Aircraft. Taken together, the 1991 military CBMs, the DGMO hotlines, and the 1949 Karachi Agreement regarding the CFL/ LoC in Kashmir provide both countries with a robust code of conduct for regulating the two militaries.

The India-Pakistan military CBMs were followed by border agreements between India and China in 1993 and 1996. As part of these agreements, both nations agreed to keep their border military presence "to a minimum level compatible with the friendly and good neighbourly relations," not to "undertake military exercises in mutually identified zones beyond agreed levels," and to "give the other notification of military exercises" along the border.[8] At the time, these agreements were hailed as a veritable no-war pact and an example of conventional force restraint between the two largest militaries in the world.[9]

A series of meetings between India and Pakistan took place in the late 1990s as envisaged in the Gujral Doctrine, although no substantive conclusions were reached. Even after the nuclear tests in 1998, Prime Minister Atal Bihari Vajpayee extended the spirit of the Gujral Doctrine by taking the peace initiative by bus to Lahore, where India and Pakistan signed the historic Lahore Agreement in February 1999—only for it to be derailed by the Kargil conflict within a matter of months.[10] In December that year, an Indian Airlines plane was hijacked and flown to Kandahar in Afghanistan. The hijackers demanded the release of Kashmiri militants from Indian custody, and the crisis was only resolved when India acceded to their demands.[11]

To Vajpayee's credit, and despite numerous crises with Pakistan, throughout his tenure from 1998 to 2004 he never gave up hope of rapprochement and achieving a lasting peace. He invited President Musharraf, the architect of the Kargil crisis, to a summit meeting at Agra in 2001 which very nearly succeeded—a joint statement and final agreement had already been prepared for signing when dissension within Vajpayee's BJP government forced the prime minister to back out.[12] Musharraf faced skeptics and detractors within his own administration as well. Hence, even though the Agra summit represented a significant next step after the Lahore Agreement, strategic enclaves on both sides once again frustrated this peace initiative, and the opportunity to achieve a stable future on the Subcontinent was lost.

Despite the failure in Agra and the 10-month military standoff in 2001–2002, Vajpayee stands out in Indian history as a leader who genuinely desired peace. He agreed to a LoC ceasefire in 2003 and met with his Pakistani counterpart Musharraf on the sidelines of a SAARC summit just before he left office. As a result of their meeting, India and Pakistan issued a joint statement about plans to start a composite dialogue alongside SAARC's Islamabad Declaration on January 6, 2004. Later that month the BJP lost the elections in India, which brought the Congress Party to power under Prime Minister Manmohan Singh. Musharraf and Singh continued working to carry the momentum forward.

The period between 2003 and 2008 (the era of Musharraf, Vajpayee, and Singh) was probably the time when the region came closest to peace, stability, and détente. Using back-door channels, Musharraf and Singh established a roadmap for conflict resolution on Kashmir. However, this would turn out to be the last time there was a sustained attempt at peace in the region. New Delhi procrastinated too long to seize the initiative, and the terror attacks in downtown Mumbai on November 26, 2008, effectively derailed the whole process.

The Demise of Attempts at Peace

Shortly before the Modi regime came to power in 2014, Pakistan's prime minister Nawaz Sharif took the initiative to begin discussions on a longstanding Indian demand for "most-favored nation" (MFN) status, which would have opened up trade and generated economic activity between the two countries—something Prime Minister Singh had always desired to accomplish before leaving public office. However, amidst growing predictions that the BJP would win the 2014 elections, Modi's campaign managers privately approached Pakistan's leaders and suggested holding off trade talks with the incumbent Indian National Congress (INC) government and even hinted that in the event of coming to power, the BJP would revoke any agreements made.[13]

Islamabad was caught in a quandary. Should it speed up reaching an agreement with the INC-led government or wait until after the elections?

Many in Pakistan argued it was unwise to trust the Modi government and suggested that a trade deal agreed under the watch of Prime Minister Singh had better chances of success, given his economic credentials and desire to leave behind a legacy of peace. Trade normalization with India would have buried the bitterness of the 2008 tragedy in Mumbai, restored Pakistan's international image after decades of terrorism and internal crises, and given the Sharif government a positive start to its third term in power. Prime Minister Sharif procrastinated, deciding to take a chance and wait until after the elections were over, whereby he missed the boat and with it the chance for peace—just as Manmohan Singh had lost the chance when Musharraf was promoting peace efforts via the back door in 2007–2008, shortly before losing power himself.

In December 2015, in yet another dramatic twist, Narendra Modi made a surprise visit at a private wedding of Nawaz Sharif's family in Lahore. The sudden euphoria of peace lasted barely a week, however, and was promptly stifled by a terror attack on an Indian air force station in Pathankot on January 2, 2016, in Indian-administered Kashmir. The Indian security forces commenced a series of suppressive military operations, including the assassination of the popular Kashmiri militant leader Burhan Wani in July, resulting in a new wave of uprisings in the region —typified by the attack on the Indian police station at Uri and India's surgical strike in response.

Since then, India and Pakistan have drifted so far apart that bringing them back onto a peaceful track would now be a colossal undertaking. Indeed, even as Islamabad was trying to put the jihadi genie back in the bottle and seeking rapprochement with India (as outlined in chapter 6), India was encouraging its own proxies to act against Pakistan and teach it a lesson. In the meantime, Pakistan's attention remains focused on its western borders as its military braces against the instability in Afghanistan following the US withdrawal. A ray of hope emerged out of the gathering storm clouds in the spring of 2021, when India and Pakistan reinstated the ceasefire along the LoC in Kashmir.[14] Nonetheless, given the rollercoaster history of crisis and false starts for peace on the Subcontinent, people in both nations (and across the world) remain skeptical of a lasting peace agreement between these two nuclear-armed rivals.

India and Pakistan at the Crossroads

Stephen Cohen doubted whether efforts to induce normalcy between India and Pakistan could succeed, and in frustration he declared that "nothing can be done."[15] Yet, both Cohen and many other experts on South Asia surmise that the international community has a significant role to play in preventing the worst outcomes in a nuclear-armed region; in the face of sufficient global pressures, India and Pakistan will eventually be forced to reach a *modus vivendi* for coexistence. Such a future is suggested with cautious optimism, in the hope that a sustained peace process would bring better times—after all, there is a history of initiatives attempting peace and there are myriad confidence-building measures already in place.[16] In Cohen's final assessment, conflict between the two nations is likely to drag on in a "regional cold war" with sporadic military crises involving hot skirmishes and "hurting stalemates."[17] He notes many Indians (and some Americans) believe that Pakistan has been "fatally wounded" in trying to meet the "challenges of the modern era" and India should just "wait it out" until "Pakistan collapse[s]" and India becomes the "dominant power in Southern Asia."[18]

For three quarters of a century, such premonitions have allowed South Asia to drift away from its "tryst with destiny," and nobody can be sure at present which direction India and Pakistan will finally take. I derive three potential strategic futures for the region which I call "the Good, the Bad, and the Ugly," and I analyze each one in turn to determine the possible trajectories and likely wild cards that could impact the future of the Subcontinent—and with it the fate of nearly a quarter of all humanity.

THE "GOOD" PATH: ACHIEVING A MODUS VIVENDI

Seeking accommodation with each other and reaching some form of *modus vivendi* is the only feasible pathway for ending this enduring regional cold war. Any other course is fraught with risks and unacceptable consequences for the whole world, and the absence of any new strategic dialogue between India and Pakistan is perpetuating these conditions of instability. Non-state actors operate freely in the region, while both countries make dubious claims about their connections with the rival state's security organs. Growing asymmetries in conventional and strategic forces are leading to a regional arms race, constantly evolving military doctrines, the acquisition of diverse dual-use delivery systems in the arsenals of both countries, and a lowering of nuclear-use thresholds. The existing CBMs, nuclear risk reduction measures (NRRMs), information-exchange mechanisms, and various other "tools of maintaining direct communications" are inadequate for sustaining peaceful relations between India and Pakistan over the long term.[19] In addition, transformations at the geopolitical level alongside rapid technological maturations mean these nuclear-armed neighbors need to introduce major reforms domestically if they truly desire to live together in peace.

In September 2013, speaking at the United Nations General Assembly, Prime Minister Nawaz Sharif reaffirmed Pakistan's commitment to a sustained dialogue with India and to "build[ing] on the Lahore Accord signed in 1999, which contained a road map for the resolution of our differences through peaceful negotiations."[20] He added: "Our countries have wasted massive resources in an arms race. We could have used these resources for the economic wellbeing of our people. We still have that opportunity."[21] Five years later, his successor Imran Khan made a similar offer to India, stating: "if India takes one step forward, we will take two."[22] On both occasions, India responded negatively.[23]

Under Modi, New Delhi's approach toward Islamabad presents a significant departure from the 1990s, when India was willing to engage with both China and Pakistan and there existed a strong desire for peace and security between all three countries. Should the BJP government now consider responding positively to the renewed offers for a peace and security deal to break this logjam, India and Pakistan will have to pick up the threads from where Prime Ministers Vajpayee and Manmohan Singh and President Musharraf left them before the Mumbai terror attacks in 2008. One possibility would be to revisit the proposals and process that led to the original Lahore Agreement in February 1999 and return the region in both letter and spirit to the situation that prevailed at the turn of the millennium.

Strategic Restraint Redux: Previous Proposals

In October 1998, Pakistan made a formal proposal titled "Strategic Restraint Regime" (SRR) to India during a bilateral dialogue that was a continuation of the "Composite Dialogue" that Prime Minister Gujral had initiated in 1997. The SRR concept offered both countries a pathway for conflict resolution and a voluntary regime of restraint that included several CBMs and NRRMs and comprised three intertwined sets of proposals covering conflict resolution, conventional force restraint, and nuclear restraint.

Conflict resolution requires that both countries agree to an overarching political framework for resolving conflicts and promoting peace and stability. Restraints on conventional forces and nuclear weapons are interdependent variables that would prevent the eruption of a sudden military crisis or war and keep nuclear weapons in recessed mode, allowing both countries to maintain a minimum credible deterrence posture and eschew an arms race. The SRR suggested five principles to proceed: (1) the creation of a political climate and culture of conflict resolution conducive to reducing tensions; (2) proportionate and balanced obligations on all sides; (3) recognition of conventional force imbalances and structural asymmetries; (4) creation of institutionalized mechanisms to prevent escalation during crises; and (5) recognition that either state could withdraw from the SRR arrangements if supreme national security interests so demanded.[24] New Delhi was not amenable; Indian negotiators began by arguing that the proposals were typical Western concepts that were not applicable to the realities of the Subcontinent.

Nevertheless, both countries negotiated a memorandum of understanding (MOU) that adopted substantive principles from the SRR concept paper that formed part of the historic Lahore Agreement signed by Prime Ministers Vajpayee and Sharif. However, the subsequent military standoff in 2001–2002 made it impossible for the peace process to commence, and it was not until the back-door negotiations between President Musharraf and Prime Minister Manmohan Singh (2004–2008) that any substantive moves were made. Nonetheless, these partial agreements left a framework and a promise for future leaders to begin a process toward conflict resolution and turn these principles into a formal mechanism for peace.

A New Peace and Security Architecture
Although prior failures have frequently dampened hopes for a *good* future between India and Pakistan, new opportunities continue to arise, and all they need are enlightened national leaders who are prepared to adapt to the new environment and willing to take bold steps for peace. The 1999 Lahore Agreement, although modest in scope, anticipated the difficult road ahead and suggested bilateral consultations on security and disarmament, a review of existing communication channels, and periodic assessments of the existing CBMs.

Hence, to move the peace process forward, intractable issues between India and Pakistan need to be put on hold or on a slow track while the two countries seek to reduce tensions and create a positive environment. This will enable their respective militaries to redirect their efforts toward the many security contingencies they currently face. The Pakistani military needs to deal with neutralizing the existing terror infrastructure within its territory and in the borderlands with Afghanistan, while the Indian military focuses on its border issue with China and multiple internal contingencies. If New Delhi fails to disassociate itself from its historic rivalry with Pakistan it will struggle to establish regional leadership, and this will damage its global standing.

In recent years, Pakistan's strategic thinking concerning the promotion of low-intensity conflict has seemingly shifted. The loss of some 75,000 lives in Pakistan due to acts of terror over the past two decades is evidence of the counterproductive returns from feeding and harboring extremist forces for security objectives. At the same time, it is not possible to cordon Pakistan off completely to prevent cross-border attacks, and nor can it be assumed that all terrorist acts in India necessarily originate from Pakistan. In addition, Pakistan is aware that any use of its conventional forces is fraught with escalatory potential. For decades now, there has been a dangerous nexus between low-intensity conflicts leading to a conventional armed forces response, or the use of conventional forces escalating toward the deployment of nuclear weapons, to no end but increased violence and a dangerous situation for all. The only logical approach to deterrence stability is mutual strategic restraint accompanied by sustained dialogue. It is time for fresh thinking.

A new framework for peace and security in the region is needed—one that recognizes the significant shifts in the global and regional strategic landscape. Failure to reach a deal on Kashmir in the Musharraf-Manmohan Singh era resulted in strengthening the hardliners in both countries, derailing prospects for a bilateral settlement, and perpetuating further tensions. The imperative now must be to create a constructive political climate of reduced tensions, which could be achieved in several stages, as follows:

- new normalization mechanisms are needed to enable greater people-to-people contact, religious tourism, direct trade, and other forms of economic and cultural investment;
- India and Pakistan must reverse their policies of sub-conventional violence and the use of force as a security policy tool.

- existing CBMs and NRRMs still have value, but new thinking around CBMs is required to limit the use of conventional forces and guarantee nuclear stabilization;
- both countries need to develop institutional mechanisms to prevent crisis-triggering events;
- India and Pakistan should create a bilateral framework that insulates bilateral stabilization measures against other regional concerns, particularly those relating to China and Afghanistan;
- both countries might consider engaging in a trialogue with China to build trilateral strategic CBMs in the future.[25]

It is time for India and Pakistan to couple economic progress with restraints on nuclear weapons and conventional forces. Direct economic trade and investment removes many obstacles and could transform South Asia from a hotbed of warring tribes, secessionism, terrorism, and boundary disputes into a hub of trading states wherein economic connectivity replaces the security-intensive geopolitical space. The broad contours of a revised regional strategic restraint arrangement might be drawn by mixing some old thoughts together with some new ones.[26]

Conventional Force Restraint

The Indian and Pakistani armies face threats from several directions, not just from each other. They have been engaged in high-altitude mountain warfare, deployed against each other along the LoC, for over 70 years. At the same time, they are involved in counterterror and counterinsurgency operations, and they have a multitude of other security contingencies as well.[27] This history of wars on the Subcontinent and the nature of the military crises between India and Pakistan warrant the crafting of an effective agreement on conventional force restraint.

With little understanding of the other's military doctrine, India and Pakistan have entangled themselves in a cycle of sub-conventional war resulting in conventional responses, which in turn runs the risk of escalation leading to a nuclear response. Finding an exit strategy out of the impasse is a huge challenge; it is therefore time to consider new strategic confidence-building measures for the region that will encompass technological developments as well. Strategic CBMs are overlapping nuclear and conventional measures that formalize the non-deployed status of nuclear weapons.[28] For these to be introduced, India and Pakistan must first create favorable conditions. One approach would be for New Delhi and Islamabad to consider reversing India's "proactive strategy" or Cold Start doctrine, and in return Pakistan would reverse its stance on tactical nuclear weapons (TNW) (which arguably was developed as an answer to Cold Start).[29] Both Cold Start and TNWs provide diminishing returns and come with significant shortcoming and risks, as identified in previous chapters.

Another initiative India and Pakistan could take is to revisit the 1949 Karachi Agreement on the LoC and other border agreements and consider replicating some portions of the 1996 border agreement between China and India. The 1996 agreement is by far the most elaborate conventional force agreement in the region that enshrines principles of "mutual and equal security" and mutual understanding on military force deployment, and which specifically pledges that "neither side shall use its military capability against the other side." Another important element within this agreement pertains to categorizing offensive weapons, as part of which both sides agreed to prioritize withdrawal and to "exchange data on military forces" to reduce overall deployments.[30]

Pakistan's 1998 proposal for a Strategic Restraint Regime included several suggestions for conventional force restraint that were identical to those India agreed with China in 1993 and 1996. Specifically, the proposition that India and Pakistan identify their respective offensive conventional strike forces and demarcate mutually agreed low-force zones along the border areas. Should there be a requirement to move additional forces into these low-force zones, mutually agreed mechanisms could be devised to notify each other and then revert to the agreed force level once the need had passed. India and Pakistan already have agreements on the prior notification of military exercises and non-intrusion of air space that were reached in 1991 to prevent a repeat of the 1986–1987 Brass-tacks Crisis.[31] These conventional force restraint measures are intended to create appropriate conditions to formalize the non-readiness and non-deployment of nuclear weapons, reduce nuclear competition, and prepare the ground for robust deterrence stability.

While India remains reluctant to conclude a bilateral conventional force restraint agreement with Pakistan[32]—for reasons of internal politics and domestic security—there are five common themes that China, India, and Pakistan have previously agreed on in separate bilateral agreements. These are: (1) to resolve all disputes through peaceful and friendly consultations; (2) to reduce the military presence at the border to an agreed minimum level compatible with the terrain, road communications, and infrastructure; (3) to categorize offensive/strike forces and offensive weapons, identify low-force zones, and limit military exercises and notify their timings to all parties; (4) to exchange military force data and establish leadership and military hotlines; and (5) to formulate joint working groups to review, clarify, and resolve all issues covered by the agreements under the guidance of the civil and military leaderships.[33] Should India agree to introduce strategic CBMs with Pakistan as well, these bilateral conventional force CBMs could be turned into mutually negotiated trilateral conventional force CBMs by bringing China into their ambit.

As New Delhi's concerns with Beijing increase following the 2020 border skirmishes, it would make good sense to soften relations with Pakistan and encourage normalization. Conventional force restraint would be a good place to start in the short- to medium-term. In the long term, asymmetrical proportional force reductions—along the lines of the 1990 Treaty on Conventional Armed Forces in Europe (CFE; concluded during the last years of the Cold War)—could be feasible and would bring real prospects for stability and peace on the Subcontinent.

Air Force Restraint

Political scientist Christopher Clary notes that there is a widening imbalance in air force capabilities between India and Pakistan which is affecting qualitative and quantitative disparities.[34] This aspect has become more pertinent since the 2019 Pulwama-Balakot crisis, with both air forces now on increased alert, prepared for any new aerial adventure. Irrespective of the crisis itself, most of the Indian air force infrastructure has been located at its western border with Pakistan, which increases the probability of air-space violations and a rapid escalation in response.

Again, India's proactive defense doctrine is based on joint land and air operations, which might include targeting alleged terrorist camps over the LoC/international border and could end with mass casualties in Pakistan. As witnessed in February 2019, the Pakistani air force will strike back if India attacks, and an escalatory spiral may result. Despite the protocols agreed in 1991 on the notification and limitation of flights along the border, they have not prevented violations of air space. The existing CBMs pertaining to air operations could be reinforced by the creation of no-fly zones and a direct communication channel between air force officers.

Maritime Restraint

Prior to the Pulwama-Balakot crisis, maritime issues, while important, were not as contentious as the Siachen Glacier and Kashmir disputes on the ground. However, now that India has deployed its nuclear submarine INS Arihant in the Arabian Sea alongside conventional naval assets (including an aircraft carrier and a conventional submarine), maritime CBMs have become far more critical. In a seminal joint study carried out by two retired Indian and Pakistani admirals some pragmatic steps were proposed; these include resolving maritime disagreements such as the Sir Creek dispute and the repeated capture and release of fishermen, and other similar incidents at sea.[35] The Sir Creek issue can be resolved on the basis of the thalweg principle, which demarcates river boundaries along the most navigable channel for large ships traveling downstream.[36]

Solving the Sir Creek dispute would enable delineation of the extension of maritime boundaries extending from Sir Creek into the sea, which would simultaneously resolve the issue of fishermen's livelihoods and facilitate collaborative efforts for dealing with piracy.

Furthermore, the current absence of bilateral maritime communications increases the probability of serious incidents at sea. To avoid this, Pakistan and India might draw from the 1972 Incidents at Sea Agreement (INCSEA) between the Soviet Union and the United States.[37] An INCSEA-type agreement becomes even more important as India and Pakistan introduce sea-based nuclear capabilities. Continued air space violations and the prospect of more incidents at sea indicate the need for properly implementing existing CBMs as well as negotiating new ones.[38]

Nuclear Restraint

If India and Pakistan were to agree some of the restraints on conventional capabilities suggested here, then a nuclear arms race could be eschewed, which would limit and regulate the development of weapons that are deemed to be strategically destabilizing. Once there is greater trust, strategic CBMs could also include sharing information on the peacetime garrisons where strategic missile units are stationed, avoiding flight-testing during tense or hostile periods, and extending the existing flight-testing notification agreements to include cruise missiles. In addition, as leading nations on the Subcontinent, India and Pakistan might consider giving a negative security assurance to all SAARC nations.

Another confidence-building measure for SAARC countries would be if India and Pakistan were to consider mutual commitments not to mate warheads with their delivery vehicles during peacetime. Almost a decade ago, the late Indian scholar Brigadier Gurmeet Kanwal and I proposed advancing transparency through the voluntary mutual elimination of redundant and obsolete short-range ballistic missiles (Hatf-I and Prthvi-I) from their deterrence posture. We surmised that missile components age silently and become obsolete much faster than one might realize and concluded that missile systems stored for long durations erode and could be dangerous if put to operational use. We recommended that future eliminations might therefore include Pakistan's Hatf-II and India's Prithvi-II.[39]

Risk-Reduction Centers and Cooperative Monitoring

For the effective notification and implementation of conventional and nuclear restraint measures, institutional channels of communication are extremely important. India and Pakistan do not have established protocols, and rarely does either country use the existing hotlines properly during periods of increased tension or military confrontations. So far, only the armies have dedicated hotlines (e.g., between the directors general of military operations), but these do not encompass air and naval operations. As the number of hotlines grows, and as technological innovations increase in cyberspace and elsewhere, new CBMs and cooperative-monitoring arrangements are becoming increasingly necessary. It would therefore make sense to establish centralized risk-reduction centers in Islamabad and New Delhi.

Unfortunately, history reveals many missed opportunities that could have changed the future of the region, and the present situation is no different. At the time of writing, stubborn resistance from the strategic enclaves and political dithering on both sides is once again allowing the window of opportunity to close. As has been seen time and again, these missed opportunities for peace invariably become harbingers of the next crisis, leading to a continuum of painful stalemate in bilateral relations.

THE "BAD" PATH: TOWARD A REGIONAL COLD WAR

In the three decades since the end of the Cold War, India has demonstrated two opposite potentials. On the one hand, it has displayed cumulative national power and strong credentials as a secular plural nation and the largest democratic state in the world; on the other, it has failed to settle problems with its neighbors and consequently has been unable to establish regional leadership. The recent decline of democratic values in India in tandem with the rise of Hindu nationalism is eroding India's reputation as a leading nation in Asia.[40]

Faced with a volatile domestic situation and increasingly frequent military crises with Pakistan and China, the worry for India is that the region could revert to the instability of the 1980s and early 1990s. Thus far, India and Pakistan (and China) have exercised strategic restraint by containing these crises between them; however, if these trends continue, South Asia will become a tinderbox on the brink of a military crisis that could escalate into a major war.

Although shifts in the international system favor India, its internal security problems have increased manifold. Having won a huge majority in the 2019 parliamentary elections, the BJP government began its second consecutive term making sweeping constitutional changes that have had a dramatic impact on Indian state and society. The Modi 2.0 regime is pressing Hindu majoritarianism in domestic reforms and openly challenging India's democratic, pluralistic, and secular characteristics.[41] Under Prime Minister Modi, India seems to be on a similar trajectory to that of Pakistan under Muhammad Zia-ul-Haq in the 1980s. Pakistan knows only too well, however, how radically Zia-ul-Haq's dictatorship changed the fabric of Pakistani society, the consequences of which are still being felt today.

India's Bleeding Wound at the Core and the Periphery

India's internal problems, overlaid by cross-border crises, are not just a major concern for it domestically but also leading increasingly to regional conflicts in India's neighborhood. Of particular concern is the continued challenge of finding a viable solution to India's "Pakistan problem," which is now compounded by border crises with China and Nepal. These multiple crises, some of which are of India's own making, will likely distract India from becoming a "net security provider" in the Indo-Pacific region or taking its desired place in the global order.[42]

The Naxalite movement in the eastern Indian states (also referred to as the Red Corridor) continues to pose intermittent security challenges that periodically spill over into neighboring Myanmar (Burma) and Bangladesh. Additionally, in December 2019, the BJP government announced a new Citizenship Amendment Act (CAA), which is perceived as targeting minorities—particularly Muslims—and prompted mass nationwide protests before the COVID-19 pandemic forced the country to shut down. In India's volatile northeast, in the areas of Assam and Arunachal Pradesh, the CAA affects thousands of Bangladeshi Muslim workers, who have been declared non-citizens or illegals; this is creating a new basis for crisis with Bangladesh.[43] Meanwhile, China claims the Indian state of Arunachal Pradesh for itself as part of South Tibet.

India's biggest challenge remains in the disputed territory of Kashmir. In its first term, the Modi government brought a fragile coalition to power in Srinagar, and then used excessive force to suppress the continuing insurgency. This escalated further in 2016, and the situation has deteriorated continuously ever since. [44] According to the London-based International Institute for Strategic Studies, approximately 490 people died in Kashmir in 2018 alone, "making it the deadliest year for Kashmir in a decade," and "more than 1,400 ceasefire violations were recorded along the Line of Control between India and Pakistan, displacing tens of thousands of civilians."[45] In February 2019, as India's national elections neared, the situation in Kashmir was boiling up when the Pulwama suicide attack on an Indian military convoy occurred; this then triggered India's aerial strike on Balakot and the subsequent resurgence of violence in Kashmir and along the LoC, which continues to date.

After the BJP won a sizeable majority in the 2019 elections, the Modi regime saw an opportunity to press forward with the BJP's long-promised agenda of revoking Jammu and Kashmir's semi-autonomous status—a special status enshrined under Articles 35A and 370 of the Indian constitution. On August 5, 2019, India revoked the two articles and announced it was separating Ladakh from Jammu and Kashmir, creating two regions. Prior to the announcement, the BJP government deployed tens of thousands of troops and paramilitary forces into the region and literally locked down the entire Kashmir Valley.[46]

Modi's message seemed clear: He was forewarning Pakistan that Indian- administered Kashmir was no longer a disputed territory between them, irrespective of any interpretation of past UN resolutions or India-Pakistan bilateral accords such as Simla in 1972 and Lahore in 1999. Finally, Modi was signaling to his international audience that India is on the move and will assertively and aggressively claim land to which it believes it has a sovereign right—in other words, any territory that India perceives to be under "occupation" by Pakistan or China. India is also demonstrating its assumed right of access to the border with China, regardless of the sovereign claim of any intervening landlocked border states—Nepal, Sikkim, and Bhutan—that are dependent on India.[47]

In May 2020, a new crisis erupted between India and China on the eastern Ladakh border, and by mid-June it had turned bloody, with several deaths on both sides in the Galwan Valley. During this crisis, tensions were also running high between India and Nepal over the tri-junction region with India and China in western Nepal, an area known as Kalapani.[48] Similar tri-junctions exist in eastern Nepal and in Bhutan. The cause of these regional tensions and skirmishes can be traced back to the bungled boundary demarcations established during the colonial era (i.e., the Durand, Johnson, and McMahon Lines, see chapter 1), which continue to be a source of conflict fueled by territorial nationalism.

Following the outbreak of COVID-19 in 2020, the crisis in Kashmir has seemingly abated. However, there is little likelihood of a return to normalcy, and as far as Pakistan is concerned, any future dialogue with India is contingent on it reversing the 2019 actions in Kashmir.

Pakistan's Agonizing Recovery from Decades of War and Instability

By 2021, after years of continuous military operations, the Pakistani military had significantly suppressed the terrorists' activities on its soil and unraveled their networks while managing to balance against India. The past two decades have taken a heavy toll on the country's security forces, however. Although Islamabad's alliance with the United States in its global "war on terror" brought the country some economic benefit, on balance, Pakistan has paid a huge political, economic, and military price. It is generally estimated that Islamabad has suffered economic losses amounting to hundreds of billions of dollars and lost over 75,000 human lives to terrorism as the war in Afghanistan spilled over into Pakistan.[49] Worse still, as the US-led "war on terror" became more protracted, Washington and Islamabad lost trust in one another. The United States blamed Islamabad for providing safe havens and support to the militants operating in Afghanistan, while for its part, Pakistan accused the United States of lacking any real understanding about the decades of crisis in the region and for giving India space in Afghanistan from which to operate against Pakistan. This has always been a fundamental concern which lies at the core of Pakistan's grievance with Afghanistan.

As great power competition intensifies, the United States is reevaluating its security calculus—seeking new strategic partners and contemplating new roles for old ones like Pakistan. After nearly two decades of terrorism, insurgency, war, and myriad instabilities in the region, the United States decided to negotiate with the Taliban and to exit from Afghanistan— apparently without foreseeing the mad scramble to leave that unfolded in August 2021 as the Taliban swept through the country to take control —leaving Afghanistan and its citizens to an uncertain future. During this time, despite being at the center of the war against terror in Afghanistan, Pakistan has seen its importance to the United States steadily decline. In future, Islamabad will likely continue to leverage its geostrategic significance to balance the United States and China. More than anything,

Pakistan needs to put its own house in order so it can halt the cycle of perennial crisis with India.

Nuclear Learning and Crisis Stability

The world at large expected India and Pakistan to discern the revolutionary change that the introduction of nuclear weapons produced in the regional security environment. Since independence, both countries have followed maximalist political ends—such as the full liberation of Kashmir from the other or India's desire for hegemony in South Asia. These lofty objectives, conceived in the pre-nuclear era, have dragged on into the nuclear era, where their continuation is fraught with greater risks than before and the costs far exceed any potential benefits.

To their credit, despite becoming embroiled in several military crises since their nuclear tests in 1998, both India and Pakistan have avoided letting them deepen into a major war. Yet, both fall shy of reversing their adversarial policies, of transforming goals, changing mutual perceptions, and overhauling their doctrinal thinking. Instead, they have simply altered their behavior and tailored their strategic plans to adapt to the new circumstances while maintaining the same old belligerency.[50] This stubborn resistance to change has perpetuated the high-tension status quo. Under these conditions, a slow arms race continues, as both countries focus on acquiring new weapons and technologies and the crises between them proliferate.

India and Pakistan have dissimilar concepts around nuclear deterrence, resulting in misaligned military doctrines and force asymmetries. India has officially declared a no-first-use doctrine, but it has also consistently flirted with the idea of "modifying its long-standing declaratory doctrine"— of shifting to a first-use strategy against Pakistan while maintaining a no-first-use strategy vis-à-vis China.[51] Furthermore, India's investment in diverse nuclear-capable delivery systems, and its sophistication in terms of surveillance systems, missile defense systems, and sea-based capabilities—reinforced by a series of public statements from active politicians as well as serving and retired military officials—all indicate that a first-strike posture, rather than a "retaliatory" strike nuclear doctrine, is becoming India's official stance.[52]

In contrast, Pakistan has deliberately maintained ambiguity and eschewed any clear declaration of its official nuclear policy, although it has unambiguously declared that its nuclear weapons capability is solely aimed at deterring India from a conventional or nuclear attack. Pakistan's public articulations of its national command-and-control system indicate the operational integration of conventional and nuclear forces and a readiness to make the first strike if its National Command Authority (NCA) determines India has crossed Pakistan's nuclear red line. Compared to India, Pakistan is lagging in intelligence, surveillance, and reconnaissance (ISR) technologies, space technology, and new information technologies—all of which rely on modern command systems and credibility of their deterrence capability.[53] These differences have led to an offense-defense imbalance in the region, which exacerbates the strategic instability.

While technological maturations continue in both states, albeit at a varying pace and with varying resource inputs, these developments are outpacing strategic doctrinal development as both nations face significant dilemmas in terms of formulating a credible strategy. India is no closer to knowing how to terminate a limited conventional war without crossing Pakistan's nuclear thresholds—thresholds that Pakistan deliberately keeps as ambiguous and unclear as possible. Pakistan believes that its nuclear capability fully offsets its conventional asymmetry with India, However, this strategy creates a serious quandary for Pakistan. If it indicates a high nuclear threshold, this will give India plenty of time and space to use its conventional forces against Pakistan; conversely, if Pakistan signals a low threshold, India might take a chance and call its bluff. Either way, there is a significant risk that deterrence might fail in this game of chicken and result in a nuclear exchange.[54]

In sum, a situation of continuous regional cold war, a slow arms race, and unresolved tensions is likely to prevail. Given that both sides seem determined to test the other's will again and again, sporadic military crises will continually threaten to broaden and deepen as well as increase in frequency. This scenario of an unending cold war represents the *bad* future for South Asia. Conventional force deployments would persist along the LoC with sporadic outbreaks of violence raising tensions along the international border. If these trends continued, forward military garrisons would gradually be reinforced in peacetime—with air bases constantly on alert and monitored amidst the fear of a surprise cross-border air attack from either side. In such a tense situation, it would not be surprising if these states moved their nuclear weapons, hitherto unmated and un-deployed, into a state of readiness during peacetime. The border between India and Pakistan would resemble the Iron Curtain between the countries of the Warsaw Pact and NATO in Europe during the Cold War.

International concerns over a serious military confrontation between the Subcontinent's nuclear-armed neighbors are unlikely to abate anytime soon. There are only two pathways away from this bad future scenario and the seemingly unending tense relations between India and Pakistan —things could either get worse, with all the terrible consequences that this entails, or events could take the dramatically opposite course toward lasting peace and security. At the time of writing, there is a complete breakdown in bilateral dialogue between the two querulous neighbors and an absence of any external efforts to normalize their political, social, and economic relations. For now, at least, peaceful relations between them is apparently a bridge too far.

THE "UGLY" PATH: ACQUIESCE OR COLLAPSE

A strategic future that unambiguously stamps India's supremacy on the region is usually premised on the complete acquiescence or collapse of its nemesis, Pakistan. As Cohen wrote, such a future vision is based on the belief that strategic competition with India, internal ethno-religious fissures, civil-military discords, and a prostrate economy would wear Pakistan down to such an extent that it would no longer be in a position to challenge the status quo. In effect, this war of attrition would resolve the last of India's three legacies from Partition—the problem of Pakistan —that C. Raja Mohan identified as having stymied India's great power ambitions ever since independence.[55]

In December 2000, a study on global trends by the US National Intelligence Council made several predictions about the world in 2015. Regarding South Asia, the study projected the rise of India, "albeit more factionalized by the secular-Hindu nationalist debate," and it anticipated the decline of Pakistan due to:

> lawlessness, corruption and ethnic friction... [that] would produce little change in the face of opposition from entrenched political elites and radical Islamic parties... altering the make-up and cohesion of the military... In a climate of continuing domestic turmoil, the central government's control probably will be reduced to the Punjabi heartland and the economic hub of Karachi.[56]

India is certainly rising as forecasted, but its rise is accompanied by troubles internally and externally. Similarly, Pakistan has suffered just as anticipated, and streaks of instability persist. However, far from reaching its predicted doom, the Pakistani nation has demonstrated an unwavering resolve to overcome the challenges and adversities it faces. As Maleeha Lodhi, a highly respected scholar and Pakistan's former ambassador to the United States, United Kingdom, and United Nations, confidently notes:

> Resilience has been part of Pakistan's story from the country's inception, obscured by the single-issue lens through which outsiders have lately viewed the nation... the strength and stability of its underlying social structures [have] enabled the country to weather national and regional storms and rebound from disasters— natural and manmade.[57]

Ugly Stability and Perpetual Crisis

Sensing its political power after repeated electoral victories and emboldened by the absence of international censure regarding its discriminatory policies against minorities and human rights abuses in Kashmir, New Delhi has upped the ante with Pakistan.[58] The international community was silent over the Indian air force attack at Balakot in Pakistan in February 2019 (as well as the subsequent retaliation by the Pakistani air force and shooting down of Indian aircraft), which has set a bad precedent.[59] India has unquestionably been emboldened to take up a more belligerent stance vis-à-vis Pakistan in future. Equally, Pakistan's armed forces now feel confident they could aggressively give a *quid pro quo plus* response to any future venture by Indian forces.[60]

Should an equally emboldened ultra-right leadership emerge in Pakistan that matches the regime in India, the region's worst political nightmare would come true and the inevitable crises and wars on the Subcontinent would follow an uncharted path. Although Pakistani voters have repeatedly rejected hardline fundamentalist parties at the ballot box and it is currently unlikely that there would be an Islamist takeover there, recent events in Afghanistan illustrate the foolhardiness of making too many assumptions. In such a hypothetical clash of two hardline governments, the region's new jihadi forces would be unleashed with extremist vigor to "liberate" Kashmir and their suppressed "Islamic brothers" from the "tyranny" of a Hindu nationalist government. In such a scenario, jihadi volunteers would reignite Kashmir by targeting Indian security forces. India is already openly supporting the separatist movements in Baluchistan and elsewhere in Pakistan and would be sure to reciprocate if its security forces were targeted. In sum, both countries could wreak havoc on each other with asymmetric means.

In an *ugly* scenario, Islamist vigilantes in Pakistan would destroy religious sites and lynch minorities for alleged blasphemies. There would be an escalation in surgical strikes across the LoC, and they could well become a regular feature with artillery fire, armed or unarmed unmanned aerial vehicles, helicopter attacks, and frequent air space violations. Sadly, the region has seen several such ugly cycles of cross-border communal bloodbaths and exodus, evoking haunting memories of Partition.

Limited Wars and the Potential for Escalation

To date, all military crises in the region have remained limited, although Pakistan and India have both climbed the escalation ladder. Several factors contributed to crisis de-escalation, most notably US intervention, deterrence, and fortuitous off-ramps. Even so, there is little assurance that either country could confidently discern the other's strategic thinking and intent. The most worrisome aspect of India-Pakistan crises is the probability of either country misreading and/or underestimating the scope of the other's willingness to use force and escalate. At some point, assumptions of escalation control could go horribly wrong, and in the absence of bilateral communications, any future crisis between the two nuclear-armed neighbors might lead to the nuclear red line being crossed much sooner than intended.

The next crisis on the Subcontinent is most likely to emanate from Kashmir, which is currently heavily suppressed due to Indian military action and the COVID-19 pandemic of 2020. Kashmir could erupt under either of these pressures, and the world would find itself facing an all too familiar crisis. If India repeats its surgical strike on Pakistani soil and there are actual dead bodies—unlike in 2019—retaliation-in-kind by Pakistan is guaranteed. The choice of weapons and nature of the escalation could be different than 2019, however. For example, either side might use long-range precision missiles to avoid cross-border flights with piloted aircraft. Thus far, and fortunately, dual-capability missiles have not been used in any India-Pakistan crisis—yet.

It is unlikely that a future India-Pakistan military crisis would be restricted to land, however. Once again, the February 2019 Pulwama-Balakot crisis portends the future. Should the Indian navy choose to deploy INS Arihant and other sea-based strategic deterrence forces on patrol during a new crisis, or attempt another naval blockade of the Pakistani coastline, a maritime incident is almost assured. In the worst case, a naval battle could erupt, leading to the sinking of a submarine carrying nuclear weapons and crossing Pakistan's quasi declared red line of economic strangulation.

At the time of the Pulwama-Balakot crisis, it was unclear whether INS Arihant was carrying nuclear warheads, nor whether the submarine was on a routine voyage or had been deployed specifically to deter Pakistan from using its nuclear option. Regardless, Pakistan assumed it was the worst case. During his keynote address in London in February 2020, former SPD Director General, retired Lieutenant General Khalid Kidwai, characterized India's actions as "strategic recklessness" and concluded that INS Arihant "was certainly carrying canisterised ready-to-go nuclear missiles." In his analysis, "Since there were no credible reports of India's first-strike weapons based on land and air being readied, one wonders whether India contemplated the use of nuclear weapons from a second-strike platform even before its first-strike options."[61]

In a similar vein, India believes that the meeting of Pakistan's NCA at the height of the 2019 Pulwama-Balakot crisis was clear nuclear signaling. It is not known publicly if there was a nuclear alert or movement of strategic arsenals. Nonetheless, the growing conviction on both sides about the other's nuclear readiness in a crisis could easily lead to the adoption of worst-case assumptions and actual nuclear consequences.

STRATEGIC RISKS AND THE FOG OF WAR

Strategic modernization in both countries continues at a varying pace, as analyzed in the chapters of this book. The tenuous strategic stability and current balance in the region could likely erode in the future as ISR systems become more sophisticated, additional ballistic missile defense systems are acquired, and outer space becomes ever more militarized (with India considerably ahead concerning the latter). Although India justifies these developments as balancing against China, they have a direct impact on Pakistan, which consequently rushes to acquire active and passive countervailing measures of its own.

Given the doctrinal dissonance and asymmetry in modernizing their arsenals, there is a huge risk that India and Pakistan could enter into a nuclear war either due to misconceptions about the other's resolve or as a consequence of escalating tit-for-tat military actions. At present, their strategic weapons are not mated or on alert, and their conventional forces are not deployed at the border but held in peacetime garrisons; however, these conditions could easily change if cross-border tensions continue or intensify. Three potential threats can be identified in this regard.

First, India and Pakistan may effectively fortify their border, much like the East-West divide in Europe during the Cold War, keeping their air forces on continuous combat patrols and/or deploying cross-border drones and lethal autonomous weapons in operations. It is possible that nuclear weapons could then be mated with their delivery systems and surreptitiously made ready under silos, while road mobile systems could be dispersed to avoid detection and targeting. One major uncertainty in such deployments is the ambiguity over dual-capability warheads —these could be secretly intermixed and concealed alongside the full mobilization of conventional forces, creating a much denser fog of war. If there was an outbreak of hostilities, any launch using such a dual-use strategic delivery vehicle could provoke an unpredictable response and the whole shape of battle could change dramatically.

Second, the gap between India and Pakistan's strategic weapons arsenals is increasing in India's favor. Although India has declared a no-first-use policy, it is developing counterforce capabilities that would support a first-strike option, reinforcing perceptions that India is nuancing its doctrinal position vis-à-vis Pakistan. Given that Pakistani planners never considered India's no-first-use commitment a serious one, these doctrinal declarations inspire little confidence regarding stability.

Third, there are exaggerated calculations about India and Pakistan's respective nuclear stockpiles that are often used for the purpose of propaganda. Such notions exacerbate threat perceptions and fuel the race to produce fissile material and increase nuclear arsenals further. The effect of all these concerns would be to hinder the economic development of both countries, especially Pakistan, as it struggles to defend two borders and weather a multitude of domestic crises as well. Worse than this, however, in any future war between India and Pakistan, the likelihood of them falling into an unintended nuclear war once they embark on the slippery slope of escalation and military momentum cannot be ruled out.

If relations between India and Pakistan maintain their current trajectory, then both the bad and the ugly future scenarios could turn from being mere hypotheses into nightmare reality. After seven decades of separation, the mutual antagonism between India and Pakistan has seemingly increased and their historical connections weakened, particularly among the millennial generation in an era of digital information and social media.

Both India and Pakistan have engaged in mass disinformation campaigns and propaganda against the other. Moreover, the rise of right-wing forces and hypernationalism in both countries is slowly erasing all memory of the common ties and history which have shaped the Subcontinent over several centuries of cultural synthesis. Today, political, and ideological forces in both countries are emphasizing the differences that pull India and Pakistan apart—their national culture, history, and religion—and repudiating everything that can bring people together—musical and cultural activities, holy places, sports, and a shared history of pain and glory.

This book has shown how the uncompromising strategic enclaves in Pakistan and India have persistently thwarted attempts at peace, from Simla in 1972 to Lahore in 1999, and from Agra in 2001 to the back-door diplomacy of 2004–2008. Nonetheless, India and Pakistan can still avoid the path to an ugly future if they choose to bring an end to the current (bad) situation and turn toward a more hopeful (good) future for the Subcontinent, and for the whole world.

Notes

1. "Albert Einstein Quotes About Peace," https://www.azquotes.com/author/ 4399-Albert_Einstein/tag/peace.

2. Arzan Tarapore, "The Crisis after the Crisis: How Ladakh will Shape India's Competition with China," *Lowy Institute Analysis*, May 6, 2021 (Sydney: Lowy Institute, 2021).

3. Bruce Riedel, "Hardening Alliances: India-America and Pakistan-China," Brookings, May 11, 2015, https://www.brookings.edu/opinions/ hardening-alliances-india-america-and-pakistan-china/.

4. "Fact Sheet: The Indus Waters Treaty 1960 and the Role of the World Bank," World Bank, https://www.worldbank.org/en/region/sar/brief/ fact-sheet-the-indus-waters-treaty-1960-and-the-world-bank.

5. "India and Pakistan Agree Not to Hit Nuclear Plants," *Los Angeles Times*, January 1, 1989, https://www.latimes.com/archives/la-xpm-1989-01-01 -mn-289-story.html.

6. "Confidence Building and Nuclear Risk-Reduction Measures in South Asia," Henry L. Stimson Center, July 14, 2012, https://www.stimson.org/ 2012/confidence-building-and-nuclear-risk-reduction-measures-south-asia/.

7. *Los Angeles Times*, "India and Pakistan Agree Not to Hit Nuclear Plants."

8. Swaran Singh, "China-Indian CBMs: Problems and Prospects," *Strategic Analysis* 20, no. 4 (July 1997) 543–559, https://www.idsa-india.org/an-jul-4.html.

9. "Agreement between the Government of the Republic of India and the Government of the People's Republic of China on Confidence-Building Measures in the Military Field Along the Line of Actual Control in the India-China Border Areas," Peacemaker UN, 1996, https://peacemaker. un.org/sites/peacemaker.un.org/files/CN%20IN_961129_Agreement%20 between%20China%20and%20India.pdf.

10. "Lahore Declaration," Nuclear Threat Initiative (NTI), https://www.nti. org/learn/treaties-and-regimes/lahore-declaration/.

11. One of those released was Maulana Azhar, who would later establish Jaish-e-Muhammad (JeM), a jihadi organization with its headquarters in Bhawalpur, Pakistan.

12. This was related to me by Pervez Musharraf, former president of Pakistan, Rawalpindi, Pakistan, April 12, 2014. In Musharraf's words, as he

was leaving Agra, Vajpayee said to him in polite Urdu: *"Mujhe kuch aur waqt deejye* [give me some more time]."

13. Stated by Pakistan's former Foreign Secretary during a US-Pakistan Track II Strategic Dialogue held at Stanford University in August 2016.

14. Joanna Slater, "India and Pakistan Announce Cease-fire for the First Time in Nearly 20 Years," *The Washington Post*, February 25, 2021, https://www.washingtonpost.com/world/asia_pacific/india-pakistan-ceasefire-kashmir/2021/02/25/02335b38-773c-11eb-9489-8f7dacd51e75_story.html.

15. Stephen P. Cohen, *Shooting for a Century: The India-Pakistan Conundrum* (Washington, DC: Brookings Institution Press, 2013), 174–175.

16. Cohen, *Shooting for a Century,* 167–178.

17. Cohen, *Shooting for a Century,* 167, 174–175 .

18. Cohen, *Shooting for a Century,* 175–176.

19. "Confidence-building Measure (CBM)," *Glossary of Terms for Conflict Management and Peacebuilding* (Washington, DC: United States Institute of Peace, 2011), http://glossary.usip.org/resource/confidence-building-measure-cbm.

20. "Nawaz Sharif Speech at the UN," September 27, 2013, https://www.scribd.com/document/171451538/Nawaz-Sharif-Speech-at-UN.

21. "Nawaz Sharif Speech at the UN."

22. Imtiaz Ahmad, "If India Takes One Step Forward, We Will Take Two: Set to be Pakistan's New PM, Imran Khan Talks Peace," *Hindustan Times*, July 27, 2018, https://www.hindustantimes.com/world-news/pakistan-elections-victorious-imran-khan-sends-peace-overture-to-india/story-bGGm77kWobmbGun4GnPKgJ.html.

23. Shubhajit Roy, "Pakistan govt, Army, parties on same pagewhen it comes to India ties: Imran Khan," *Indian Express*, November 29, 2018.

24. Feroz Hassan Khan, *Eating Grass: The Making of the Pakistani Bomb* (Palo Alto, CA: Stanford University Press, 2012), 297.

25. Feroz Hassan Khan, "Time for a Trialogue: The Need for Restraints Involving India, China and Pakistan," *Global* Asia 16, no. 2 (June 2021), https://globalasia.org/v16no2/cover/time-for-a-trialogue-the-need-for-restraints-involving-india-china-and-pakistan_feroz-hassan-khan.

26. For a detailed analysis, see Feroz Hassan Khan, "Strategic Restraint Regime 2.0," in *Deterrence Stability and Escalation Control in South Asia,* ed. Michael Krepon and Julia Thompson (Washington, DC: Henry L. Stimson Center, 2013).

27. Feroz Hassan Khan, "Break the Impasse: Direct Talks Between Army Chiefs," in *Off Ramps from Confrontation in Southern Asia,* ed. Michael

Krepon, Travis Wheeler, and Liv Dowling (Washington, DC: Henry L. Stimson Center, May 2019), 154–161, https://www.stimson.org/wp-content/files/file-attachments/OffRamps_Book_R5_WEB.pdf.

28. Khan, "Strategic Restraint Regime 2.0."

29. Christopher Clary, "Deterrence Stability and the Conventional Balance of Forces in South Asia," in *Deterrence Stability and Escalation Control in South Asia*, ed. Michael Krepon and Julia Thompson (Washington, DC: Henry L. Stimson Center, 2013).

30. "Agreement between the Government of the Republic of India and the Government of the People's Republic of China."

31. India and Pakistan signed the Agreement on Prevention of Air Space Violation in 1991. For a brief summary of recent CBMs, see "Confidence-Building and Nuclear Risk-Reduction Measures in South Asia," Henry L. Stimson Center, June 14, 2012, https://www.stimson.org/2012/confidence-building-and-nuclear-risk-reduction-measures-south-asia/.

32. Syed Ali Zia Jaffrey, "Enhancing Deterrence Stability on the Subcontinent: The Case for Conventional Deterrence," Stimson Center, April 8, 2020.

33. Feroz Hassan Khan, "Trilateral Strategic Confidence-Building Measures in South Asia," in *Asia-Pacific Leadership Network Conference*, ed. Peter Hayes (forthcoming), paper presented in December 2020.

34. Clary, "Deterrence Stability."

35. Hasan Ansari and Ravi Vohra, "Confidence Building Measures at Sea: Opportunities for India and Pakistan," Cooperative Monitoring Center Occasional Paper No. 33 (Albuquerque, NM: Sandia National Laboratories 2003): 5, https://www.sandia.gov/cooperative-monitoring-center/_assets/documents/sand2004-0102.pdf.

36. The thalweg principle has been usefully employed in disputes between Guyana and Suriname and between Benin and Niger. Sikander Ahmed Shah, "River Boundary Delimitation, and the Resolution of the Sir Creek Dispute between Pakistan and India," *Vermont Law Review* 34, no. 357 (2012): 367–369, https://lawreview.vermontlaw.edu/wp-content/uploads/2012/02/shah.pdf.

37. "Agreement between the Government of the United States of America and the Government of the Union of Soviet Socialist Republics on the Prevention of Incidents on and over the High Seas," Bureau of International Security and Nonproliferation, US Department of State, May 25, 1972, http://www.state.gov/t/isn/4791.htm.

38. Muhammad Ali, "Maritime Issues between Pakistan and India: Seeking Cooperation and Regional Stability" (Master's thesis, Naval Postgraduate School, 2012), 1–4.

39. Feroz Khan and Gurmeet Kanwal, "Let's Stop Being MAD, Move to CBMs," *Times of India*, September 11, 2011, https://timesofindia.indiatimes.com/home/sunday-times/all-that-matters/Lets-stop-being-MAD-move-to-CBMs/articleshow/9939854.cms.

40. Mujib Mashal, "In a Region in Strife, India's Moral High Ground Erodes," *New York Times*, November 6, 2021.

41. Sadanand Dhume, "How Democratic is the World's Largest Democracy," *Foreign Affairs*, September/October 2021.

42. Cohen, *Shooting for a Century*, 63.

43. Alyssa Pong, "The Impact of India's Citizenship Amendment Act on Bangladeshis in India," The Organization for World Peace, February 22, 2020, https://theowp.org/the-impact-of-indias-citizenship-amendment-act-on-bangladeshis-in-india/. See also Faisal Mahmud, "India-Bangladesh on a Diplomatic Tightrope," *Asia Times*, January 7, 2020, https://asiatimes.com/2020/01/india-bangladesh-on-a-diplomatic-tightrope/.

44. Max Bearak, "In Kashmir, Indian security forces use pellet guns that often blind protestors," *The Washington Post*, July 12, 2016; *IISS Armed Conflict Survey 2017* (London: Routledge-Taylor & Francis Group for the International Institute for Strategic Studies, 2017), 253-261.

45. *IISS Armed Conflict Survey 2018* (London: Routledge-Taylor & Francis Group for the International Institute for Strategic Studies, 2019), 252.

46. "Conflict Between India and Pakistan," Council on Foreign Relations, Global Conflict Tracker, July 21, 2020, https://www.cfr.org/interactive/global-conflict-tracker/conflict/conflict-between-india-and-pakistan.

47. Constantino Xavier, "Interpreting the India-Nepal Border Dispute," *Upfront* (Brookings Institution blog), June 11, 2020, https://www.brookings.edu/blog/up-front/2020/06/11/interpreting-the-india-nepal-border-dispute/.

48. Nepal accuses India of meddling in Nepalese politics to oust the current government—specifically Prime Minister Khadga Prasad Sharma Oli—from power. Some in India allege that Nepal is only standing up to India because of encouragement from China, although there is no proof of this. See Xavier, "Interpreting the India-Nepal Border Dispute."

49. Islamuddin Sajid, "Pakistan PM Recalls Sacrifices Made in US War on Terror," Anadolu Agency, November 19, 2018, https://www.aa.com.tr/

en/asia-pacific/pakistanpm-recalls-sacrifices-made-in-us-war-on-terror/
1315757.

50. Feroz Hassan Khan and Ryan Jacobs, "The Challenges of Nuclear Learn-
    ing," in *Nuclear Learning in South Asia: The Next Decade*, ed. Feroz Has-
    san Khan, Ryan Jacobs, and Emily Burke, (Monterey, CA: Naval Post-
    graduate School, 2014), 3–15Error! Hyperlink reference not valid..

51. Christopher Clary and Vipin Narang, "India's Counterforce Temptations:
    Strategic Dilemmas, Doctrine, and Capabilities," *International Security* 43,
    no. 3 (Winter, 2018/2019): 7–52, 51, https://doi.org/10.1162/ISEC_a_00340.

52. Clary and Narang, "India's Counterforce Temptations," 23.

53. Feroz Hassan Khan, *Nuclear Command, Control and Communications
    (NC3): The Case of Pakistan* (Berkeley, CA: Nautilus Institute, 2019),
    https://www.tech4gs.org/nc3-systems-and-strategic-stability-a-global-
    overview.html.

54. Khan, *Nuclear Command*.

55. C. Raja Mohan, "India and the Balance of Power," *Foreign Affairs* (July/
    August 2006), https://www.foreignaffairs.com/articles/asia/2006-07-01
    /india-and-balance-power.

56. National Intelligence Council, *Global Trends 2015: A Dialogue about
    the Future with Nongovernment Experts* (Washington, DC: National
    Intelligence Council, 2000), 66, https://www.dni.gov/files/documents/
    Global%20Trends_2015%20Report.pdf.

57. Maleeha Lodhi, ed., *Pakistan: Beyond the Crisis State* (New York: Colum-
    bia University Press, 2011), 2.

58. For example, "India ramps up pressure against Pakistan after UN
    blacklisting," AlJazeera.com, May 2, 2019, https://www.aljazeera.
    com/news/2019/5/2/india-ramps-up-pressure-against-pakistan-after-un-
    blacklisting.

59. Sameer P. Lalwani, Elizabeth Threlkeld, Sunaina Danziger, Grace Easterly,
    Zeba Fazli, Gillian Gayner, Tyler Sagerstrom, Brigitta Schuchert, Chloe
    Stein, Akriti Vasudeva, "From Kargil to Balakot: Southern Asian Crisis
    Dynamics and Future Trajectories," Asia Policy Paper, Stimson Center,
    February 2020, page 2, https://www.stimson.org/wp-content/uploads/2
    020/02/2020-2-SA-Crises-Consequence-PolPaper-1062.pdf.

60. Khalid Kidwai, "Deterrence Stability" (presented at the South Asian
    Strategic Stability: Deterrence, Nuclear Weapons and Arms Control
    Workshop, London, February 7, 2020), https://www.iiss.org/events/202
    0/02/7th-iiss-and-ciss-south-asian-strategic-stability-workshop.

61. Kidwai, "Deterrence Stability."

Conclusion

As noted earlier, this book's main premise flowed from the multi-authored study in 2001 that attempted to discern South Asia's strategic trajectory by 2020. The advent of nuclear weapons capability ought to have impelled India and Pakistan to embrace a cooperative future with the emphasis on conflict resolution and regional détente. Instead, deep-rooted cognitive biases, territorial nationalism, and widening power asymmetries have dragged the Subcontinent away from reaching its true potential. The historical baggage and complex political, social, and economic variables not only make it difficult to provide accurate future predictions but also dampen hopes of achieving real peace and security in the region.

As the locus of geopolitics on the twenty-first-century chessboard pivots toward Asia, the Subcontinent is the strategic linchpin in the looming great power competition. With approximately a quarter of the world's population living on its territory, including the highest concentration of Hindus and Muslims, the Subcontinent's great economic potential and strategic significance is not lost on the world. At the same time, its dangerous propensity for crisis and war, with the potential to escalate into a nuclear exchange, is especially worrisome and continues to cast a dark shadow over South Asia's strategic future.

Given the more than a century of combined Hindu-Muslim struggle to free the Subcontinent from the yoke of colonialism, the international community is baffled at the failure of modern South Asia to evolve into a stable geopolitical region. Scholars, policymakers, and those familiar with the region note how greatly the Subcontinent's past civilization—with its rich culture, immense resources, and abundant talent—contrasts with the general deprivation, lack of development, religious dogma, and multiple forms of instability seen today. These negative trends stem primarily from the anachronistic rivalry between India and Pakistan. In short, the more these two major players dedicate their energies toward thwarting the national objectives of the other, the more they suffer jointly. Despite this, neither side is able to find a viable solution to its problem with the other. As Stephen Cohen surmised, "because theirs is a paired-minority conflict," India and Pakistan are unable to find "regional normalization."[1] He concluded that without a new stimulus or outside intervention to compel change, both sides would still be "shooting each other for another century."[2]

This book has analyzed the deep-rooted cognitive and structural factors that have been the primary drivers in shaping India and Pakistan's grand strategies and casting the Subcontinent adrift. It also questioned whether India and Pakistan have the wherewithal to achieve their grand strategic aims—for India to attain global power status and for Pakistan to emerge as a model Muslim middle power. I conclude that neither country has achieved its true potential because both continue to punch above their weight and are fixated on their mutual rivalry rather than the good of the region. In their desire to outbid each other, Indian and Pakistani policymakers have repeatedly brought South Asia to the brink of annihilation.

If India and Pakistan are ever to achieve their dream—to become the great power in Asia as envisioned by Lord Curzon more than a century ago—they need to reach a *modus vivendi* for cooperative coexistence and positive integration. Given that both these nations possess nuclear weapons, conflict between them can be classified as limited war to date. However, the differences in their respective security postures, security apparatuses, and political structures could lead to serious miscalculations and escalation if they continue to support low-intensity conflict. Even if the non-use of nuclear weapons is maintained in future conflicts, it is clear their nuclear capability has neither improved the security situation nor reduced tensions in South Asia.

At the time of this writing, normalcy is returning to the world as the pandemic subsides and more and more people are being vaccinated.

Meanwhile, we are witnessing two major geopolitical developments that will significantly shape South Asia's future for years to come. First, just as US forces were completing their withdrawal from Afghanistan at the end of their twenty-year war on terror, Taliban forces entered Kabul in a surprise move on August 15, 2021, causing the Afghan government to collapse and President Ashraf Ghani to flee with his closest advisors. In the face of Afghanistan's likely descent into chaos, the potential for the crisis to spill over into Pakistan—with all the wider implications for the Subcontinent that entails—remains a prime concern. Second, although India and Pakistan have reinstated the ceasefire on the LoC in Kashmir through backchannel contacts, violence in Kashmir has nonetheless returned. Any glimmer of hope that India and Pakistan might commence a new peace process, having both suffered so much during the pandemic, has once again been extinguished.

In the larger sweep of geopolitical shifts, the *entente cordiale* between Pakistan and China continues to develop, although progress on the CPEC project has slowed due to several reasons, including the global pandemic. Meanwhile, the strategic partnership between India and the United States is broadening and deepening, particularly as the US aims to rebalance in the Indo-Pacific region.

While these geopolitical alignments are reshaping world politics, technological maturations of the twenty-first century are constantly presenting new challenges and changing the character of war. The addition of disruptive technologies such as autonomous weapons systems —especially hypersonic missiles and lethal unmanned aerial systems (drones)—into the mix poses a serious threat to the precarious stability brought about by nuclear weapons in South Asia. Drones are "low-cost and disposable" and avoid the mass spilling of blood; they offer the advantage of "constant surveillance combined with a precision armed strike" in a single system. Drones are providing both a "coercive advantage and the ability to limit the use of force," as displayed during the Armenia-Azerbaijan crisis in May 2021.[3] The advent of lethal autonomous weapons systems and other technological innovations in crisis-ridden South Asia would increase both the inevitability and the pace of a future crisis. There could be additional dangers too; machines would challenge political decision-making and control over forces, and once military operations commence, the speed of the machines and their precision would overwhelm the command-and-control systems in place.[4]

Finally, the economic impact of the COVID-19 pandemic on future globalization trends and military modernization is still uncertain; however, as resources become increasingly scarce, this is likely to have an impact on military and nuclear strengths. Sadly, it does not appear that the world has seen an end to violence in South Asia, and the prospects for peace, détente, and stability—the *good* future—remain firmly out of reach. The Subcontinent today is still very much adrift.

NOTES

1. Stephen P. Cohen, *Shooting for a Century: The India-Pakistan Conundrum* (Washington, DC: Brookings Institution Press, 2013), 174–175.

2. Cohen, *Shooting for a Century*, 195.

3. Amy Zegart, "Cheap Fights, Credible Threats: The Future of Armed Drones and Coercion," *Journal of Strategic Studies* 43, no. 1 (2020): 6–46, https://doi.org/10.1080/01402390.2018.1439747.

4. Aamna Rafiq, "Lethal Autonomous Weapon Systems (LAWS) and State Behavior: Global and Regional Implications," Arms Control and Disarmament Center Report, Webinar April 7, 2021 (Islamabad: Institute of Strategic Studies Islamabad, April 2021), https://issi.org.pk/report-webinar-on-lethal-autonomous-weapon-systems-laws-and-state-behaviour-global-and-regional-implications/.

INDEX

Praise for the Book

"*Subcontinent Adrift* provides a comprehensive account of the India-Pakistan competition after 75 years of independence, three bloody wars, and numerous near-miss nuclear crises. Professor Feroz Khan, former Director in Pakistan's Strategic Plans Division, gives us a vivid account of the region's tragic history, the domestic and international roots of rivalry, a spiraling nuclear arms race, and the many failed bids for peace and normalization. He offers a compassionate and lucid analysis of South Asia's past and present and valuable insights into South Asia's possible futures, ranging from the reassuring to the outright terrifying."

—Peter Lavoy, former Senior Director for South Asia,
National Security Council

* * * * *

"The Indo-Pakistani rivalry has receded in international consciousness in recent years—sometimes for good reason. But the underlying sources of instability persist. Feroz Khan's sympathetic survey of this competition aptly highlights why the quest for a lasting peace cannot be neglected any longer."

—Ashley J. Tellis, Tata Chair for Strategic Affairs,
Carnegie Endowment for International Peace

* * * * *

"On the heels of his masterly account of the growth of Pakistan as a nuclear weapons state, *Eating Grass*, Feroz Khan turns to explaining the strategic imbalance in South Asia that feeds the unending hostility between India and Pakistan. In this compact and compelling analysis, he illustrates the historical and militaristic thinking on both sides that feeds enmity while hobbling the ability of both countries to achieve internal and external peace and development. Khan's cogent new book should be seen as a warning that armed conflict or use of terrorist proxies will not solve the problems facing the teeming millions in South Asia—they will only exacerbate them."

—Shuja Nawaz, Distinguished Fellow, South Asia Center, Atlantic Council

* * * * *

"This is an important volume on the India-Pakistan rivalry by a veteran scholar-practitioner on South Asian security issues and comes as the two countries celebrate 75 years of independence. It takes a historical overview of their rivalry with a comprehensive discussion of the evolution of their military strategies, situating it in the domestic and international political contexts. Professor Feroz Khan brings decades of experience as a senior military officer and as a highly respected academic expert to give well-considered projections of various strategic futures. For scholars, policy professionals, and students, this book provides a rich and timely perspective on the subcontinental dyad."

—Sharad Joshi, Associate Professor, Middlebury Institute of International Studies at Monterey

* * * * *

"A must read from Feroz Khan on the continuing simmering security dangers in South Asia and their impact on the rest of the world. Khan lays out a sensible path toward a 'good' future but then laments that a 'bad' or 'ugly' future is more likely given the breakdown in India-Pakistan relations."

—Siegfried S. Hecker, Professor and Senior Fellow, CISAC and FSI, Stanford University

* * * * *

"It didn't have to be this way—two nuclear armed neighbors constantly at each other's throats, drifting from one crisis to another, barely speaking, locked in perpetual struggle. Yet India and Pakistan share so much in common, including shared history, geography, and culture. What happened? Feroz Khan captures the deeply tragic nature of India-Pakistan relations that lead them on such different paths, one a chaotic democracy on the road to becoming a global power, the other a society still struggling to find its place in the sun. This book explains how South Asia arrived at its current circumstances, and how a better future might be possible."

—Zachary S. Davis, Senior Fellow, Center for Global Security Research, Lawrence Livermore National Laboratory

Cambria Rapid Communications in Conflict and Security (RCCS) Series

General Editor: Geoffrey R. H. Burn

The aim of the RCCS series is to provide policy makers, practitioners, analysts, and academics with in-depth analysis of fast-moving topics that require urgent yet informed debate. Since its launch in October 2015, the RCCS series has the following book publications:

- *A New Strategy for Complex Warfare: Combined Effects in East Asia* by Thomas A. Drohan
- *US National Security: New Threats, Old Realities* by Paul R. Viotti
- *Security Forces in African States: Cases and Assessment* edited by Paul Shemella and Nicholas Tomb
- *Trust and Distrust in Sino-American Relations: Challenge and Opportunity* by Steve Chan
- *The Gathering Pacific Storm: Emerging US-China Strategic Competition in Defense Technological and Industrial Development* edited by Tai Ming Cheung and Thomas G. Mahnken
- *Military Strategy for the 21st Century: People, Connectivity, and Competition* by Charles Cleveland, Benjamin Jensen, Susan Bryant, and Arnel David
- *Ensuring National Government Stability After US Counterinsurgency Operations: The Critical Measure of Success* by Dallas E. Shaw Jr.
- *Reassessing U.S. Nuclear Strategy* by David W. Kearn, Jr.
- *Deglobalization and International Security* by T. X. Hammes
- *American Foreign Policy and National Security* by Paul R. Viotti

- *Make America First Again: Grand Strategy Analysis and the Trump Administration* by Jacob Shively

- *Learning from Russia's Recent Wars: Why, Where, and When Russia Might Strike Next* by Neal G. Jesse

- *Restoring Thucydides: Testing Familiar Lessons and Deriving New Ones* by Andrew R. Novo and Jay M. Parker

- *Net Assessment and Military Strategy: Retrospective and Prospective Essays* edited by Thomas G. Mahnken, with an introduction by Andrew W. Marshall

- *Deterrence by Denial: Theory and Practice* edited by Alex S. Wilner and Andreas Wenger

- *Negotiating the New START Treaty* by Rose Gottemoeller

- *Party, Politics, and the Post-9/11 Army* by Heidi A. Urben

- *Resourcing the National Security Enterprise: Connecting the Ends and Means of US National Security* edited by Susan Bryant and Mark Troutman

- *Subcontinent Adrift: Strategic Futures of South Asia* by Feroz Hassan Khan

For more information, visit www.cambriapress.com.